D0852351

ALSO BY COLETTE DOWLING

The Frailty Myth

The
Frailty Myth

WOMEN APPROACHING
PHYSICAL EQUALITY

COLETTE DOWLING

 Random House • *New York*

Copyright © 2000 by Colette Dowling

All rights reserved under International and Pan-American Copyright Conventions. Published in the United States by Random House, Inc., New York, and simultaneously in Canada by Random House of Canada Limited, Toronto.

RANDOM HOUSE and colophon are registered trademarks of Random House, Inc.

Grateful acknowledgment is made to the following for permission to reprint previously published material:

Doubleday, a division of Random House, Inc.: Excerpt from *Schoolgirls,* by Peggy Orenstein. Copyright © 1994 by Peggy Orenstein and the American Association of University Women. Reprinted by permission of Doubleday, a division of Random House, Inc.

Human Kinetics: Excerpt from "Learning Life's Lessons in Tee Ball," by Melissa Landers and Gary Fine, from the *Sociology of Sport Journal* 13 (1), 1996. Used by permission.

Library of Congress Cataloging-in-Publication Data

Dowling, Colette.
The frailty myth: women approaching physical equality/
Colette Dowling.
p.   cm.
Includes bibliographical references and index.
ISBN 0-375-50235-1 (acid-free paper)
1. Women—Psychology.   2. Sex differences.
3. Women—Physiology.   4. Sex role.
HQ1206 .D683   2000
305.3—dc21   00-028093

Random House website address: www.atrandom.com

Printed in the United States of America on acid-free paper

23456789

First Edition

Book design by Jennifer Ann Daddio

For Rachel, Gabrielle, Conor, and Susan

Acknowledgments

It's always interesting, after finishing a book, to look back and note the many people whose energy and ideas and personal passions have in one way or another contributed to it. I'd like to thank my brother, Dr. William Hoppmann, a psychotherapist in Pittsburgh who specializes in EMDR treatment of people suffering from trauma—including athletes for whom trauma interferes with sports performance. Bill has always been on the cutting edge of his profession, and my discussions with him over the years have had a big influence on my thinking and writing.

My dear friend Dr. Barbara Koltuv read early work on *The Frailty Myth* and, like a true Jungian, encouraged me to loosen up and fly beyond my sources. I talk about many of my ideas with Barbara and always come away from our conversations enriched.

Val Tekavek, a professor at Bard College, is my writing buddy, the first one I've ever had, and it's been a revelation and a blessing to share my work with her. Val is a wonderful and generous writer and teacher who has helped me enormously in the struggle with themes, and ideas, and the best and simplest ways of talking about them on paper.

I am indebted to many scholars whose research and writing have provided deep background for my own thinking. There are far too many to list here, but I would like to single out a few who, it seems to me, are navigating a sharp course in a new direction. They are sports historian Susan K. Cahn; Patricia Vertinsky in the School of Human Kinetics at the University of British Columbia in Vancouver, Canada; Jackie L. Hudson, a movement analyst and teacher of biomechanics at California State University–Chico (and who lists among her credentials the fact that she taught herself the fallaway jump shot by observing and imitating older players when she was a preteen in Gruver, Texas, but that she was denied the opportunity to compete in youth-league baseball because she was female); and psychiatrist and trauma theorist Judith Herman, M.D., of Harvard Medical School. I found visionary the work of Martha McCaughey, who teaches at Virginia Tech, in developing a theory of what she calls "physical feminism." Dr. Barbara Sherwin and Dr. Ethel Siris, a psychologist and an endocrinologist, respectively, have shaped my thinking about the relationship of hormones to physical strength in women.

It was in seeing how different things have been for my two daughters, Gabrielle and Rachel, that I came to recognize my limitations in having been educated before the Title IX amendment to the Civil Rights Act demanded equal rights for women on the playing fields of America. Through their inspiration and encouragement, I have increased the physicality of my own life, and I thank them for helping me to see what's possible for women.

Finally, I thank my agent, Ellen Levine, who has stood behind me for many years, and many books. She thought I would like working with Susanna Porter, my editor at Random House, and she was right. Not only has Susanna paid meticulous attention to the various drafts of my manuscript, she basically required of me a higher level of writing. This book would have been an entirely different one without her help, and I can't thank her enough for her intelligence, her persistence, and her belief in what I was doing.

Contents

Contents

Introduction

Not long after I began work on this book, my daughter Rachel came home from the office one night to discover that her boyfriend's father, a thug in disguise, had rented a truck with the intention of removing her belongings from his son's New York apartment and taking them to a small studio I keep in the city. His son was too young for this relationship, Dad believed. He felt he was losing control over his son and he needed someone to blame.

Recognizing that something out of control was going on, Rachel phoned up a place that rents storage units and then asked the meddlesome father to deliver her furniture there. He refused. "There's no room in my mother's apartment," she told him. Too bad. Rachel was waiting in front of the building with a couple of girlfriends when the truck arrived. The father opened up the back doors and flagrantly dropped her television on the sidewalk. His turncoat son was with him. Rachel told the doorman to call the police. Then she jumped on the back of the truck with her arms outspread to prevent the man from destroying any more of her possessions. She held her stance until she heard the police car's siren.

For me, the image was powerful. The bold physicality of Rachel's moves implied a belief in both her strength and her rights. But the belief in her body was crucial. Her strength allowed her not only to defend her rights, but to *experience* them. Within minutes the NYPD Blue arrived, and they escorted the truck, driving Rachel in the car with them, to the storage place and waited while father and son oh so carefully removed her furniture from the van.

What does it take to jump on the back of a truck and prevent two angry men from entering it and dumping out your furniture? What, physically and mentally, is being accomplished here?

I have no doubt that a connection exists between Rachel's leap to defend herself against aggression and her experience, beginning in childhood, with competitive sports. Rachel was one of the millions of girls who began breaking new ground after Title IX, a section of the Educational Amendment Act of 1972, mandated equal funding for girls' sports. They didn't *get* equal funding for years (and often still don't), but change was in the air. Billie Jean King, after all, had accomplished the presumably impossible at Wimbledon in 1973, when she beat Bobby Riggs. As female athletic stars gained in visibility, girls around the country began pioneering the breakdown of the frailty myth—the belief that women are physically incompetent—on a grassroots level. The first broke into heretofore "boys'" sports: soccer, track and field, wrestling, and even football. The *very* first did it by becoming the only girls on the team, as Rachel had done in high school soccer.

The payoff for breaking the cultural mold would be big. By the time Rachel jumped on the back of the truck to defend her belongings, she'd grown into a woman who had internalized a belief in her strength and her ability to defend herself. Because of her physical competence, she has a sense of her body's power that eludes most women of my generation. For us, the greatest physical boldness had been walking down the middle of a city street if we got caught in a dicey neighborhood at night. We had swallowed whole the half-baked syllogism of our generation and that of many generations of females before us: Men have strength, agility, and endurance; women don't; and therefore women need men for protection.

It took years of watching my daughters develop strong, agile, competent bodies before I began to recognize that something new was happening: a further stage in the emancipation of women was under way. At seventeen Rachel took a semester-long trip, sleeping in snow caves, rappelling, telemarking, learning how to avoid "box-car" whirlpools (so named for their size) while piloting a kayak alone through white water. She came home, split up with her boyfriend, and went back to school. There was a whole life out there to be lived. In the wilderness Rachel had discovered things I had simply never learned: that in survival situations, males and females are equally important; that she was better at some physical activities than the boys; that she could counter unwanted sexual approaches from a male counselor without help from someone older. I was proud of her when she returned from the trip a stronger, more confident, more socially flexible person.

It strikes me as odd, looking back, that I never once wondered what my daughters' physical experiences might have done for *me* at that age. It was as if my daughters and I had grown up in different worlds.

And we had, more than I ever realized before beginning work on this book. And yet I'd never actually been weak. When I was a teenager I may not have liked the routines of school gym classes, but

I had *always* liked moving. I used to link arms at the skating rink with a line of boys my age, ice hockey players on their school teams. We'd charge past the Saturday skaters, forming a mighty whip as we made the turns. It amazed me—I'd forgotten this—that I wasn't afraid. "You could play hockey!" one of the boys marveled once, and I could have burst from the thrill of it, and from the pleasure of my own strength and movement. I felt unusual, though. No high school girl I knew liked doing athletic stuff with boys.

Then I went away to school to learn philosophy, and English literature, and the decorum required of Catholic girls coming of age in the fifties. I gave up my beloved tennis and ice-skating. The thrilling and strenuous use of my body came to a stop, not to be enjoyed again for another thirty years.

But my daughters never did that, never gave it up. When my older daughter, Gabrielle, left college and came to New York to begin work, she plunged into the study of seito karate. By then I wasn't surprised by her roundhouse kicks, the "guys' push-ups" she did until her knuckles bled. Hadn't she, at thirteen and fourteen, twisted and flipped her body in the air, leaping from one high bar to another in gymnastics competitions? My heart would be in my mouth whenever I watched her perform, but she had a different experience of it. She was exhilarated by her physical prowess and was becoming practiced in learning to trust her body. When, in her thirties, she put on her first pair of in-line skates and began learning to spin, jump, and spread-eagle, I thought, Of course. She will do this sort of thing all her life. It is part of who she is.

What did surprise me was my own desire surging up, suddenly, in my fifties, to take up skating where I'd left off. Then it had been ice skates. Now I wanted to do, with in-line skates, the same figure-skating routines I'd done as a girl. I probably wouldn't have tried had it not been for Gaby's encouragement. "Come on, Mom," she said, luring me to a beginner's class at Chelsea Piers, a huge sports complex on the Hudson River. "You can do it!"

Miracle of miracles, I wasn't the oldest person in the class. And I not only survived the hour-and-a-half lesson, I triumphed, learning to slalom between two rows of orange pylons on my very first try. After class there was a free-skate session with the music of James Brown pumping out over the PA system. We were outdoors, with the Hudson River a few yards away and a bloodred sunset in the sky. I was back in my sixteen-year-old body, feeling the strength in my quads and the thrilling pounding of the rhythm propelling me around the oval rink. This was not a "new me"; it was me taking back the body I'd been born with but had given up on, as I mimed what I thought were the required, if restricted, behaviors of adult femininity. It was never even clear just *what* was required of young women of my generation, but I can tell you this: Being a "true woman" in the sixties had nothing to do with playing tight end on a football field. Today a girl can actually tackle boys to the ground and not be considered a freak of nature. On the contrary, she can still be popular and considered sexually attractive, as were two placekickers on their high school football teams who were also crowned homecoming queens. And as can the thousands playing tackle football, ice hockey, and soccer.

These new young athletes are dramatically proving that physical competence doesn't compromise femininity. In fact, a belief in the competence of one's body is essential—for mental health, for physical safety, for fulfillment in relationships and success in the workplace. Yet for centuries women have been shackled to a perception of themselves as weak and ineffectual.

In the 1990s it became clear that attitudes toward physical strength and competence were changing when women's ideas about physical appearance began to shift. The vast majority of first-year college women, in one study, considered ideal a *mesomorphic* physique, with the kind of upper body muscularity that doesn't happen without substantial amounts of physical exercise. Shame about having hips and breasts and looking like sexual, grown-up women began to recede.

Female athletes were helping to spearhead the change. Florence Griffith Joyner, the greatest woman runner in the history of the world, had a body to die for and no problem flaunting it. Tinker Bell gymnasts were no longer praised for their tininess. Developing figure skaters talked openly about devising changes in their technique to address the shift in balance produced by growing breasts and hips. They didn't make their bodies stop growing to accommodate the sport, as gymnasts and skaters used to have to do; instead, they made the sport accommodate their growing bodies.

"There's something very freeing about it," twenty-year-old Shana Sundstrom told the readers of a women's magazine, speaking about the way she and her sisters, all speed skaters, felt about their bodies. "We're not trying to have bodies for society, like Kate Moss. We have big butts."

The social skeleton look had vanished. The athletic look had arrived. But the change indicated more than a trendy fashion statement. Muscularity—and a body that consumes enough nutrition to sustain it—became the expression of a new understanding of what it means to be "feminine." Physical competence was becoming central to female self-esteem. As champion volleyball player Gabrielle Reece wrote in *Big Girl in the Middle*, the only statement women used to be comfortable taking over the top was "I'm sexy." "Why not say, instead, 'I have a big intellect and bold spirit—and I can kick your ass'?" she asks.

Why not indeed! Young women of the nineties watched, thrilled, as old physical stereotypes were smashed and pioneers of female bravado like Reece demonstrated striking confidence and physical prowess. Girls began following their new, athletic role models the way groupies used to follow rock stars. Warming up to pitch a game for the Duluth Dukes, Ila Borders, the first woman to join a pro men's baseball team, prompted the chanting of thousands of girls in the stands: "I-la, I-la, I-la."

"Ila is my favorite, no question," a thirteen-year-old girl told a *New York Times* reporter, "because she shows you can just do it."

Shows, that is, that you can do it even if you're a girl. Women in erstwhile men's sports are coming to be seen not only as "normal," but as a source of pride. "Ila is going to make the big leagues," said the owner of Ila's team, the Duluth Dukes, whose own daughter wrestled on her high school boys' team. "She's going to be like Jackie Robinson being the first black man to play in the majors, or Chuck Yeager being the first to break the sound barrier."

Today's young women are developing ways of standing up—with their bodies, if need be—for their rights. It isn't brawn that allows them to do that, but something far more important: a psychological stamina that comes from *physical self-esteem*. Female strength, courage, and competitiveness are providing women a new way to live in the world. We are shedding timidity and learning to stand up for ourselves. We are accomplishing a new way of feeling secure that's rooted in our own agility, timing, and physical strength. And that is going to create social change.

When she began in-line skating on the streets of Manhattan, Rachel told me of a technique she used for seeing what the traffic coming up behind her was doing. She constantly checked the side-view mirrors sticking out from trucks. "I'm learning to take my space, Mom," she said. The very idea of her zinging through city traffic was disturbing; still, I thought I knew what she meant by taking her space. Just walk down any busy street during the workweek if you don't think men are determined to dominate public spaces. The veering to one side as a man and a woman are about to collide on a crowded sidewalk is nearly always done by the woman.

Men in the streets will not move out of the way to prevent a collision; they *expect* women to. Presumably it's a badge of their superior status. "One thing is clear: woman's body language speaks eloquently, though silently, of her subordinate status in a hierarchy of gender," feminist scholar Sandra Lee Bartky has written. And so it was for my generation and those before me.

Today, however, women are communicating with a more aggressive body language. One woman in her twenties told me that when she walks around the streets of New York, "I've stopped getting out of men's way. I just let them bang into me if they're going to." The woman in such a scenario will be jolted, but so will the man. "At the last possible moment, most men will move," the woman reported. "But some don't."

Is women's becoming more socially and economically powerful the reason men are playing the bully more flagrantly than ever? It's as if, in the anonymity of the city's canyons, men feel free to push women around, whereas they may not be able to dominate at home or in the office. Navigating city sidewalks, in any event, has become like coed ice hockey without the protective equipment.

A defensive backlash is occurring among men, whose power is threatened by the increasing legal and economic independence of women. It can be seen in men's growing "football mentality" and their homophobic response to strong female athletes. Yet there are signs that men's subtle, and not so subtle, physical one-upping of women doesn't have the same power over us it used to. Women of Rachel's generation are developing ways of standing up—with their bodies, if need be—for their rights. And getting them!

Our new understanding of what women are physically capable of challenges old ideas about the very nature of men and women—ideas that have been used to establish, and maintain, a belief in men's physical superiority. That physicality was supposedly what made men self-sufficient—and women not. It was what made men *necessary* to women, not just for love and intimacy and friendship, but for their very survival. The weakness of women was the rationale for a belief in their total inferiority—physical, mental, emotional.

The good news is that women are beginning to appreciate their bodies for their superb functionality and for the pleasure they provide. They are beginning to feel stronger in the streets and on rural country roads, able to defend themselves, and as a consequence live lives whose horizons are broader. They are experiencing a sexiness that comes not from being viewed as an object but from physical vitality.

But there are changes that have to take place if women and girls are to become strong, powerful, and physically self-confident. To this day, girls are being kept from developing their full physical potential by teachers and parents who do not recognize the harm that they're doing. Many girls are shrinking their bodies—*avoiding* physical development—in their effort to be "feminine" and acceptable to boys. By the same token, most adult women still keep themselves unnaturally weak and thus physically vulnerable—victims of men's presumed greater strength. The price they pay for clinging to an old model of femininity is great: with dwarfed development and unnecessary dependence on men, women hang back from physical freedom, constrict their lives, and sometimes even lose them!

This book is about freeing our minds of unnecessary fear and taking our space in the world, and about the history of constraint that has made this so difficult to accomplish. It is about a hidden agenda of keeping women in their place by keeping them believing in their weakness. And it is about the unrecognized backlash taking place as women have crashed through one barrier after another erected against their opportunities for physical development over the last century—until, like the fact of the emperor's nudity, the suspicion begins to arise that maybe, when all is said and done, there *is* no appreciable strength difference between men and women. Maybe, like the previously assumed difference in men's and women's intellectual capabilities, it has all been a question of unequal access to opportunity and training. New methods of performance assessment, which I write about later in the book, are clearly raising this possibility.

But this much is certain: the concept of female frailty, with its roots in nineteenth-century medicine, has had long-term damaging effects on women's health and on their social and professional status. Drawing on studies in motor development, performance assessment, and sports physiology, I will show how, by *keeping themselves physically undeveloped,* girls and women have fulfilled the myth of the weaker sex.

Until women are able to experience strength, endurance, and *pleasure* in their bodies, whatever social freedom we achieve will be limited. We will withdraw from physical challenge, coddling ourselves in a misguided belief in our frailty. As adolescents, we will begin the retreat from our sexuality, hiding from it out of fear of being harmed or exploited. We will live out our lives as if our bodies needed protection.

And haven't we done that, while our bones turned porous and our fear of male physical power grew to delusional proportions?

The psychological effects of the frailty myth are more compromising, even, than the physical. It was recognizing this in a gut way that made so many women cry when they watched the World Cup soccer finals on television in the summer of 1999. It wasn't just the physical brilliance of the players that stunned us, although certainly that was thrilling. Here were women who had not allowed themselves to be compromised—women who had stopped the frailty myth in its tracks—headed it, as it were. When I watched the semifinal game between the United States and Brazil, I was at home with my daughter-in-law and my thirteen-year-old grandson. Everything about this spectacle was mind-blowing, including the Monistat advertisement blinking on the scoreboard high above the bleachers. A treatment for vaginal yeast infections up there for all to see: to me, this said everything about the changed view of women's bodies. The huge crowd, the thousands upon thousands of young girls, the dads in the stadium cheering just as hard as their daughters—it was almost too much to take in.

But it wasn't until the final game, the following week, against China, that the full impact of what was going on hit me. That game with Brazil was no fluke. These women, who'd been training and playing together for almost a decade, were representative of a change that was culture-bending: women were being given recognition—international recognition—for their physical prowess. For their ability to outthink and outmove the opposition. For their speed, agility, aggression, endurance, and grace under pressure. Then it came to me as a kind of physical shock and thrill: I never thought I'd see this in my lifetime.

A revolutionary freedom has charged the lives of my daughters and their peers, and they are causing the rest of us to look at our lives and bodies differently. Women of all ages have begun trading in the crimped "femininity" of the past for a bold new female bravado. Today, women in their eighties are running marathons. As the different beliefs supporting the frailty myth shatter, one after the other, the change will not be trifling. It will alter the way women walk on the earth.

The Frailty Myth

ONE

The Frailty Myth

A hundred years ago, women were pushed backward in a very particular way. Just as they were beginning to demand education and political and economic power, they were stripped of the power of their bodies. Just as they began to get ideas about fighting for justice, they were required, with all the persuasion of a moral movement, to cultivate frailness. Nineteenth-century women were given to believe that weakness was their natural condition. It was a total gaslight job. There wasn't a plot. No single group could be held accountable. What made the concept so powerful was the influential mix—the various groups whose interests came together into a single compelling philosophy about woman's purpose on the planet. That philosophy—some scholars have dubbed it "the frailty myth"—became the rope that restrained women from developing physically, restricted them to small half movements, isolated them in rooms hidden from the sun, and threatened them with the worst of all punishments should they refuse to comply: the loss of their capacity to bear children.

The theory behind the frailty myth was this: Women could not be allowed to follow their own pursuits—physical or mental—

because every ounce of energy they could generate was needed for maintaining their reproductive processes. No option was offered in this matter. In the nineteenth century female confinement was considered a social necessity. Women owed it to the next generation, and the generations thereafter, to cultivate nothing but their fertility—not mind, not artistry, and certainly not body. This became known as "the cult of true womanhood." Educators, psychologists, churchmen, and physicians—particularly obstetricians and gynecologists—were its chief proponents. Men were certain that if women weren't controlled, the very species (or "race," as they called it then) was at risk. They drummed up a role for women, an idea called "femininity," an appropriate "character," an appropriate "look"—and with all of these, they persuaded women that their reason for being was essentially heroic and thus worth giving up a lot for.

For years my image of Victorian women was narrowed by stereotypes. I had been taught that women of the late 1800s were frail, overprotected creatures who didn't have much of a life. Everything they did seemed to require undue effort. As a young woman reading about Victorian "ladies," I could only imagine trying to swim in the ocean weighed down by wet bloomers and baggy blouses. The daily struggle with corsets and merry widows, the attempt to walk, much less run, in huge skirts and hats—it seemed, to my generation, pathetic. Those women had lived their lives according to bizarre rules, and courtesies, and restraint. Rags were used for mopping up menstrual blood. Sex was a joke because Victorian men didn't know the first thing about the parts of women's bodies that give pleasure. It was hard to see how the Gay Nineties could have been all that frolicsome.

Mine was, of course, a glib view of those times. To think about actual flesh-and-blood women living in that way—to contemplate the hard, merciless doctors' couches on which they lay, trying to make sense of their ailments—would have required more emotional imagination than I possessed. I chose not to relate. It was the same way I'd distanced myself from my mother's history, thinking of her life as too strangely different from my own for us to have much in common. Hers was another time; it might as well have been another country. I wanted to be safe from my mother's rural Nebraskan history, her fifteen siblings, her diabetes-ravaged mother, the farm that failed, she and her sisters were given to believe, because there weren't enough boys to do the heavy work. Because I preferred to think that my mother and I were not quite the same under the skin—just as I viewed those strange Victorian ladies—I lived for years without knowing important things, things that would have strengthened my appreciation of my own womanhood and allowed me to see myself as belonging to a family—not only a personal family, but the historical family of my gender.

Old habits die hard. In tracing the frailty myth back to the nineteenth century, I found myself at first wanting to gloss over what I was starting to see: an inevitable connection between the women at the end of that century and women of our day—a continuum of actual physical oppression in which all of us had been kept down. I wanted to be able to name the final decades of the nineteenth century as the flowering of the frailty myth and move on. But as I began to dig further into the journals, and studies, and diaries of those women, it became clear that something fundamental to growth and development had been taken from them and that the loss was not only theirs, but ours. More and more I began to see that the frailty myth hadn't died, it had only wedged its way a little further underground. I wanted to comprehend the forces keeping women from their bodies, their physical strength and spirit.

The Frailty Myth is about the social domination of women's bodies. It is about girls' and women's restricted physical development. It is about the attempt to keep them feeling as doctors, educators, and even religious leaders have intended them to feel: physically limited. Unable to run long distances. Unable to play five sets of tennis. And even more important, unable to raise a barn or (once it was invented) fix a car. Unable to go for a walk in the woods unaccompanied. Unable to exist, in short, without the muscular heft and presumed physical assistance of the other half of the species.

For centuries women have been shackled to a perception of themselves as weak and ineffectual. This perception has been nothing less than the emotional and cognitive equivalent of having our whole bodies bound. The myth of women's frailty has been so systematically entrenched that it could fairly be called a hoax. But a hoax is a conscious deceit, while myths are believed in as truth. What propels them is complicated and invisible. The frailty myth was driven by men's repressed wish to preserve dominion. To make the myth viable, society constructed elaborate ways of keeping women cut off from their strength; of turning them into physical victims and teaching them that victimhood was all they could aspire to.

Before Frailty

Historically, strength has been encouraged in women only when the economy needs it—during wars, while the men are away, or when helping to pioneer new lands. But as feminist scholarship in the past quarter century has uncovered, women in fact lived far more complicated and demanding lives over the course of the first millennium than you might imagine if you looked at the picture of "true womanhood" to which women were restricted in the nineteenth century. It was striking to learn, when it was first published in the late 1990s, that in Paleolithic times women weren't sequestered in caves, sweeping up stone dust and suckling their infants, as male anthropologists had always suggested. That particular view of Ice Age females' physical ability was the result of certain questions *not* being asked, according to Olga Soffer, one of the world's leading authorities on Ice Age hunters and gatherers. Soffer's research and that of other feminist scholars in the 1990s led to the discovery that Paleolithic women were strong and physically active, and provided up to 70 percent of family nutrition. And they weren't just gathering nuts and berries. Paleolithic women hunted small animals with bows and arrows and used nets to trap larger ones. Even the children participated in these hunts. Women and children "set snares, laid spring traps, sighted game and participated in animal drives and surrounds—forms of hunting that endangered neither young mothers nor their offspring," reports Heather Pringle in an article in *Discovery*, "New Women of the Ice Age." "They even hunted, on occasion, with the projectile points traditionally deemed men's weapons."

The new research opens to question the idea that women and families, from the beginning of human time, relied on male strength for their survival. Even the much vaunted killing of very large animals for meat, long associated with Ice Age man's superiority, was rare, owing to the sheer difficulty of slaying a six-thousand-pound pachyderm with a short-range spear, Soffer explains. "If one of these Upper Paleolithic guys killed a mammoth, and occasionally they did, they probably didn't stop talking about it for ten years."

Women's strength was appreciated and made use of in later societies as well. In the Minoan civilization on the Greek island of Crete (this flourished between 6000 B.C. and 1450 B.C.), bull vaulting was popular among aristocratic youth. Only recently have we learned that men and women worked as bull-vaulting teams.

They actually took turns, one grasping the horn of a bull to steady it while the other somersaulted over its back. "The equal partnership between women and men that seems to have characterized Minoan society," Riane Eisler wrote in *The Chalice and the Blade*, "is perhaps nowhere so vividly illustrated as in these sacred bull-games, where young women and men performed together and entrusted their lives to each other." It may sound apocryphal, but many urns and other artifacts show women's participation in bull vaulting. Yet we never heard about these Amazonian women until recently.

In ancient Greek and Roman times women hunted, rode horseback, swam, ran, and drove chariots. In Sparta, whose social organization was not typical of Greek city-states, men lived apart from women in military barracks until they turned thirty. Forced to live on their own, females became thoroughly independent. Not surprisingly, young females were encouraged to develop strength. Spartan girls were taught to foot-race, wrestle, and throw discus and javelin.

In the Middle Ages women often showed athletic courage. They jousted at one another with lances, on horseback. Some were fine archers. Others competed in a forerunner of the modern game of darts that involved throwing eighteen-inch projectiles. But however skilled they might become, they never got to the elite levels of competition. Occasionally they were invited to keep score. Often they made awards presentations. Sometimes they *were* the awards. But they could never know the thrill of victory because any important contest was closed to them. Even at the tournaments, so central a part of medieval life, women were "little more than cheerleaders for chivalry," as two sports historians have put it. This exclusion of women whenever big athletic competitions were organized continued up to and including the modern Olympics.

But left to their own devices, women happily threw themselves into the competitive fray. Roberta J. Park, who's written widely on the history of sport, says that women in the eighteenth century had prizefights with one another. In an odd kind of marital minuet, husbands and wives staged fights against other couples, using swords or quarterstaves and competing for cash prizes. Even wrestling had the odd female combatant. Margaret Evans of North Wales was reported to be such a powerful wrestler that even at the age of seventy, "few young men dared to try a fall with her," Park tells us.

In the 1700s the most popular activities of women were running and racewalking. In 1765 a young woman completed seventy-two miles from Blencogo, Scotland, to Newcastle in two days. It was worth a mention in *Sporting* magazine, in 1806, that a woman racewalker in her forties was "victorious" over a younger man. In fact, in hindsight, women had begun to mark their turf as champions of endurance marathons. Women's individual achievements at the time included walking for a month with less than ten or fifteen minutes of continuous rest, walking and running more than four hundred miles in six consecutive days, and defeating all men contestants in endurance marathons.

Women's walking races were "significantly *more* frequent than those for men," according to one researcher. In the 1820s British and Scottish girls and women between the ages of seven and eighty-five were gaining money for their families and public notoriety for themselves with pedestrian races. During the 1850s women in New York and in the Midwest performed exhibitions in saloons, walking back and forth for hours along wooden planks measuring fifteen to thirty feet. In the late 1800s the sport gained even more in popularity as media coverage of women athletes increased. Between 1876 and 1881 women's walking and running events took place on sawdust ovals in major cities throughout the United States. Reports Dahn Shaulis (University of Nevada), who made a study of nineteenth-century women's endurance efforts, "In music halls, indoor arenas, and national guard armories around the country, women walked against men, participated in multi-day women-only races, and sometimes walked solo, to break endurance records." Paying crowds of hundreds, and sometimes several thousand, watched and gambled on the women walkers. Journalists noted that to gain large crowds, women athletes were forced to attempt increasingly difficult feats, such as walking four hundred meters every fifteen minutes for thirty or forty consecutive days. Religious preachers publicly condemned pedestrian sport as "evil" and "coarse." In 1879 the Brooklyn Women's Temperance Union protested against both women walking on Sundays and the alcohol and tobacco use and gambling that took place among their spectators. These races were soon ordered closed by the New York City Police Department. By 1880 the "pedestrian industry" had all but collapsed. Schools and universities forbade females from endurance walking and running. And the modern Olympic Games excluded women from running events until 1928.

Not all physical feats were pursued for recreational purposes. In America in the 1700s, women performed backbreaking labor in helping to pioneer a new country. Many "became part of the movement to stake out new farms and towns in the western back countries," writes historian Nancy Struna, "and this meant clearing trees and planting fields and few neighbors." In the South, developing plantations required of women efforts that often were equal to men's. Mrs. Francis Jones, who with her husband carved a plantation out of the wilds of Virginia, stunned the official auditor of property boundaries when he saw how strong she was. Yet, he put in his records, she still retained that lovely female daintiness men so feared strong women would lose. Though she showed "nothing of ruggedness or Immodesty in her carriage," the auditor wrote in a 1710 report, Mrs. Francis Jones not only worked in the field, but would "carry a gunn in the woods and kill dear . . . catch and tye hogg, knock down beeves with an ax and perform the most manfull Exercises."

Following the shift from agrarianism to industry that formed the Industrial Revolution, millions of women and children moved to the cities, where they performed menial and frequently dangerous tasks in factories and mills. Again, and notably, these were times when women's physical capacities were valued by the economy—especially in light of the fact that they could be paid a fraction of what men got for doing the same work.

Then there is the sketchy and generally discounted history of women as soldiers. The ability to do battle has long been considered the ultimate proof of men's superiority and women's need to depend on them. Yet when times require it, females are employed as fierce defenders of their nations. Some, like Joan of Arc, eventually become heroines. Others remain hidden once their day is over. In the eighteenth and nineteenth centuries, women in the elite female troops of the West African kingdom of Dahomey were trained from an early age to handle weapons, be strong, and withstand suffering. "They lusted for battle, rushed into it with blood-curdling yells, reveled in it, and fought with fury and valor, seemingly immune to fear," Stanley B. Alpern, a British historian, wrote in 1999. In preparation for battle, the Dahomey amazons went into the woods for days at a time to learn to withstand hunger, thirst, wounds, and wild animals. They were "as solidly muscled as black male warriors" and demonstrated "superior muscular strength." Their weapons were muskets, machetes, and clubs, and they rarely used shields.

The Dahomey amazons, who were celibate—a key, perhaps, to their fierce independence, if not their very existence as a warrior clan—died off in the early 1900s.

Such women, the British writer Antonia Fraser tells us, often thought of themselves as "honorary males." Being regarded as men was, for them, the supreme compliment. It meant they were "strong, brave, resolute, fearless, disciplined, loyal, reliable—virtues that females were supposed to lack."

Those very qualities can be found today in African women in Eritrea, who fight side by side with men. In the long-drawn-out war with Ethiopia, every body is needed. All Eritrean girls learn to handle weapons and study military tactics and survival techniques. By the time they're old enough to be on the front, they're carrying bombs, machine guns, and rocket-propelled grenades with the best of them. Young Eritrean women today have powerful role models in their mothers, who fought in the thirty-year war for independence from Ethiopia that was won in 1991. "We liberated the country. Now you are the ones who have to defend it," the mothers have taught them. Today women soldiers in Eritrea consider themselves to be taking their country further on the road to sexual equality. After their mothers' war, females were able to enter the National Assembly and other political positions for the first time. The new ambassador to the European Union and the ministers of justice and labor are all women. It's harder to prevent women from gaining social power once they've put their bodies on the line.

Behold the Cult of Invalidism

During the times when society *doesn't* need women to labor, or to prevail against enemies, its entire attitude shifts. Strength and courage and the ability to take risks suddenly become unfeminine. *Frailty* becomes feminine. Physical prowess belongs to men alone. Such a weakening of women occurred after the Industrial Revolution, which had had a withering effect on men's identity. Once machines could do the work of manufacture and agriculture, physical strength became less valued. To salvage men's failing sense of dominance, women were encouraged to scale back their own physical development, turning themselves into restricted creatures "with relaxed, half-formed limbs," as English feminist Mary Wollstonecraft wrote. In her famous treatise at the turn of the nineteenth century, *A Vindication of the Rights of Woman*, Wollstonecraft lamented the stunting of girls. In British boarding schools they were not allowed to play freely as boys were, "but were made to walk stupidly backwards and forwards on the same broad walkway, holding up their heads and turning out their toes, with shoulders braced back."

One young narrator of an 1899 autobiographical novel spoke with sad envy of boys, and it hadn't to do with their penises:

> *The boys were lucky. They did gymnastics. They exercised. They were allowed to romp around freely in the streets and squares. Snow and ice was theirs in winter, the lake in summer.*
>
> *We girls didn't do gymnastics, we didn't swim, we didn't row. We weren't allowed to have snowball fights, not even to skate. Remember, the knitted sock was still in its heyday.*

The girls were home knitting the socks. The boys were outdoors skating in them.

Wollstonecraft was convinced that physical education is as important as mental. By not being allowed to develop "the strength of body on which strength of mind in great measure depends," girls and young women, she wrote, were being made weak. Unnaturally weak. That is, they were actually being *kept* from full physical development. And who even knew what full development was for them? Not until females were given the same opportunities as males to develop strength, this early feminist observed, would anyone know precisely "how far the natural superiority of man extends." (She was being ironic, of course, with her use of the word *natural*.)

In the 1800s sport was used as a hefty wedge to separate the weak from the strong, the proletariat from the elite. Boys in England's prestigious public schools were supposed to make a smashing show at rugby if they expected to become economically powerful men. As the century unrolled, sport played a larger and larger role in maintaining the gender hierarchy: Men were warriors who could absorb all manner of brutality on the playing field and come back for more. Women were too wan even to think about it. When organized team sports emerged, women were pushed out of the picture, restricted to horseback riding, bowling, and the occasional game of tennis, in which they hobbled about in long skirts and tight corsets.

It's hard to overstate the influence of medicine on the myth of female frailty. Protecting pubertal girls from too much mental and physical activity became a major campaign among physicians of the nineteenth century. In a widely quoted 1879 medical textbook, Thomas Emmet advised that girls "spend the year before and two years after puberty at rest." Each menstrual period should be endured in "the recumbent position," until their systems could adjust to "the new order of life."

Another male medical writer advised adolescent girls to avoid exercise altogether. Sufficient strength could be gained in the kitchen, the washroom, and the gardens—"nature's gymnasia for adolescent girls," as he so nimbly put it. (Well they might acquaint themselves with whatever gymnasia they could, for by adulthood they would need every ounce of strength they could muster for the "homely gymnastics," as housework was called.) Girls' "immature tissues and organs" were considered peculiarly unstable and vulnerable to injury. Fatigue of any part of the body could lead to fatigue of the whole.

Should bones grow ahead of muscles, strain could occur. Should heart growth lag, girls could weaken and suffer fainting spells.

Sport also carried, for women, the disturbing potential of "masculinization." Too much activity "of a masculine character causes the female body to become more like that of a man," one health educator proclaimed, and he wasn't just concerned about their appearance. Excessive exercise would have a negative effect on everything, not least, he wrote, "the genital organs, for they tend to decay."

It's hardly surprising that girls retreated to the drawing room, preferring to train themselves in needlework and other feminine arts rather than lend themselves to the possibility of genital decay. Yet, not surprisingly, persuaded to quit running and jumping and climbing trees, Victorian girls soon began to show signs of constitutional weakness. Suddenly medicine did an about-face, and became concerned about the "enfeeblement so common among pubescent girls," as one doctor put it. He proposed that girls beef up their stamina by "romping with beanbags and hoops and bathing in cold water." Too fragile for developing much more than "grace" (oddly put forth as a health goal for females of the time), girls nevertheless needed to prepare themselves for the onslaught of motherhood. Quiet walks and drives and boating, these were the "sports" for nineteenth-century girls and women—except during menstruation, when breathing was about as vigorous an activity as they could permit themselves. Then all possible precautions were prescribed to prevent girls from overdoing. Everyone got into the act—physicians (including female physicians), families, educational institutions. At Vassar girls were "positively forbidden" to do anything physical during the first two days of their periods, including going up and down stairs. Parents, in fact, were warned against letting their girls attend schools more than two stories high, lest during their menstrual periods they destroy themselves getting to the third floor.

Women who allowed themselves to become overly active could "dislodge" the uterus, "robbing future generations," as one doctor put it. This was the noble concern with which medicine legitimized its insistence on managing the female body. The possibility of vigorous physical effort taxing men's ability to produce and father children was, of course, never raised. Only women were required to sacrifice their physical development for the greater glory of the species. It was considered, historian Patricia Vertinsky tells us, "the price for having a female body."

Male organizers and promoters discouraged women from participating in games and sports. They withheld adequate facilities and programs, ridiculed women's athletic attempts, and threatened those who protested with the specter of "race suicide." If women put all their energy into vigorous sport, they would undermine not only their own health but "the future of the white race." Those in power didn't have to worry about the ruin of black women's reproductive organs, since at that time blacks were even more thoroughly excluded from organized sport than were women.

By the second half of the nineteenth century, exercise for all women, not just schoolgirls, was being carefully monitored. Physicians prescribed special regimens to keep females from wearing themselves out while still allowing them to become sufficiently robust to cope with giving birth and managing children (a tricky balance to strike, one imagines). From the time she was an adolescent until she turned forty, a woman could count on needing 20 percent of her energy for reproductive functions—menstruation, pregnancy, lactation. The Victorians believed that a calculable amount of energy was dispersed each time a woman menstruated and each time she gave birth.

It's important to note that these doctors and writers were convinced there was a scientific basis for their views. Animal studies showed males to have a highly active metabolism (catabolic), which evolutionists believed led to their larger brains. It was the female's biological fate to be inclined "to sluggishness and passivity (anabolic) and possess a more quiescent metabolism with less variation and a tendency toward emotional and irrational behavior," according to two extremely influential evolutionists. Patrick Geddes and J. Arthur Thompson, in their book, *The Evolution of Sex,* claimed that the hierarchical distinction between the sexes (the distinction, that is, whereby men were superior to women) "was based firmly upon anabolic-catabolic biology which could not be reversed." Women were fated to inferiority forever.

Many female doctors joined their male colleagues in promoting physical restriction for female patients. "Most women are able to get enough exercise just moving around the household," Dr. Elizabeth Scovil advised in her popular *Preparation for Motherhood Manual,* "and a long walk doesn't bring sufficient compensation for the fatigue it causes."

Ideas about women's bodies became increasingly peculiar. One doctor wrote, in *Popular Science Monthly,* that at puberty "the pelvis alters its shape . . . and the effect . . . is to bring the knees closer together, and to produce a weak-kneed condition and awkward running gait peculiar to women." (Apparently it never occurred to anyone that weak knees and awkward gait might be due mainly to lack of exercise.) Physicians on both sides of the Atlantic promoted a theory of menstrual disability that sharpened the stereotype of women as the weaker sex. Eventually women themselves came to view menstruation as disabling, if not actually pathological.

Yet at the same time as mainstream society was telling women to stay home and, effectively, eat bonbons, a group of moralistic health reformers had started pushing in the opposite direction. They tried to shame the "Misses Languid" of fashionable society for being out of shape. Talk about a double bind. Those maligned Victorian women were damned if they did and damned if they didn't! One of the earliest and most influential reformers was Catharine Beecher (sister of Harriet Beecher Stowe, author of *Uncle Tom's Cabin*). Beecher invented a form of calisthenics, wrote a textbook on it, and founded a girls' school in Hartford, Connecticut, in 1824, but she was no feminist mover and shaker. Beecher believed in women's subordination to men and the importance of their role as homemakers. The exercise system she developed was meant to correct female form and better fit women for work in the home. Beecher's gymnastic system was typical of nineteenth-century efforts to give females a sense of importance while at the same time keeping them in their place.

A century after British feminist Mary Wollstonecraft raised the first flag of doubt about men's physical superiority, an American feminist took up the cause of female physical development. Charlotte Perkins Gilman, born in 1860 in Rhode Island, had an avid interest in physical development from the time she was very young. She was still an adolescent when she persuaded the local gymnastics teacher to start a female-only gymnasium. She spent hours each day there, lifting weights, performing gymnastics routines, and running a seven-minute mile.

Gilman was also ahead of her time in wanting not to collapse into a dull, narrow existence once she married. Physical strength, she somehow intuited, might help her in that regard. It would turn out that she was prone to dark moods, which may have been another reason she took to daily exercise. Eventually she married and had a child, after which she went into a tailspin of depression. Again she returned to exercise, hoping to improve her outlook on life. She would go to the gym each morning at six. She also liked rowing and amazed her husband with her ability to row over four miles in under fifty minutes without tiring. Yet something clearly was amiss. Though by now she was consciously trying to fend off her mood dips with vigilant exercise (a technique used, as well, by late-twentieth-century females), no matter how hard she worked out, she eventually would succumb again. It seemed—and probably was, given what we know now from neuroscience about mood disorders—beyond her control. Gilman in any event would suffer episodes of severe depression throughout her life. But no treatment was ever as appalling to her—or as characteristic of the way physicians were "treating" the liberated "new woman"—as the so-called rest cure prescribed for her by S. Weir Mitchell, who enjoyed a reputation as the most prominent neurologist in America.

The rest cure—and this was becoming an increasingly popular prescription—was an extreme regimen of immobility designed specifically for females. Easing whatever symptoms a woman presented to her doctor required "resocializing" her to give up her ambitions and content herself with solely domestic obligations, according to Patricia Vertinsky, a historian noted for her studies of medicine's effects on the socialization of nineteenth-century women. A nervous "new woman" was sent to bed and not allowed to sit up, use her hands, or read. The "treatment" lasted up to eight weeks. Imagine being deprived of reading and writing, activity of any kind, and visits from friends.

Charlotte Perkins Gilman's story is often told in feminist writing because it so starkly reflects the kind of control medicine had over women's lives—control that diminished only gradually during the twentieth century. Women in Gilman's day would do whatever doctors told them to do, no matter how restricting or even downright insulting it might have seemed. Dr. Mitchell told Gilman to go home, give up all physical activity and social contacts, and concentrate on her domestic life. "Have your child with you all the time. . . . Lie down an hour after each meal. Have but two hours of intellectual life a day. And never touch pen, brush, or pencil for as long as you live," he told his patient. Gilman followed these directions for months, but her depression held fast.

Dr. Mitchell had plenty of support for his restrictive prescriptions. Medical convention at the time attributed women's physical and emotional complaints to the greater freedom they were beginning to gain. Increasingly, male doctors built practices around the plentiful supply of women whose menstruation, childbearing, and menopause made them prone to "nervous irritability." The medical profession was acutely aware of its power. At a meeting of the Obstetrical Society in 1867, one physician pontificated, "As a body who practice among women, we have constituted ourselves, as it were, the guardians of their interests, and—in many cases—the custodians of their honor. We are, in fact, the stronger and they the weaker. They are obliged to believe all that we tell them and we, therefore, may be said to have them at our mercy."

Eventually Charlotte Perkins Gilman would write a story about a woman who went mad because of the idleness enforced upon her by a doctor who had her at his mercy. Inspired by her disabling experience with Dr. Mitchell's rest cure, Gilman's first book, *The Yellow Wallpaper*, became famous. Everything Gilman ever wrote afterward would emphasize the importance of physical mobility for women. Her most important work, *Women and Economics*, raged against patriarchal restriction of women's intellectual and physical development and attracted attention on both sides of the Atlantic. She became a leading intellectual in the early women's movement. One can only speculate how long the "cult of invalidism," as historians came to call it, would have kept us frail if a scattering of feminists hadn't begun a movement against the system—women who had the vision to *see* it as a system and who recognized what a disabling effect it had on them.

A terrifyingly influential part of that system was the eugenics movement. One of its chief proponents was American psychologist G. Stanley Hall, an educational big shot, a writer of books and papers, a giver of speeches in high places. A founder of so-called child study, Hall claimed he had questionnaires, surveys, *facts* with which to back up his proclamations. And proclaim he did. In a 1903 address to the National Education Association, an assembly of public school leaders, Hall not only supported the idea that women's chief duty was to breed, he took it a good step further. Through a national program of physical training and a policy of selective breeding, he announced, women would be able to ratchet things up a notch on the evolutionary ladder, but first they had to turn themselves into "the fittest possible instrument for racial improvement." Getting them to this point was a huge responsibility. Neither doctors nor ministers, in Hall's opinion, were equipped to help women pull off this bit of evolutionary magic. The task fell to him and others of his ilk. Only the experienced psychologist, imbued with "genetic sense," and understanding the importance of health and muscle culture, could guide the physical development and education of the female toward "the constraint and joy of pure obligation." In return, woman had something wonderful in store. Her role would be special—in fact, nothing less than "the conduit through which the 'mansoul' might some day become a 'superman' in a 'superstate.'" Could women be expected to regulate their own health practices in this transcendent endeavor? Certainly not. It was the scientist, the psychologist, and the pedagogist, said Hall, who had "first to know, then to control," the methods whereby females could produce a new, more advanced race of men. National supremacy was a big propellant here. It would go, Hall was quite sure, "to that country that is most fecund [for] . . . the nation that breeds best, be it Mongol, Slav, Teuton or Saxon, will rule the world in the future."

The medical control of women was so solidly entrenched that almost another century had to pass before the frailty myth was upended. Even in the 1950s and 1960s mothers were warning their daughters to take it easy during menstruation. The month before I went off to college, my mother took me to the beach for a little vacation, just the two of us. It was a lovely idea, marred only by her nagging me not to go into the ocean because the water would chill me (I was having my period), setting me up, she warned, for a lifetime of terrible cramps. Of course I rebelled and took to the waves. My first period at college was so bad, I thought my mother had put a curse on me—or worse, that she might have been right.

Simply put, women in the nineteenth century and well into the twentieth were socialized "to see their bodies and view their natural functions in peculiar ways," Vertinsky concludes. They assessed the risks and benefits of physical activity in the same way Victorian doctors, and psychologists, and educators did. "Women became subject to a system intended to produce compliant beings," she believes, "and the methods that encouraged compliance began in childhood."

The Masculinity Crisis

"For the good of the race" was the rationale Hall and others used to disguise a fear too disturbing for society to acknowledge: that if women were not prevented from developing themselves physically, men's "masculinity" would be compromised. Masculinity, after all, was a concept just as fragilely contrived as femininity and one that definitely needed bolstering after the Industrial Revolution and the early stages of women's emancipation left men pondering the very point of their existence. In both England and America, changes in work and family, urbanization, and the increasing female domination of schools led to what historians and sociologists today refer to as "a crisis of masculinity." While male identity was in relatively good shape in the early part of the century (geographic expansion and rapid industrial growth "had fueled a virile optimism," as one writer put it), by the mid-1800s urbanization had gotten out of control, crushing farmers and small-business men and robbing males of the manly capacity to provide. Making matters worse was the rise of the women's movement on both sides of the Atlantic. Ambitious, feminist, sexually active, the "new woman" was signaling "the end for men's monopoly of the ballot box, the college classroom, and the professional school." Nineteenth-century notions of male superiority were clearly in jeopardy.

The founding of the Boy Scouts in 1910 was an American effort to "reverse the feared decline in manliness"—a decline the U.S. commissioner of education explained, with a fine appreciation of the centrality to masculinity of physical violence: "The boy in America is not being brought up to punch another boy's head, or to stand having his own punched in a healthy and proper manner. . . . There is a strange and indefinable air coming over the men; a tendency toward a common . . . sexless tone of thought."

By "sexless" the commissioner meant genderless. Thinking itself was losing its vital masculine edge, as men fell into a state of intellectual flaccidity long considered "feminine." Athletics not only sharpened men intellectually but were thought to strengthen "character." Through sports men were expected to develop "courage, manliness, and self-control." As, one by one, old bastions of differentiation—social, economic, intellectual—began to crumble, at least men had their physical strength to fall back on. Size, muscle power, and the courage to pit body against body in sport were all male with a capital "M." But by the end of the twentieth century those distinctions, too, would go down the tubes.

In the course of attempting to refire their faltering nineteenth-century egos, men even tried bulking up God so they could identify with the Biggest of the Big. (After all, women couldn't identify with God, could they?) A movement called "muscular Christianity" transformed the image of Jesus "from a beatific, delicate, soft-spoken champion of the poor into a muscle-bound he-man whose message encouraged the strong to dominate the weak." G. Stanley Hall, you may be sure, supported the muscular Christianity movement. "We are soldiers of Christ, strengthening our muscles not against a foreign foe but against sin within and without us," Hall proclaimed grandly in an article on Christianity and physical culture.

British and American proponents of the muscular Christianity movement equated manhood with stoicism, courage, tolerance of pain, and quick thinking under pressure. Men began lifting weights, which soon gave birth to the "he-man" mystique. If women were determined to act like men, men would up the ante: a woman could *never* be a he-man. A man could *always* develop more muscle. And this muscle would serve as a veiled threat, a reminder to any who questioned male supremacy that might makes right. And men will always have more might.

In the midst of all this social focus on male physicality, the understanding of women's health was absurdly primitive, especially considering this was only one hundred years ago. Women themselves possessed little knowledge of the workings of their bodies—their physiology, even their sexuality. What information existed was firmly in the grip of male doctors. Often they didn't trust these doctors, particularly when it came to gynecological problems, and opted to keep their illnesses untreated rather than expose themselves—literally and metaphorically. Finally, the male doctors' insistence upon control, in combination with their insensitive and overbearing treatment of women, caused women to

rebel. An 1877 article by Mary Putnam Jacobi won Harvard's prestigious Bolyston Medical Prize (with her name removed!) by
demonstrating empirically that there was nothing inherent in menstruation that made periodic rest necessary for most women.
Women were getting the picture. Many accused the male medical
establishment of "using professional authority to repress women
and curtail their activity by exaggerating, prolonging, and even encouraging their ailments, real or imaginary," Patricia Vertinsky
writes in *The Eternally Wounded Woman,* her examination of medicine and nineteenth-century females.

The trap of the frailty myth was peculiarly like that produced by
the institution of slavery, in which slaves were *made* dependent on
their masters and subsequently were assessed as weak-minded and
helpless. Think of medical men as the masters of the late nineteenth
century. You can imagine that they wouldn't want women entering
their domain. But women wanted access to information, and one
way or another they were going to get it.

Individual women had been trying to break into medicine since
the mid-1800s, without, as you might suspect, a great deal of encouragement. In America, Harriett K. Hunt was the first woman to
attempt to become a doctor. She apprenticed herself to physicians
in order to learn, refusing to be deterred after her application was re-
jected twice by Harvard Medical College, in 1847 and 1851. The
first stage of the women's movement was gathering steam. Women
were becoming interested in the possibility of having women doctors
attend to them. At the First Women's Congress, in 1874, Mary Putnam Jacobi rallied interest in the "immense influence" female doctors would have in "dissipating the stupid prejudices which had for
so long concealed from women the general physiological knowledge
which was most important for them to know."

"Stupid prejudices"? Things were beginning to pick up.

Out of Confinement

Late-nineteenth-century feminists and physicians took opposite stances on physical development and women's health, with feminists openly protesting the absurdity of all the constrictions. "Physically rather weaker than men we undoubtedly are," Viscountess Harberton remarked dryly, "but why exaggerate this weakness by literally so tying ourselves up in clothing that the muscles in some parts of the body dwindle till they become useless?" "Rational dress" was the new motto of reformers like Harberton, who complained that long skirts, heavy materials, and corsets not only endangered women's health but made them vulnerable to accidents. Bloomers, knickerbockers, and other bicycling costumes became popular, soon to be abandoned in favor of shortened skirts.

At its peak of popularity in the late 1890s, cycling promised the "new woman" thrilling liberty. "There is a new dawn, a dawn of emancipation, and it is brought about by the cycle," trumpeted an article in *Lady Cyclist* magazine. "Free to wheel, free to spin out into the glorious country, unhampered by chaperon or even more dispiriting male admirer, the young girl of today can feel the real independence of herself, and while she is building up her better constitution, she is developing her better mind."

Bicycling allowed women to get rid of their corsets and strengthen their abdominal muscles. Strong leg muscles, they were now advised, would improve pelvic tone. Even the uterine muscles would shore up, making labor easier. So promised—at least temporarily—the doctors of the day. Suddenly the bicycle could be counted on to "rescue thousands of women who otherwise would have qualified for invalidism," as one physician announced. "Cycling, it appeared, had come along just in time to rehabilitate British and American women,"

Vertinsky comments. But no sooner had the Victorian health police approved bicycling for women than its very popularity created fresh alarm. Once again doctors became worried about women's historical propensity to overdo. They began blaming cycling for spinal deformities and strained hearts. Some even claimed women were too weak to carry their weight on their wrists or sustain their weight on the pedals.

The most vigorous medical debate, of course, had to do with bicycling's effects on women's reproductive capacities. Cycling during menstruation could produce "incalculable harm." Uterine displacement and spinal shock were rueful possibilities. Faulty saddles meant potential damage to perineum and vulva. Abdominal muscles that had grown firm were suddenly viewed as likely to worsen labor, not aid it. Taking the moral high road, doctors expressed concern that friction from the saddle would cause ladies to masturbate.

Another menace of physical exercise was the dread "bicycle face"—strained and grim it was, not at all the "tender and loving gaze" men found so soothing. But by now it was really too late for such dire warnings. Not even fear of bicycle face could counteract the thrilling effects of getting on a bike and taking off. Technology played a role in women's physical emancipation. In 1885 the lower "safety bicycle" replaced the high bicycle with the huge front wheel and gave women the mobility to get about by themselves for the first time. Soon they ditched the confining skirts, put on bloomers, and started really taking off.

It wasn't long before women began pursuing more strenuous activities. In 1890, only two years after the first ascent of Mount Rainier, Fay Fuller became the first woman to climb the peak. Soon after the Sierra Club was founded in 1892, women made up nearly half the club's membership. In 1905 a Sierra Club group that included forty-six women succeeded in climbing Mount Rainier. One by one peaks toppled as women made their first ascents, all duly reported in club journals and popular magazines.

The thrill of exploration had gotten into women's blood. In 1910 the first group of women entered the Grand Canyon, picking their way down a trail called Bright Angel, wearing split skirts they'd rented to accommodate riding mules. Women's new feats of glory were tapping into ancient fears about women who refused to be frail. "Are Athletics Making Girls Masculine?" the *Ladies' Home Journal* asked in 1912. The implication was quite clear: To be "masculine" (that is, to be strong and adventurous) was to risk becoming nonmarriageable.

Even cheerleading, which began in the late 1800s, was considered too rambunctious for females. It actually originated as an activity for males. When women first tried cheerleading, around the time of World War I, they were seen as intruding upon male turf and in danger of becoming "masculinized." By the 1940s and 1950s, males were dropping out of the activity in droves, most likely because the appearance of women was putting their machismo at risk. At this point—*voilà!*—cheerleading became "naturally" female. The switching back and forth on "gender appropriateness" of any given sport only reveals how artificial the concept of gendered sport really is. For the longest time, track and field was considered *the* quintessentially "male" sporting event, almost as macho as football. To keep it "male," women had to be kept out. And they were. I'll discuss at length the systematic exclusion of women from "men's" sports in chapter 5, "Can I Play?: The Struggle to Get into the Game." For now, suffice it to say that fear for their masculine identity motivates men to do everything they can to prevent women from appearing equally capable, physically.

The extremes to which they have gone seem ludicrous today, when we have seen so dramatically just how athletically brilliant women can be. Anything and everything was used to "prove" that women couldn't cut it physically. The dastardly effect of athletics on women's abilities to be mothers, for example, was continually proclaimed. Hockey playing (and this was just field hockey, mind you, not ice hockey) could deprive girls of the future ability to breast-feed. *How* this would happen was not spelled out, although we can surmise it had to do with getting hit in the breast by stick or ball.

Women's breasts have been standard symbols of women's fragility through the ages. "Amazon" is thought to derive from *a-mazos,* meaning "breastless," and taken from the myth that Amazon warriors amputated a breast to facilitate drawing the bow. Unfortunately, women themselves have fallen prey to the myth that breasts undermine athletic performance. The winner of the shot put in France's 1917 National Athletic Championship, Violette Gouirand-Morriss, had both breasts removed in the hope that it would improve her performance.

Still, by the end of the nineteenth century women were enjoying a more vigorous and varied sports life than anyone could have imagined a century earlier. They lived longer and had fewer children, better health, and better medicine. In spite of the dampening effects of "true womanhood" and the cult of invalidism—or perhaps because these cults were so debilitating and extreme—the First Wave of feminism, which began in the early nineteenth century, gave way to a Second Wave beginning in the twentieth that endorsed "a new model of able-bodied women."

As the new century got under way, social forces were gathering that would temporarily overcome men's fear of women encroaching upon their masculinity: war especially—war being the great gender bender. When national security is at stake, women are not only encouraged but expected to take on men's jobs. It's considered their "war effort." World War I presented women with opportunities they'd never had before. Work they would otherwise have been criticized for attempting was suddenly something they were quite strong enough for. With the men away at war, who else was going to work in the factories and keep the country—and the war machine— running? The struggle to protect the nation overshadowed the question of mere gender, allowing women to step out into the world and gain new skills without threatening men's security. Frailty as a measure of femininity went up in smoke.

Still, the war image of woman as builder and machine maker was grafted tenuously, at best, onto the Madonna image (as in Madonna and child). "Rosie the Riveter," the national symbol of the good patriotic woman, was portrayed as the little wife, blond ringlets peeking out from under her work kerchief as she brandished her welding iron. Women were good in a pinch, in other words, but physically no threat.

So World War I temporarily obliterated the significance of gender difference. Non-war-related jobs previously held only by men also suddenly opened to women. The nation's vast parks, which until then had been masterfully organized and guarded by men, were for the first time entrusted to women. Hired as park rangers and camp directors, they organized and guarded perfectly well, of course. They also found the experience of being out on their own radicalizing. It wasn't long before outdoorswomen started introducing girls to the rugged challenges of life outside the home in the hope they would learn "independence and fearlessness." Girls' camps, stashed in the woods of our great national parks, were regarded as "social incubators" for the development of "a new type of woman." But when the war was over women were summarily relieved of their jobs so the men could have them back. Such radical projects as conditioning girls to become independent and fearless would not be taken up again until the Third Wave of feminism began, in the late sixties and early seventies.

By the mid-1880s physical education programs in all eastern U.S. women's colleges and universities, and many in the Midwest as well, offered sports or gymnastics for women. The teachers of physical education decided that *they* should be the ones to decide what was in girls' best interests. Their power ("similar to a mother's control over her daughters," one historian observed) was not to be underestimated. They envisioned a world of "women's sports" that would be different from men's—a world, not incidentally, that would be theirs to create and control. Female phys ed teachers, however unwittingly, would end up contributing to the frailty myth. For various reasons, some of which may have been self-serving, these educators didn't want girls going all out to develop themselves. They wanted to see *difference* between men's and women's sports, not sameness, in part to ensure that their jobs were unique and would not be taken over by men. "Girls' rules" were invented. Basketball, a favorite sport of young women's, was pruned into a scaled-down version of the men's game. "Rough and vicious play seems worse in women than in men," remarked coach Senda Berenson at Smith College, where women's basketball got its start in 1892, ". . . and the selfish display of a star by dribbling and playing the entire court" was not to be tolerated. Girls were restricted to playing on half a court and were allowed only three dribbles before they had to pass the ball. *Stars* were not allowed.

From 1880 onward, phys ed teachers "had a tightly knit structure" that persisted in the schools for decades. They were able to retain, says historian Joan Hult, "an almost monopolistic hold over girls' and women's sports and athletics in higher education, and to a lesser degree in high schools and the public domain." Their agenda? To limit competition, to have women governing athletic programs, and to encourage a "feminine approach" to sports.

It wasn't that women phys ed instructors were against *all* competition, they said, only the "wrong kind." In 1923 a survey found that 93 percent of them were opposed to intercollegiate play for women. Women claimed they weren't cut out for competition; they also insisted that "play for play's sake" was superior to the male style of competing in sports, which overemphasized winning and elitism at the expense of the majority.

It's hard to know how much of the protest against the aggressive "men's model" of sport had to do with the kinder, gentler philosophy of women's sport and how much had to do with female physical education teachers wanting to hang on to their turf. These women "saw themselves as having jurisdiction over women's physical education and athletics on all college campuses," writes Hult. "They had a missionary zeal to control and direct women away from varsity and Olympic opportunities."

Ironically, as sports became more important to girls and young women, men began to infiltrate—just what the female phys ed teachers had been guarding against. Coaches in the men's Amateur Athletic Union (AAU) started female athletics programs. Physical educators and other women leaders, among them Lou Henry Hoover, President Hoover's wife, became alarmed. In 1928 the women's division of the National Amateur Athletic Federation, led by Mrs. Hoover, actually opposed women's participation in the Olympics. This group concerned itself with potentially "harmful" methods of physical training and enjoined the phys ed teachers to get girls to hew to its cautionary standards. It published antivarsity and anti-Olympic literature and promoted the alternative "recreational" model of athletics.

It seems odd, from the current perspective, to think that female educators were so strongly against competition for women. Yet remember how deeply inculcated the frailty myth had become. If women physicians were still subscribing to it as the twentieth century rolled along, how surprising can it be that educators did? But attempting to keep women out of competitive sports, no matter what the motivation, would turn out to be a futile effort.

The years of World War II became pivotal in changing the attitudes of women themselves toward athleticism. Because the labor market needed strong, healthy women, the government supported competitive fitness programs. The War Department itself backed competitive sport, producing elite-caliber female athletes as well as male. Young women recruits competed in athletics in the armed services. By the end of the 1940s, the phys ed teachers, the amateur athletic establishment, and popular culture were all supporting competitive women's sports. Even the pristine, private girls' school gymnasia opened their doors to competition.

By the 1950s female high school students were competing against one another in leagues and tournaments. In the Catholic girls' high school I attended, gym and swimming classes were required several times a week. There were varsity and junior varsity field hockey games for which we wrapped our hockey sticks with surgical tape to soften the blows. We had swim meets and basketball tournaments. All were ruled by one gym teacher/coach. With her sturdy little legs and graceless swagger, Miss Smits wasn't like anyone we knew. The fact that she wore the same uniform we did, a maroon tunic halfway to her knees, with bloomers underneath, only enhanced our sense of not wanting to be like her. Miss Smits, we found out, wasn't married. Sometimes we speculated about her in an unkindly fashion. We didn't know anything about lesbianism in those days; our worst imagining was that Miss Smits slept in her tennis shoes. The trouble we had with her was this: she didn't really seem interested in us. As she ran about umpiring games with sharp blasts on her whistle, shouting at us to "hurry it up," she wasn't *with* us, an empathetic adult, a nurturer of young talent. She was in a gym-teacher world of her own.

On balance, I suppose we were lucky to have had Miss Smits. Some girls going to Catholic schools in that era got their physical education from nuns. "When I was young in the Dark Ages," says the mother of a nine-year-old soccer-playing daughter, commenting on the stunning change in women's sports over the last several decades, "the nun who coached us would pin up her long blue sleeves, hold an instruction manual in front of her, and pray."

Well, at least Miss Smits knew the rules. She and the thousands like her in schools across the country represented a cultural force in America, a force for a professional, if "feminized," physical education for girls. To give credit where it's due, girls' physical education at that time was part of a movement in process. It would lead to further changes. It gave us a taste. It made us want more.

By 1960 a cultural revolution was under way that ended up affecting society's entire attitude toward women and sports. The counterculture's emphasis on physical freedom, bodily pleasure, and leisure created indirect encouragement for female sport and fitness activities. At the same time, the television era made sports more popular than ever. An expanding consumer economy created a multibillion-dollar sporting industry. Virtually all those billions went to men's sports, but times were clearly changing. A *Ms.* magazine article in 1973 titled "Closing the Muscle Gap" linked women's athletic achievements to a revolutionary change in gender relations: "By developing her power to the fullest, any woman, from Olympics star to the weekend tennis player, can be a match for any man she chooses to take on. More importantly, she will inherit the essential source of human self-confidence—pride and control over a finely tuned body. That alone would be a revolution."

The idea of any woman being physically a match for any man was prescient, but it would take close to another quarter of a century before women actually began to close the "muscle gap." Vestiges of the frailty myth persisted, even after girls began taking up team sports with a vengeance in the 1970s; even after the Olympics became a showcase for women athletes in the 1980s; and even after women began outdoing men in endurance marathons in the 1990s and plunging victoriously into the contact sports—ice hockey, football, rugby—for so long considered ineffably "male." As I'll show in the following chapters, men were often ambivalent, at best, about women's increasing physical competence and entrance into high-level competition.

At a dinner party in the summer of 1999 I was raving about the new physical development of women—I didn't imagine it a controversial subject, it was a week after the American women's soccer team had won the World Cup—when my host, a gynecologist, furrowed his brow and said, "Yes, but Colette, those women are all getting osteoporosis."

Excuse me? "Those" women? *All?*

"Only women in extreme endurance sports," I corrected him. "And not *all* of those."

He could see he was going to have a discussion on his hands and desisted in deference to his wife's dinner party. But this sort of globalizing concern, this lumping of all women into the medical danger zone, is overzealous and restrictive—out-and-out nineteenth century in tone. On my way home from the party I thought, My God, the cult of invalidism lives on.

Shattering the Menstrual Myth

The myth that women should restrict their physical activity lest they compromise their ability to bear children lingered long into the twentieth century. Notably, however, it was not until women, by the millions, had entered the new sports movement that medicine formalized its requirements. In 1985, for the very first time, a panel of the American College of Obstetricians and Gynecologists introduced guidelines for exercise during pregnancy. The document stated that a pregnant woman's heart rate should not exceed 140 beats per minute, strenuous activities should not exceed fifteen minutes' duration, exercise should not be performed in the supine position after the fourth month, the Valsalva maneuver (straining while holding your breath) should be avoided, and maternal core temperature should not exceed 38 degrees centigrade. Although the panel claimed the guidelines were well grounded in medical fact, detractors took issue, saying that the guidelines were not based on empirical data. That a pregnant woman's heart rate should not exceed 140 bpm seemed particularly unreasonable, not supported by controlled laboratory or clinical study.

As will happen in medicine, instead of serving as a guide for individuals (as the professional organization later stated its suggestions were originally intended), the document became the standard to which all exercise programs were held. However, the controversy did spark nine years of research and many studies. In the end, the medical community acknowledged that it had no evidence of any contraindications to exercise during a normal pregnancy. The new data made clear that women who exercise during pregnancy do not have a greater risk of complications than women who do not exercise, and they may, in fact, have a lower risk. In 1994 the American

College of Obstetricians and Gynecologists published a "technical bulletin" rescinding all its previous advice and stating, "There are no data in humans to indicate that pregnant women should limit exercise intensity and lower target heart rates because of potential adverse effects," which included any potential "deleterious effects on the fetus." In fact (guess what?), exercise was helpful in preventing health problems associated with pregnancy—excessive weight gain, insulin resistance and impaired glucose tolerance, poor posture and low back pain, and susceptibility to anxiety and depression.

The myth of reproductive vulnerability—which had included exercising during and after pregnancy and during menstruation—couldn't have been more dramatically toppled than it was by the German runner Uta Pippig during the 1996 Boston Marathon. The race was a dramatic event to begin with, as Pippig was favored to win a third time, which would be a first. But adding to the drama was "the unprecedented obviousness" of her menstrual bleeding and pain, Elizabeth Kissling wrote in *Sociology of Sport Journal*. "The runner's period began early in the race, and throughout it she suffered cramps and severe diarrhea."

Kissling, a sociologist at Eastern Washington University, was particularly interested in the press reports after the race and how (mostly) male sportswriters stumbled all over themselves trying to decide what to say and what not to say, and how. Pippig's experience wreaked havoc with the ages-old taboo on speaking openly about menstruation. How could the newspapers ignore it? Pippig—so frequently written about as blond, beautiful, and "feminine"—didn't stop running when the blood came. She didn't stop when the cramping and diarrhea began. At each water stop she did her best to clean herself up, then kept on running. She ran until the end. She ran while Kenya's spitfire Tegla Loroupe passed her. Then, after the twenty-four-mile mark, Pippig came from behind to overtake Loroupe and win the race, win it for the third year in a row, win it looking "a mess," as one reporter described her.

Kissling studied the sports pages of forty-five newspapers, "reading closely for tone, to assess underlying attitudes, assumptions and values." There were three basic ways in which Pippig's menstruation had been handled by the press, she found. One was not to mention it as the source of Pippig's difficulties. Another was by using language so explicit that the report became clinical in its detachment. The third was to exaggerate and overemphasize menstruation's "debilitating" effects. Interestingly, nearly half the newspapers failed to mention menstruation in their coverage—as in this almost throwaway line from the *Los Angeles Times*: "Uta Pippig was sick for almost 25 miles on Monday, then was nursed back to health by some loud Bostonians."

Other reports (the *Boston Herald*'s and *The Washington Post*'s among them) equivocated, attributing Pippig's difficulties to "stomach" problems. *Newsday* and *The Detroit News* said Pippig had considered dropping out of the race because of cramps, but they neglected to mention that menstruation was the cause of the cramps. Finally there were the hysterics who covered the event as Pippig's victory over menstruation rather than over the other racers. Michael McGee's article in the *Boston Herald* labeled Pippig's body "dysfunctional" and her menstrual difficulties as "meltdown." Same paper, another reporter: "There is no delicate way to put this. Pippig had female issues at the worst possible time. She was in pain. She was a mess."

Female issues. Isn't that seemingly casual but dismissive phrase no less a put-down than the "quiescent metabolism" with "a tendency toward emotional and irrational behavior" that the authors of *The Evolution of Sex* expressed a hundred years earlier, in 1889? Elizabeth Kissling concluded that most of the coverage of Uta Pippig's race perpetuated the menstrual myth, not only in its language but in its implication, as Michael McGee put it, that perhaps Pippig should have "do[ne] the sensible thing and pull[ed] off to one side."

Quit the race, that is. Acceded to meltdown in the interests of feminine decorum.

Still, both Pippig's accomplishment *and* the media's coverage of it represented a victory for women. All forty-five papers pointed out that Uta Pippig's pain didn't stop her from winning the twenty-six-mile Boston Marathon. *That* was a major breakthrough. "Pippig's victory makes it just a little bit harder for anyone to argue that menstruation is disabling or that women can't compete athletically because of it," Kissling wrote.

The women of the generation before Pippig—my generation— were taught not only to restrict themselves physically during menstruation, but to hide any evidence of it at the risk of utter shame. Those were powerful lessons, the shame lesson being even more debilitating to us, perhaps, than the restriction lesson. For menstrual shame, I believe, is profoundly related to women's feelings of physical inferiority—and to their acceptance of secondary status. Menstrual shame is not just physical shame or gender shame; it is identity shame. To read of Uta Pippig's throwing caution to the winds in order to finish what she set out to do is myth-toppling. To think of her running for miles—past spectators, reporters, and television cameras—all bloodied and messy, boggled my mind. It made me just want to throw my arms around her.

When I was sixteen I played varsity badminton at my Catholic girls' high school up on a hill outside Baltimore. In one memorable game with a visiting school I leaped about in my whites, reveling in my smashes and volleys and sly drop shots, thrilled by the movement, the sweat, the ultimate victory. Then, in the locker room after the game, the crash—the bright red blood on the back of my shorts. My mind shot to the gym balcony with its gallery of onlookers, other students, boys—even worse than boys, nuns. And all that time, me playing with the mark of the beast on my backside.

Nothing could have been more mortifying. I couldn't speak of the incident to anyone. It would have been admitting to such a weakness, such a flaw, such stupidity. If girls could do nothing else in this world, they were supposed to be able to keep their blood from showing. The embarrassment came from the cultural implications of menstruation, not from modesty. To bleed every month. What could be a greater sign of frailty?

The frailty myth has had profound effects—physiological, psychological, emotional. Many women have grown up alienated from their bodies, not knowing the extent of their strength and endurance and not daring to try to find out. But just as physical weakness has been learned, so can it be unlearned. And that is happening today, as women acknowledge the price they have paid for their weakened bodies—and are no longer willing to pay.

By the end of the twentieth century much of the menstrual myth—with the help of women like Uta Pippig, physician Mary Jacobi, and feminist writer Charlotte Perkins Gilman—had been decimated. It took women's protests to get medicine to actually study what effects menstruation has on the body. In researching the relationship between menstrual cycle events and exercise, as we've seen, scientists have found that physical activity *doesn't* threaten the menstrual process; on the contrary, it helps regulate it.

Exercising during pregnancy *doesn't* threaten the mother or child. In fact, not exercising leaves the pregnant woman open to medical problems she can prevent if she's fit.

The relationship of exercise-induced amenorrhea (abnormal absence or suppression of menses) to bone density (to which the gynecologist was referring when he said, "Those women are all getting osteoporosis") is complicated and not completely understood. The problem is best addressed by testing individual athletes for hormone levels and bone density, not by issuing blanket proscriptions against intense exercise. Many health benefits have been found for exercising females, so care must be taken not to overpresent the cases of women who harm themselves by going to extremes. Girls who are physically active, as we'll see in the next chapter, decrease their likelihood of developing chronic disease later in life. They lower their chances of getting breast cancer. And they meet the crucial goal of achieving peak bone mass during adolescence.

Today women are discovering the long-range effects of physical competence and strength in their lives. "I learned from sports that I can be pushed down and get right back up again," said a thirty-year-old college professor and lacrosse player. "That knowledge gives me a strong, almost scary capacity to succeed."

Tenacity and grit may be the greatest dividends to come from shattering the frailty myth. Women clearly *feel* stronger when their bodies are stronger. They no longer need men for protection. They are their own warriors, capable of defending themselves, capable of standing up to anyone, capable of going wherever they want. Equal opportunity to develop ourselves physically, and the capacity to be no less safe, or fearful, in the world than men, will be the last frontier for women. It seems obvious now, but maybe that's because women are approaching physical equality for the first time: as long as we remain physically oppressed, we can't be free.

TWO

The Incredible
Shrinking Woman

The newspapers loved it. The First Lady had been practicing with the President all weekend in the Rose Garden, but when she threw the opening ball of Chicago's 1994 baseball season, tough, savvy, always-besting-her-husband Hillary stepped forward on the wrong foot and muffed it. The frailty of her throw was painful, especially when compared with her husband's. And compare the media did. Both *The New York Times* and *The Washington Post* lined up two photos side by side on their front pages. One showed Bill rearing back before whipping forth the opening ball for Cleveland; the other showed Hillary on the same day, looking pathetic in Chicago. A knowing, sportsmanlike assessment of the dynamic duo in the *Atlantic Monthly* described the President throwing as a lefty. He "had turned his shoulder sideways to the plate in preparation for the delivery," James Fallows wrote. "He was bringing the ball forward from behind his head in a clean-looking throwing action." Hillary, by cruel comparison, stood facing the plate. "A right-hander, she had the elbow of her throwing arm pointed out in front of her. Her forearm was tilted back, toward her shoulder. The ball rested on her upturned palm."

Oh God, I thought, reading this. I could only imagine where things went from there, the First Lady wobbling forth her paltry pitch, an ill-concealed smirk spreading throughout the stadium as the men bonded in jocular superiority. Bottom line, they're thinking, Hillary isn't so tough after all. Bottom line, she throws like a girl.

When I began work on this book, I was interested in finding out how women's frailty had become so fundamental an idea that it was—and to a great extent still is—regarded as self-evident, a fact no less obvious than Hillary Clinton's weak pitch. How was this myth actually transmitted to girls, and by whom? I wanted to know, because I had begun to discern how much the frailty myth had impaired my own life.

I was in the first generation of women to become mentally educated (in the mass movement toward college that began in the 1950s). I was *not* in the first generation of women to become *physically* educated. My daughters are in that generation. The education of their bodies went beyond rote calisthenics and half-court basketball—way beyond. It allowed for the possibility of elite training, competition, and full development of musculature. A body so developed was on display for the world to see when Brandi Chastain stripped down to her black sports bra the moment the American World Cup team made its final winning point against China. That was a body to grace its cover, the editors of *Newsweek* decided, a body with quadriceps, biceps, and lats. A body that was built not by StairMaster, but by running up and down a soccer field and doing weight training. A body that defied objectification. The huge banner splashed across the *Newsweek* cover read GIRLS RULE!

In my generation a body like Brandi Chastain's would have been inconceivable. Even if one could have imagined such muscle on a woman, it would have been thought freakish. Acceding to the femininity demands of our era, we backed off from physical development. Keeping "small" was our legacy from the nineteenth century. The cult of the he-man, defining men, and the cult of frailty, defining women, may have originated in the nineteenth century, but they flourished long into the twentieth. For the cults to work, men had to *make* themselves strong and women had to *make* themselves weak. To keep the distinction between male and female eminently apparent, to make the whole gender arrangement crystal clear, an abilities gap had to be fabricated. Women's brains, in the nineteenth century, were believed to be weaker than men's; so, too, were their bodies. But of course neither belief is true. Women's intellectual equality has slowly been acknowledged during the course of the last century. Their physical equality is another matter.

What do I mean by physical equality? I mean equal opportunity to become physically educated; equal opportunity to compete in sports; equal opportunity to develop muscular strength. Last but not least, I mean equal opportunity to learn how to defend ourselves. Make no mistake: society's resistance to women having physical equality is huge. It's like Custer's last stand. If women should ever demonstrate that they're just as strong, agile, and enduring as men, the whole game would be up.

Becoming Feminine: The Gender Effect

Gender is a fascinating subject because so much gets determined by a concept that is basically "socially constructed" or made up. These fabricated ideas about gender influence everything, from the way we think about behavior to who ends up running the show. No one really knows what differences, if any, there are between the *essence* of what it is to be female and the *essence* of what it is to be male. But the very tenuousness of the distinctions, due to our gender conditioning (as we'll see), makes people uncomfortable. We're driven to keep male and female as opposite—as "different"-seeming—as possible.

After the Industrial Revolution society saw a waning of the importance of strength differences between men and women and the concurrent rise (as shown in the last chapter) of the he-man and the female invalid. Those distorted concepts of masculine and feminine held sway all the way through the twentieth century until Ken and Barbie sprang from the plastic womb of Mattel in the 1960s, and even beyond. Feminist moms have always deplored the macho and femme proclivities of Ken and Barbie and didn't want them in the house. Forget it. Their little girls *want* these caricatures of grown-up "man" and grown-up "woman"—Ken the he-man and Barbie the wan one (however perkily turned out). The very extremity of their sexual personae somehow makes them comforting.

But as the nineties drew to a close, some social scientists (if not little girls) seemed to be putting the entire notion of "difference" on the chopping block. If they weren't killing it off entirely, they were certainly challenging old assumptions. Do men and women really have different traits, different ways of feeling and thinking about things? they questioned. Do men and women have different physical capacities? Do they fatigue and recover at different rates? Can one endure activity longer than the other? Is one more courageous, more daunting, more willing to take risks? The very raising of those questions, when I first encountered them, seemed strange—the psychological equivalent, for a woman raised Catholic, of having given birth to a dozen kids when the Pope ups and announces that birth control is okay. What? *Now* you tell me? For years my generation had tried to adjust to the restrictions deemed appropriate for our gender. Now social scientists were suggesting that femininity and masculinity, at least as arbiters of social behavior, were relatively meaningless concepts. The seed and the egg, now *there's* a difference. But femininity and masculinity? They are totally manufactured concepts.

As a young woman in the 1960s, I worried that I'd never really be able to *get* the essence of femininity. Dress, behavior, and feelings were as carefully circumscribed for my generation as sex, but the "rules" of femininity kept changing. Fashion said pantsuits were in; tradition (and many male bosses) said they were out. Satisfying work for women was in—but not at the expense of the fragile male ego. There was much discussion of sex and whether or not women were having "true" orgasms. The whole game kept us hopping.

The elusive femininity was important to us mainly because we thought of it as a necessary commodity in attracting appropriate, fully developed, mature adult males. (It was one of the less than solacing revelations of the feminist movement that such men were in woefully short supply.) Being sufficiently "feminine" was a concept my generation had cut its teeth on, grown up with, lived our entire lives by. (Being sufficiently "masculine," of course, was an equally stringent and limiting requirement for males.) A female could not be said to have reached mature adulthood if she had not, along the way, acquired this mysterious trait. One could never be sure *when* it had taken hold, or *whether*. Yet the mandate was clear: Femininity meant bowing to one's fate, limitations and all. It was a hierarchical thing, a status thing, and it came with a quid pro quo: Women had to get comfortable with being number two, or they wouldn't be able to have "true" orgasms. "True" orgasms were vaginal orgasms, the vagina being the last outpost of "true womanhood." You think those clitoral orgasms are fine? some therapists would say to their female patients. They're not. Clitorally stimulated orgasms were considered clinically infantile. The originator of this chilling sexual threat, which had tremendous staying power, was Freud. He said, "[T]he clitoris must give up to the vagina its sensitivity, and, with it, its importance, either wholly or in part. This is one of the . . . tasks which have to be performed in the course of the woman's development."

The bombastic "true" orgasm was reserved for women who "transferred" their clitoral sensitivity to their vaginas. For this to be possible, a psychological trick of sorts had to take place. Basically women had to give up any thoughts of being number one. They had to appreciate—and trust—men and stop trying to be like them. This shrinking of their social status and potential for power was the price they had to pay for sexual fulfillment.

Not until the 1960s, when feminists—and the sex researchers William Masters and Virginia Johnson—finally started crediting the importance to female sexuality of the clitoris, did women's orgasms, and how they were produced, suddenly become less mysterious. With the aid of minuscule intervaginal cameras, used in Masters and Johnson's laboratory at Washington University in St. Louis, the physiology of the female orgasm was finally studied. And what do you know? The little clitoris (a kind of shrunken analogue of the penis, in the eyes of Freudians) actually had more nerve endings than the penis! In the world-rocking words of Masters and Johnson, in their groundbreaking *Human Sexual Response,* "women's . . . physiological capacity for sexual response infinitely surpasses that of man." Thus 1966 was a breakthrough year for Number Two. Women, it turned out, were, or could be (if men only knew anything about sex), the queens of multiple orgasm. They could go on all night.

One can see why men might be motivated to tame them. One can also see why the clitoris, once out of the closet, became an organ of political consequence for feminists, who grasped that it wasn't just lack of information that had compromised women's sexual fulfillment for aeons. There was power riding on the myths about women's "inadequate" sexual response. In some societies surgically removing the clitoris is the method of controlling women's sexual response (and diffusing their potential power). A more "civilized" method was simply ignoring, or explaining away, the truth about women's sexuality.

Difference, in any event, is the main thing. Without difference you cannot have hierarchy, or one up, one down. You cannot have better and worse, strong and weak, superior and inferior. Hierarchy is how social inequality is maintained, and "masculinity" and "femininity" are about hierarchy. Supposedly "natural" differences between men and women are used to validate the differences in the amount of social power they hold. *Bodies*—men's "stronger" bodies and women's "weaker" bodies—are used to explain differences in behavior, which in turn are used to explain why men naturally have, and need, more power. Hierarchical power differences are the persistent bugbears provoking much of the scholarly interest in gender—and "gender theory," as it is known. Today the "sex differences" that have been used for so long to support hierarchy (or what used to be called "patriarchy") are being punctured like so many fragile balloons. In the process we are learning a great deal about how and why women's bodies have been controlled and their physical development restricted, all to protect men's interests as "the stronger sex."

In the effort to nail down the elusive "masculinity" and "femininity," social scientists, like astronomers searching for black holes, are forever creating scales—the Bem Sex-Role Inventory, the Sex Role Behavior Scale, and the Sex Role Identity Scale, to name a few. These are used as assessment tools to learn where, on a supposed masculinity-femininity continuum, a given individual lies. Since the scales produce few significant data, researchers are always looking for "new, more 'sensitive' ways to measure masculinity and femininity," Yale psychologist Anne Beall tells us. But working from prior assumptions can make scholars sloppy. When gender-role scales were revamped for the widely used Minnesota Multiphasic Personality Inventory (MMPI), no one thought to check whether they were actually valid for another decade. Independent researchers who finally got around to making the evaluation decided the MMPI's vaunted new gender scales revealed far more about personality traits than they did about masculinity and femininity. "Overall," the researchers confessed, with scholarly understatement, "they do not hold as much promise as hoped for."

Oh dear. But just *what* was the magical promise such tests were supposed to yield? Over 40 percent of men score above the median on traits considered feminine, and over 40 percent of women score above the median on traits considered masculine—a substantial overlap if one is looking for attributes to define femininity and masculinity. Scholars of gender difference constructed these scales, Beall reveals, by selecting questions that men and women responded to differently and then making up a scale accordingly. "The responses that males gave were called masculine and the responses females gave were called feminine," wrote Beall, who was blowing the whistle on the scale makers, who in essence were *creating* the difference they were supposed to be discovering. Nineteenth-century concepts of "masculine" and "feminine" remained entrenched in the twentieth, she explains, because investigators *never questioned* "the theoretical justification for such traits and just assumed the existence of masculinity and femininity, even though many of the scales were not quantitatively reliable." In such a way can psychologists both create and validate their own theories.

"Sex inventories," as social scientists call them, fail to predict much about psychological functioning, but they continue to be used for making diagnoses of people's psychological abnormalities. People's actual mental health is assessed through such artifice. *Women's mental health*, for most of the twentieth century, was held to be contingent upon their degree of femininity—and *that* was contingent upon their views of the importance of having a penis. Remember the ancient penis envy theory? The truth is, it's still around. And it is closely intertwined with the frailty myth, in that it posits women as less potent than men. *Penis,* in this penis envy construct, was a kind of code word for physical superiority whose power was virtually God-given. Men's bodies were better than women's. The female's central psychological "task," as psychoanalysts (and, later, developmental psychologists) thought of it, was to accept her lesser status, to stop envying men their greater power, and to see that true fulfillment would come—and come only—in both accepting her fate and devoting herself to the one great possibility she *did* have, which was becoming a mother.

As you can see, this thinking was little different from the "woman as breeder" theory so dear to the hearts of nineteenth-century eugenicists. In the twentieth century psychoeducators downplayed the superman talk of G. Stanley Hall and his crowd, but the ongoing ideology of man as superior was still there to be gleaned in everything written, everything seen, every nuance of women's relationships with men, whether intimate or professional.

Nietzsche described strength as "a feeling of dominion in the muscles . . . of strength as pleasure in the proof of strength, as bravado, adventure, fearlessness, indifference to life and death." He didn't exactly have women in mind when he wrote those words. Male identity relies not only on being strong, but on being able to give the impression of being strong—on being able to "project a physical presence that speaks of latent power," as one of the new gender-studying sports sociologists put it.

In learning to become female, girls, on the other hand, are taught to project a physical presence that speaks of latent vulnerability. Today researchers are studying the peculiar decline in physical competence that takes place as girls grow older. Some attribute the decline to what they call "emphasized femininity." They mean exaggerated femininity. Self-imposed restraint. False weakness.

What I'm concerned with in this chapter is the fallout from the frailty myth—what girls and young women today are seeing and hearing and doing—that keeps them on the path of learned weakness. That puts at risk not only their physical ambitions but their very lives. That encourages them to shrink themselves—*and then says it's in their nature to be shrunken.*

Learned Weakness

"Emphasized femininity" begins in the cradle, and it is something girls are taught. A study of parents interacting with their twenty- to twenty-four-month-old children found they treated boys and girls differently in significant ways. Boys were more likely to be left alone in play or joined neutrally by parents. Girls got constant comment, whether praise or criticism, as if parents weren't comfortable allowing them to just explore on their own. Typically boys got a positive response for playing with blocks, a negative response for dallying with dolls. Girls got positive reactions when they played with dolls, asked for help, or passively watched television. They got *negative reactions for running, jumping, and climbing.* How surprising can it be to learn, then, that in children as young as two and a half, boys perform better on power and force?

The parents had little idea that they were reinforcing passivity in their girls. "Parents are not fully aware of the methods they use to socialize young children," the author of this study pointed out.

When little girls are not given equal opportunity to play—or if they withdraw from opportunity because of what they've learned about what is "appropriate"—they fall behind in learning motor skills. Strength and agility come from *doing,* after all. "One's sense of oneself as an active person is developed precisely through experiences of mastering one's body and realizing one's intentions in physical movements in and through space," the French philosopher Maurice Merleau-Ponty wrote. *I, I can,* and *I cannot* are all "embodied" experiences. You *feel* in your body that you aren't able to do something, or you *feel* in your body that you are. And arriving at those feelings comes in the course of doing the movements.

Many girls get the message early that athletic competence isn't expected of them. They don't feel physically competent to begin with, and unless someone takes pains to convince them otherwise, they assume their frailty is inborn. Boys are stronger, more agile, more athletically talented. It's "nature"—just one more difference between being a boy and being a girl.

Given the power dynamics of gender difference in our society, is it any wonder that kids are taught that their social status demands adhering to sharp boundaries between female and male, boundaries that place restrictions on appearance, voice, dress, and behavior? "The media, parents, teachers, and peers tell children in many obvious and subtle ways that if boys are one thing, girls are its opposite," Margaret Carlisle Duncan, a professor at the University of Wisconsin, told the President's Fitness Council on Girls and Sport. Children begin using gender labels reliably between twenty-one months and forty-four months. Children internalize the gender categories presented them and "practice" the corresponding behaviors, miming the roles society labels feminine or masculine. By age three they know the rules of gendered behavior and start thinking it's wrong for people to engage in cross-sex activities. By age four they already identify playing with dolls, picking flowers, skipping, and dancing as appropriate for girls and sports and fighting as appropriate for boys. Only recently have researchers begun to study the price that girls in particular are paying for the extreme focus on gender—a focus, Dr. Duncan warned, that invariably will shrink girls' physical expectations for themselves *unless* parents, teachers, and other influential people in girls' lives work hard to counter the conditioning.

On average, girls are two years older than boys when they start participating in sport. That means they're behind from the get-go in learning the skills needed for physical competence. This disadvantage—again, perceived as "natural"—is enough to dissuade many girls from trying further. Seventy percent of children reject organized sports before age thirteen, but the fallout rate of girls is six times that of boys.

"Stereotype threat," as sociologists call it, has the potential to seriously undermine performance. For example, if you make a young woman who's good at math more aware of being female, she'll do less well on math tests. Race stereotypes work the same way. All you have to do to lower the score of a bright black kid on a test of academic ability is give him or her, before the tests, a short questionnaire that includes the question "Race?"

"Gender threat," as I'll call it, operates similarly. Suggest to a girl that she is acting like a boy and she'll pull in her movements like a turtle retreating into its shell. Because vigorous movement and expansive use of space are coded as "masculine," girls avoid them. They adopt their own specific gestures and movements—a kind of frailty reper-toire: delicate, restrained movements (crossing the legs, folding the arms)—and unconsciously take up as little space as possible.

Preschool boys still handle *more* tools, throw *more* balls, con-struct *more* Lego bridges, build *more* block towers, and tinker with *more* mechanical objects than do girls. The type of recreation chil-dren participate in is neatly gender-divided by the time they enter first grade. A study of the playground activities of approximately three hundred boys and girls in the first to fourth grades found boys playing large, self-organized games like basketball, while the girls hung out in groups of twos or threes, talking. I find it amazing that so little has changed in the twenty years I've been reading these sorts of studies. But today researchers are beginning to see that these dif-ferences aren't "natural"—effects of some biologically determined hierarchical structure. And for the first time they're suspecting that gender bias actually affects girls' motor development.

A great deal of evidence confirms that girls are often given little encouragement in physical movement. Fathers have long been known to have more physical contact with infant sons than daughters, and this apparently hasn't changed. Researchers in the 1990s found them still rough-and-tumbling with their sons and coddling their daughters. Both parents continue to overhelp small girls. In one study, moms and dads of toddlers were seated in the middle of a room, surrounded by a barricade of soft cushions. Their toddlers were left outside the barri-cade, trying to get in. The researchers noticed that parents were more likely to urge boys to climb over barricades. The girls they just lifted over. "Different sets of play behaviors begin to evolve for males and females at very early ages and primarily under the direction of parents and caregivers," noted Tonya Toole and Judith Kretzschmar, two pro-fessors of movement science, in a review of studies making gender comparisons of motor skills in children. "Beginning in infancy, both parents elicit gross motor behavior more from their sons than from their daughters."

Even in preschool, boys get significantly more positive feedback for high-activity play. Because they haven't been trained to "play small," boys will instigate large motor activities on their own, researchers believe. Preschool girls, on the other hand, tend to avoid large motor activities. It's finally being recognized that unless these activities are built into the school curriculum, girls don't get the large-muscle stimulation they need. Girls must be encouraged if they're going to get the physical stimulation they require for normal development. But they're not being encouraged—at least not in school. A number of studies in the 1990s found gender biases in physical education classes, with teachers giving more positive evaluation of physical competence to boys than to girls. The teachers' perceptions, wrong though they may be, lower girls' feeling of adequacy and predilection for participating in physical activities. A 1992 study by Sheila Scraton found that in spite of the "different but equal" ethos prevalent in girls' schooling in the United Kingdom, physical education for girls is always regarded as less important than for boys. Scraton wanted to find out if the historical biases toward girls' physical development (the cult of female invalidism, recall, was rampant on both sides of the Atlantic earlier in the century) are still present in contemporary teaching. Her open-ended interviews with PE advisers, heads of girls' PE departments, and other staff led her to the dismal conclusion that the contents and methods of physical education classes today remain "traditional"— essentially still centered on supposed "standards" of feminine behavior and physical appearance. The teachers she interviewed had strong assumptions about perceived differences in the "natural" physical abilities of girls and boys—assumptions that directly influenced their teaching. They tended to accept a sexual division of labor and basically believed that women's "natural" function was motherhood, Scraton found. To their way of thinking, women are less powerful, aggressive, active, and strong than men—and this is either "natural" or simply culturally inevitable. Accordingly, they attributed girls' tendency to drop out of physical education to their changing bodies.

Shocked by the continuing pervasiveness of these limiting beliefs, Scraton concluded her study with a call for change in physical education, including training courses to alert PE teachers to gender biases that limit girls' interest in and performance of physical activities.

Parents as well as teachers tend to stifle aggression in girls and encourage it in boys. This leads to the development in boys of a sense of entitlement and an increasing tendency to dominate. By fourth grade, researchers have found, boys have already begun to associate their self-esteem with aggressive acts and to feel less guilt about aggression than girls.

Sports teach boys to use their bodies in skilled ways, and this gives them a good sense of their physical capacities and limits. They develop the capacity for forceful movement by learning coordination and follow-through, and how to use physical leverage. Girls' movement patterns are often incomplete because they don't learn to generate torque when executing a throw, a swing, or a tackle. Lack of torsion (which essentially is what is meant by "lack of follow-through") results from failing to put the whole body into the motion. Girls often hold themselves back from full, complete movement. Although it's usually something girls are unaware of, they actually learn to hamper their movements, developing "a body timidity that increases with age." In a widely cited collection of essays, *Throwing Like a Girl,* Iris Young describes this held-back state as "inhibited intentionality." As girls become young women, their restricted movement patterns are reinforced. "Constrictive clothing and 'dignified' postures," admonishments for speaking and laughing loudly—all of these "contribute to 'shrinking' behavior in women," a physical movement analyst wrote in a textbook on the history of women in sport.

Two out of three girls in the United States don't participate in school athletics, the National Council on Research for Women found. And only half take high school phys ed classes. Trained to halt the development of their bodies at puberty because of the cultural proscription against females being strong, girls weaken themselves unnaturally. In adolescence most stop using their bodies and start using appearance for whatever power they're going to exert in the world. The majority of high school girls are interested in a different kind of body culture. To the detriment of their health, they take up "disciplinary practices" that produce a body of a certain size. A body of a certain configuration. A body that says, "I topple easily." Sadly, these girls have little idea of the trade-off they're making, much less its consequences.

It's femininity training that makes women cultivate being "small and narrow, harmless," writes feminist philosopher Sandra Lee Bartky, who has devoted her career to the study of gender. She points to fascinating 1980s photographs by the German photographer Marianne Wex, who liked to document men's and women's body postures in day-to-day life. Women in a station waiting for trains, for example: Wex found them sitting with arms close to the body, hands folded together in their laps, and toes pointing straight ahead or turned inward. Their legs were conscientiously pressed together. The women in Wex's photographs are tense, their bodies taking up little space, Bartky points out, while the men are "expanding" into the space around them, sitting with arms and legs flung out, crotch visible, in what she calls the "proffering position." Women are trying to hide their sexuality, men to display it.

Similar comparisons can be seen in the way men and women walk, body-watching scholars note. A man has "more spring and rhythm to his step; he walks with toes pointed outward, holds his arms at a greater distance from his body and swings them farther; he tends to point the whole hand in the direction he is moving." In contrast, the circumspect woman holds her arms closer to her body, palms against her side. "If she has subjected herself to the additional constraint of high-heeled shoes," writes Bartky, "her body is thrown forward and off balance: the struggle to walk under these conditions shortens her stride."

It's gender training that turns girls obsessive about "femininity," gender training that deprives them of the natural use of, and pleasure in, their bodies. By adolescence, girls feel compelled to exaggerate their difference from boys, believing their social acceptance depends on it. Since the very definition of a popular boy is to be strong, physical, and athletically talented, many a girl will avoid developing these capabilities. The learned weakness that we saw was part of the gender training of Victorian females has persisted, if in a less extreme form, over the past century. It has put a hold on the physical development of too many girls, and this affects the rest of their development as well.

"Physical sport and activity are not simply things young girls do *in addition to* the rest of their lives, but rather, they comprise an interdependent set of physiological, psychological and social processes that can influence, and in varying degrees sustain, girls' growth and development," reports the University of Minnesota's Center for Research on Girls & Women in Sport.

Motor development, as we'll see, stimulates cognitive development. The brain requires physical activity to create the neural circuitry that permits complex thinking. It doesn't take becoming an elite-level athlete to grow a lively brain, but it *does* take moving hard and breathing hard. The body, in short, has to be put to use. The brain can't develop in a hollowed-out husk.

Throwing Like a Guy:
The Mystique of Innate Ability

An early notion about motor abilities—and one that's still widespread among people not familiar with the research—was that motor skills are the result of a single, all-encompassing ability—a kind of body IQ. "Athletic ability," "coordination," "motor ability"—whatever the term used, the implication was the same: If a person had a strong *general* motor ability, he would do well at almost any motor task. If Johnnie could throw, that is, it was a foregone conclusion that he could hit, catch, kick to a fare-thee-well, and punch out an opponent's lights if need be. If a boy did one thing well, he was assumed to have "the Power" and likely would be encouraged to try developing other skills. The reverse was how it was seen for girls. If Jenny *couldn't* throw (or hit or catch), it was assumed she was useless in every physical domain. Jenny wouldn't get the chance to try other sports—in part because teachers had written her off as hopeless and in part because she'd written herself off.

The idea that motor ability was "general" came out of the same research on cognitive abilities done in the 1930s that produced the concept of a "general" intelligence—the capacity to act purposefully, think rationally, and deal effectively with one's environment. This hypothesized "general" mental ability—which supposedly could be measured and was called "intelligence quotient," or "IQ"—was thought to be important for success in every mental arena. Ultimately, as we know, the theory of IQ didn't hold up, as researchers came to a more sophisticated understanding of how minds work. "Instead of a single dimension called intellect, on which individuals can be rank-ordered, there are vast differences among individuals in their intellectual strengths and weaknesses and also in their styles of attack in cognitive pursuit," writes Howard Gardner in *Multiple Intelligences*. Gardner, a cognitive psychologist at Harvard, was the first to identify the existence of what he called "body-kinesthetic intelligence"—I call it physical intelligence. It refers to the fact that our bodies learn, and we learn through them.

The rigid, unidimensional view of intelligence began unraveling in the 1950s and 1960s, when both general intellectual ability *and* general motor ability came to be seen as inaccurate and limiting. Franklin Henry, a psychologist at the University of California at Berkeley, discovered that different motor abilities are specific to particular tasks and function independently of one another. You could be great at throwing but lousy at sewing, for example. Or, like a brilliant neurosurgeon named Charlie Wilson (he was profiled in *The New Yorker* in 1999), you could have performed three thousand resections of pituitary tumors as small as 18 millimeters in diameter and still not be able to get off a good game of tennis. Wilson is good at other sports, but with tennis, for some reason, he has a problem with mental imaging. He just can't *see* the game in his mind.

Those who *can* see the game of tennis in their minds don't necessarily all see it in the same way. Partly it's a matter of the particular skills an individual has developed. Negotiating the wind, for example, is something one tennis player might have learned and another not. Martina Hingis was able to "recalibrate" inside "a virtual wind tunnel," as one onlooker put it, watching tennis balls behaving like stunt kites at the U.S. Open following Hurricane Dennis. Her opponent, Anke Huber, hadn't learned this skill. Hingis credits her wind-management finesse to her coach and mother, Melanie Molitor, who's been teaching her since she was an infant. It's a practiced skill that gives Martina the capacity to keep up with the erratic flight of a wind-driven ball. "You don't get born with that thing," she told a reporter. "You learn it."

———

The way in which movements are organized through the central nervous system and then executed by the body is called "motor control." The scientific study of this ability dates back to the early 1900s, when researchers were doing time-and-motion studies in the effort to get more efficiency out of assembly-line workers. Physical educators became interested in the implications for sports performance of early ideas about motor control. Growth, maturation, and motor performance began to be studied, and a new subarea called "motor development" emerged that focused on how movement is *learned*. For decades, however, behavioral scientists interested in complex forms of motor performance, and neurophysiological scientists interested in how brain neurons control movement, were working in totally different camps.

A merger between research on neural control and research on motor behavior didn't get under way until the 1970s. Glimpsing the important relationship between *how people move and what's going on in their brains,* researchers began to study how humans code and store movement data, how the brain represents movement in memory, and how individuals process information about motor "errors" in such a way that learning occurs. Eventually the study of motor development brought scientists to the astounding concept that males' greater physical skills were chiefly the result of learning and practice. They were not a matter of "superior" physiology.

In the 1980s those who were studying motor skills became interested in the gender differences in acquiring them. The distinction between the ability to *learn* a movement and the ability to *perform* it seemed relevant when making motor skill comparisons between males and females. Since it had been discovered that performance skills are actually learned, a salient question was now pressing: To what degree were scores on motor skills tests being affected by differences in what subjects had *learned,* and to what degree did they reflect "natural" differences in male and female abilities?

First, motor development researchers had to clarify what an ability actually is. They decided it's a relatively stable trait having to do with biological processes of growth and maturation, one that remains more or less unchanged by practice. A *skill,* by comparison, *is* modified by practice. Essentially it is learned. The much ballyhooed skill of throwing a baseball is *learned.* Boys aren't born with it.

Finally, as the mystique of motor brilliance was penetrated, a more democratic understanding grew about what people can do on a baseball field, say, whether they're boys or girls, blacks or whites. The average person who hasn't been taught how to throw properly will follow an "ipsilateral pattern," which means using just one side of the body. If a person is right-handed, his or her inclination when throwing will be to step forward on the right foot. Most boys as well as girls will throw ipsilaterally when they start out. It's part of teaching them, says Marty Ewing, a Michigan State sports psychologist. "When girls start throwing, it's more like, 'Well, she's a girl, and it doesn't matter.' But boys get to that point and the father says, 'Oh, my God, he's throwing like a girl!' " Then Dad goes to work to improve his son's throwing skill. "Step forward on the opposite foot and swing your torso into it"— that's the all-important advice the kid gets. It allows him to produce the "contralateral" pattern that makes possible a powerful, whiplike series of movements. How to execute the contralateral pattern is *not* part of some quintessential male mystery. It's a learned skill—a skill available to anyone who is taught it and practices it.

Studies from the 1950s found boys to have greater ability to "move with an integrated body pattern" during throwing, catching, and kicking. This, we now know, is something boys were being taught, not a part of their genetic code. While one can observe differences in throwing patterns between boys and girls as early as age three, researchers in the 1980s were beginning to interpret this as girls just being slower to develop "good" form. In the 1990s they finally figured out that "slower to develop" really was a question of girls just not being *taught* good form. When a right-handed thrower is taught how to step forward on her left foot, she finds that her body swings automatically as she brings her arm through, pushing energy through her lower body to her upper body and then to bicep, forearm, and wrist. What a breakthrough!

Part of what's involved in developing motor control is solving what Nikolai Bernstein, an influential Russian physiologist, called the "degrees of freedom" problem—figuring out ways of organizing the different parts of the body so the task can be accomplished. Imagine that you are asked to make an overhand throw that lands the ball as far away as possible but as close as possible to a straight line running in the direction of the throw. If you try this with your dominant arm, you'll probably do okay. But if you use your *non*dominant, or unpracticed, arm, you're likely to restrict the range of motion of the limb's joint angles. That was Hillary's trouble. For her—but not for Bill, because he was practiced at it—the opening pitch for the ball game presented a degrees-of-freedom problem. Remember how she pointed her elbow out in front of her, with her forearm tilted back toward her shoulder? Such a constricted gesture comes from "freezing" the amount of movement one allows oneself. This is how novices try to solve the problem of performing an unaccustomed physical movement or sequence of movements. By limiting the degrees of freedom (and this is done unconsciously), one keeps the task rudimentary, so that the brain doesn't have an overwhelming amount of motor information to organize. Gradually, as the skill is practiced, the mental organizing becomes easier and the player is able to let go of the unconscious restraints she puts on her range of motion. Hillary had the right idea in choosing to practice her throw ahead of time, but a weekend just wasn't enough to "thaw" (as motor behavior experts call it) the lifetime of freezing that resulted in that pathetic little underdeveloped pitch.

So now we have it. Throwing "like a girl," running "like a girl," or hitting "like a girl" is little else but freezing. Females have been kept stuck at this awkward stage because cultural proscription against using their bodies discouraged them from practicing enough to reach "thaw." The assumption that females differ in some fundamental way—in the construction of their shoulders, say, or in their general muscular development—that makes it hard for them to throw a ball correctly (or do anything else in sport) is part of the frailty myth. The girl is given to believe she can't throw, and one day she tries to and fumbles, then she *knows* she can't, so she stops trying. For girls in our culture it's a classic sequence. Yet there is no inherent biological reason for girls not to throw as far, as fast, or as hard as boys do.

Okay, but what about boys' muscles; what about their frames? Aren't boys just plain bigger than girls from the get-go?

No, they're not, and it's a reflection of our preconceptions about male strength that we imagine that they are. Boys, before puberty, are neither taller nor heavier than girls. Some studies have found greater elbow- and knee-joint diameters and larger estimated arm and leg muscles in boys. But researchers today question whether these differences are biological or are caused by the fact that boys begin practicing gross motor movements early on—and girls *don't*.

There's a remarkable amount of literature comparing throwing in girls and boys. Only recently, though, have sports scientists attempted to investigate possible *environmental* causes for the performance differences. One fascinating 1996 study looked for a possible training effect to account for gender differences. Researchers wanted to know what the influence of *practice* might be. To find out, they made a comparison of dominant and nondominant arm throws. Videotapes were made of three age-groups of kids (seven to eight years, nine to ten years, and eleven to twelve years) performing forceful overarm throws with both their dominant and nondominant hands. The dominant-hand results were typical of those reported in earlier studies. One of these, for example, reported second-grade boys as throwing 72 percent faster than second-grade girls. But when the use of the nondominant hand was compared, what do you know? There were *no* differences in how fast boys and girls threw!

What could this mean? Simply, that *practice* is what gave boys superior throwing skills. If gender differences in performance were, in fact, "strongly related to biological factors," these researchers argued, "then gender differences should persist when children throw with their nondominant arm." In fact, performance differences between the use of boys' dominant and nondominant hands were so huge, it strengthened the authors' theory that practice, and practice only, is what gives boys the edge.

Until we were allowed to develop our mental powers in the halls of higher academe, everyone thought our brains were weaker than men's. They still think our bodies are weaker. Sports sociologists interested in how gender differences in physical development are maintained have begun to talk about the political implications of "learned weakness" and are asking pointed questions. *Why* aren't girls taught to throw? Who is really afraid of getting their toes stepped on here?

Most people today still think males have more physical potential than females. It's a bias that was supported by the literature of the seventies, eighties, and even early nineties, which claimed to show that men outperform women in various athletic skills—strength, pursuit tracking, ladder climbing, throwing, jumping, and running. But by the end of the 1990s many of the old studies began to be seen as inconclusive. "It is difficult to know whether or not these differences have to do with gender per se," wrote two experts on motor learning. "Rather than simply documenting that males are or are not different from females on some task, a more fruitful approach is to ask what the sources of these effects, if present, may be."

Agreed. That *would* be more fruitful. Is it biological sex causing the difference in male and female sports performances, or are other factors at work? This question is only now being addressed with any vigor, mostly because of the historical assumption that any gender difference showing up in physical skills had to be the result of male strength and female frailty. What *else* could it be?

Plenty, the new research tells us.

Comparisons
(Or, Are We Fated to Be Weaker?)

When comparing males' and females' physical capacities, the consideration of one single variable—the amount of skill practice—is critical. What appears as difference in boys' and girls' abilities is often nothing more than a difference in training, studies are finally beginning to reveal. The secret is coming out of the closet.

Two social scientists working together in the 1990s produced some interesting research when they compared sports skills of girls and boys from kindergarten through eighth grade. It became increasingly clear, as the studies progressed over the course of several years, that the question of which gender is more skilled is not easily answered—and given the way boys and girls are socialized, it may not even be relevant.

This was the first time a team of researchers had ever compared a number of motor skills in boys and girls *and included the all-important variable of how much sports participation each child had engaged in prior to the study!* That single variable makes all the difference in assessing skill for the simple reason that skill *changes* according to the amount of practice. If a child has never thrown a ball before, there's no question he'll be clumsier and less effective than the kid whose dad has been playing catch with her in the backyard since she was three.

First, the researchers, S. A. Butterfield and E. M. Loovis, analyzed the influence of age, sex, balance, and sport participation on the development of throwing skills in children. Boys they found to be better at throwing than girls in every grade, from kindergarten through eighth. The two most influential variables were "sport participation" (or amount of experience) and "sex." That is, if you were a boy, you performed better, *and* if you had more experience in throwing, you performed better. The distinction the study *didn't* address was this: Since boys enjoy higher sport participation, in general, than girls, did their testing better have to do with their being boys or with their being more practiced? Was it possible these girls were unskilled throwers simply because they hadn't learned and hadn't practiced?

Next, the researchers studied catching. Again, "mature catching development" was influenced by sex: "Boys performed better at all grades, except in Grade 8 all girls and boys showed mature catching patterns." Wait a minute. If girls were lagging behind from kindergarten through seventh grade, how, suddenly, did they match boys' catching skill in the eighth grade? Did they finally gather the requisite amount of experience—say, in the summer between seventh and eighth grades? One truly significant question remains: If they had been getting the same amount of training and practice as boys beginning in kindergarten, would their catching skills have been comparable to boys' all along? It's likely. There is nothing inherently different in the physiological makeup of girls and boys that would account for differences in overarm throwing—or, for that matter, differences in any physical skills.

No one has yet tested what effect beliefs about gender appropriateness have on the development of particular motor skills. Maybe girls perceive catching as less macho than overhand throwing, so they don't feel they're compromising their femininity by executing a good catch. Only give them enough practice—and they're off and catching. (The Loovis and Butterfield tests stopped at eighth grade, so we don't know what happened to the girls' catching skill after that.)

Kicking was the third skill studied, and imagine! This time the boys didn't outperform the girls until sixth grade. Because of its association with macho-to-the-max football, kicking, one would think, would be a skill girls would avoid like a pestilence. By grade six most have entered puberty, when their concerns about gender appropriateness go through the roof. This conceivably could weaken girls' ambitions to kick on a par with boys. (On the other hand, the cultural perception of kicking as a male-only skill has shifted dramatically since this study was published, in 1994, owing to the popularity of girls' and women's soccer and to increasing numbers of girls playing football. One can only speculate how girls would fare in a kicking study done today.)

Last but not least, Loomis and Butterfield studied side-arm striking (as in a tennis swing). Here again there was the notable phenomenon of girls lagging behind the boys five years in a row until fifth grade, when suddenly their "mature striking development" is at par. Equally remarkable is the fact that their side-arm striking *stayed* at par for only a year. In sixth, seventh, and eighth grades the girls were back behind the boys again. One little window of parallel skill, and then boom, down they shrink, as if the experience of being physically equal were too much to bear.

It isn't only the brain that determines when and whether an individual can grasp a ball or swing a leg with force. The development of the muscles themselves contributes to motor dexterity and speed. The child who is muscularly underdeveloped, we might deduce from studies such as this one, will be at risk of delays in motor development. "Muscle maturation may impose a rate-limiting envelope for all motor tasks which is particularly evident in rapidly alternating movements," two scientists wrote in a study published in the British medical journal *Lancet*. That is, the *speed* at which someone can perform a physical task is limited by muscle development. This study was published under the title "The Maturation of Motor Dexterity: Or Why Johnny Can't Go Any Faster."

What we really need to know more about is how *Jenny's* motor dexterity matures. For example, one study found that six-year-old girls were 3.5 percent slower in distance running than six-year-old boys. "With astounding predictability the girls fell another 2.7 percent behind each subsequent year," says Jackie Hudson, a movement analyst at California State University. Half the year-to-year change in performance was attributed to the boys' improvement; the other half had resulted from the girls' deterioration. But what was making the boys get better? asks Hudson.

I think the more important question is, What was making the girls get worse? Was an increasing difference in body fat the problem? No. An inch-for-inch comparison of fitness norms for children found that boys and girls gain fat at about the same rate between the ages of six and twelve. Hudson wonders, Are boys possibly learning effective technique and girls ineffective technique?

Keeping these muscle and skill comparisons in mind, let's remember what happens to very young girls. Could it be that girls are staying in the doll corner at three and four and five because that's where they think they belong—and because nothing else is being offered them? And if they *do* spend all their time in the doll corner, what possibly will be the effect on their muscle development? It seems logical to suspect that their muscles might mature later, or less, than boys'—and for the not very edifying reason that they've been dissuaded from *using* them. This is the question that hasn't been addressed straightforwardly: Do girls experience delays or perhaps even truncation of motor development because of their gender conditioning? Is disuse producing a bonsai effect?

The 1970s took the study of movement further. The underlying mental or neural events that support (or produce) movement were the subject of the day. As sophisticated new imaging techniques developed, the way body and brain work together became the compelling focus of research. By the 1990s scientists were able to look directly at the brain while different motor skills were being performed. They could see, for example, that specific abilities weren't necessarily handled by only one part of the brain, and that some problems of coordination originate in the cerebellum, others in the basal ganglia. In any event, the scientific understanding of motor behavior's extraordinary minuet with the brain had catapulted, by century's end, way beyond physical educators' relatively crude methods of assessing their players' abilities. Coaches were still picking potential football players on the basis of, How high can you jump? How many pounds can you bench-press? How fast can you sprint? "The sum of the scores in these tests is considered predictive of athletic performance," says Malcolm Gladwell, writing in *The New Yorker* on "physical genius." But he notes that the closer one looks at motor behavior, "the less it can be described by such cut-and-dried measures of athleticism."

Yet until fairly recently these were the measures scholars themselves used in looking at motor skills. Certainly when it came to measuring gender differences, which is our concern here, the bluntness of the testing methodologies produced gross results, results that had little to do with the actual ability to learn a sport. Who could throw farther, a boy or a girl? Who could hit harder? Who could do the best job delivering the celebratory pitch on the opening day of baseball season? These questions were posed not just by newspapers and the general public, but by those attempting to arrive at scientific answers. But the scientists sidestepped the whole issue of what it took to *learn* these skills and—most important—whether females had an equal opportunity to learn.

Culture, or environment, is a major influence on skill development. In tests to examine agility, coordination, and static and explosive strength in almost four thousand individuals between the ages of three and eighty, living conditions explained 22 percent of variance. Culture explained 26 percent. Gender was not looked at in these tests, but the data certainly provoke us to ask, What might happen to Jenny's motor development if the amount of time she got to spend in the doll corner was limited, just as kids whose parents don't want them growing into passive, brain-dead couch potatoes have their television time limited? Would she possibly spend more time in physical activity?

Maybe it's not good for girls to be spending so much time in their fantasy worlds of playing Mommy taking care of Baby and vice versa. The activities children pursue etch themselves on the neural pathways of the brain. We don't want our kids just plopping themselves passively in front of the television. But we assume that girls sit quietly in the doll corner because it's "natural." It isn't. Running and kicking and throwing are "natural," and girls are being weaned away from these activities—and into the doll corner—before they're out of diapers.

A few years ago a friend's three-year-old son was teaching me the proper way to throw a Frisbee. (It's never too late.) He analyzed my throwing and showed me what to do. When I got it right, he pumped his little arm in the air and shouted, "I *gave* you the Power!" His statement was influenced by his love of Power Rangers, but I was charmed nonetheless, for it was as clear as the nose on his face—he knew it, and I knew it: Getting a Frisbee to arc beautifully over a summer lawn may seem magical, but it isn't. It simply requires knowing what to do with your body—a certain positioning of shoulder and elbow, a deft flick of the wrist. When you have this information, you have "the Power." When you don't, you don't.

Once teachers and coaches spy differences in the performances between boys and girls, they tend to accept them as physiological. Then their expectations of the two sexes change, and the type and quantity of instruction they offer change concomitantly. "Girls generally are provided with less (or lower-level) instruction, encouragement, and opportunity for practice and performance of their motor skills; subsequently their personal expectations generally are lowered," note Toole and Kretzschmar.

The gender training so vigorously foisted on girls is disabling to them, Dr. Duncan told the President's Council on Physical Fitness and Sports, "both in absolute terms and in relation to boys." To put it plainly, "girls don't get the formative experiences they need" if they are going to be able to use their bodies powerfully. When they do get the necessary experiences, they blast the gender gap to smithereens. Consider the following rescue scenario. A sick man who is driving to a doctor's office with his seven-year-old daughter suddenly passes out at the wheel. Drivers in neighboring cars watch in horror as the Honda station wagon begins to roll backward. Then, remarkably, the girl manages to budge him over enough so that she can get her feet onto the brake and gas pedals. She drives four blocks on a four-lane highway to Howard University Hospital, where she stops the car and runs into the emergency room for help. Her father, who'd had a 105-degree fever when he collapsed, credits her with saving his life.

Latia Robinson, the little girl, was later photographed for *People* sitting smiling and proud behind the steering wheel of the family car. Her back was straight, her chest open, her gaze direct. She told a reporter she'd been able to drive because her father had been letting her sit in front of him and steer since she was five. Latia's rescue of her father is a story of physical intelligence in action. Think of what her feat required: the multitude of connections among eye, hand, foot, and brain, the minuscule calculations and constant feedback that allowed her to move the car safely through traffic. Howard Gardner, the multiple intelligence theorist I referred to earlier, would call what Latia accomplished "solving a body-kinesthetic problem." Physical problem solving may not at first glance appear to be as mentally demanding as solving a mathematical equation, but consider: Simply hitting a tennis ball requires complex body-kinesthetic problem solving. The brain has to calculate not only the initial velocity of the ball, but the effects of the wind (as Martina Hingis can tell you) and the progressive decrease in velocity after the ball bounces. The brain is constantly giving orders, based on refined and updated information, to the muscles. To return a serve of average speed, you've got only about a second in which to do all this. Imagine, then, the body-kinesthetic complexities of driving a car, the continual calculations as Latia drove among other cars, her regulation of speed and ongoing negotiation of traffic signals, her assessment of distances in mirrors, and all of this while her body was executing the movements involved in accelerating, braking, and steering.

When I came across Latia Robinson's story, I had already been delving into the effects on females of being taught to trust their bodies. I knew that young women growing up in the last two decades had benefited from a different legacy than that given those who had grown up before the seventies: they had a wholly different sense of their bodies. The photograph of seven-year-old

Latia—self-confident, strong, and independent—suggested just *how* different.

It also illustrated how young a girl can be and handle a tremendous number of complex motor skills smoothly and automatically— if she's had the training and experience. As Martina Hingis says, "You don't get born with that thing. You learn it." Latia had practiced, over and over, with her dad. She had learned the various movements involved in driving a car so well that her body could go on automatic; her brain had already mastered the tasks.

Are there gender differences in motor performance during the early childhood years? In summary, yes. But as long as the system of education remains as it is, it's hard to know the extent to which these differences are merely socially, or environmentally, created. Toole and Kretzschmar offer major caveats: Differences between boys' and girls' motor performances will *continue* to exist, they remind us, as long as the following conditions remain:

1. The differences are viewed as *biologically* based and are therefore accepted as unavoidable and unchangeable.
2. Different *expectations* are found, with respect to play behavior and standards of performance.
3. Differential *treatment* is given, in terms of encouragement to perform, instruction in technique, and opportunities for practice.
4. Activities are *labeled,* whether by name or by model, as "gender-appropriate" or "gender-inappropriate."
5. The *reward* system continues for boys and terminates for girls in middle or late childhood.

Sadly, there is a connection between girls' lack of opportunity and training in physical skills and what happens to them when they get older. Comparisons in overarm throwing in men and women have been studied up to the age of ninety. Women's overarm throwing patterns tend to remain "immature." In a group sixty-five to seventy-six years of age, 77 percent of the females and 11 percent of the males displayed immature patterns in the action of the trunk and arms, Toole and Kretzschmar reported. These immature patterns were presumed to be the reason men this age threw faster than women. So, if a child has not developed mature movement patterns in early childhood, will she eventually develop a mature pattern by older adulthood? Based on the relatively few cross-sectional studies that have been done on older adults, the answer would be no. "Women are still using immature patterns in later life and producing lower throwing velocities and distances than men," Toole and Kretzschmar report, noting that no data show whether the older women tested had ever gotten any throwing instruction since childhood.

Note, however, that women *do* improve in running as they get older. While young boys develop a mature stage of running sooner than do young girls, by age fifty performance differences have evened out. Women, at fifty, are little different from men in sprint stride velocity and stride length. This brought up, for the above scholars, the interesting issue of practice. "Do young girls practice running (or play using the running pattern) as much as young boys?" they ask. "If not, it may be that environmental factors contribute wholly to gender differences in early childhood."

At the very least, the fact that gender differences in running can be reduced with practice in older age is very positive. By the same token, "disuse phenomenon," as they call it, radically affects the quality of old age. Older women have poorer balance than older men, and as a result fall more often and break hips and ankles and wrists at a far greater rate. But when they are young, females are better at balance tasks than young boys! So what happens to this advantage as women age? Probably disuse—or lack of exercise—causes the decline in balance in older women. They do not, over their life span, continue practicing the play behaviors and daily skills that contribute to better balance.

We know, from the history of female physical education in the last century, that women who are older today experienced a discriminatory restriction from the full use of their bodies. But Toole and Kretzschmar see change happening and conclude their report on an optimistic note. "Hopefully, with the acceptability of exercise, fitness, and sport to all individuals at all ages, gender differences in movement patterns throughout the lifespan will disappear and quantitative differences in power, strength, speed, and reaction time will slowly diminish."

As I read these studies I found myself becoming more and more excited. Everything going into performance can be quantified, measured, made visible. The mystique of innate inability has been penetrated and the truth revealed: high performance for women is eminently achievable. The more unbiased the instruments used to understand and assess performance, the clearer it became. Studies show gender to be barely relevant as a predictor, or limiter, of athletic performance. What really counts are acquired skills, trained muscles, and movement efficiency that comes from refined technique.

Shrinking Bodies, Shrinking Brains

It doesn't take a gender scientist to imagine what the frailty repertoire might do to girls' sense of physical competence. In a survey of third- to sixth-graders, girls scored only 2 percent lower than boys on a battery of motor skills tests, but they self-rated their skills as 14 percent lower. By the time they enter first grade, girls have already decided their athletic ability is zilch compared to boys'. Nine-year-old boys and girls are virtually identical in anaerobic performance, one study shows. Yet girls don't think so. Their false perception of physical competence is reminiscent of their false perception of their weight. The groundwork for body disturbance in girls—and this includes not just body image, but how they *use* their bodies—is laid early. Then, at puberty, the gender effect tightens like a vise.

The effects of learned weakness are as profound as they are underrecognized. Participating in sports, after all, promotes identity development in girls. It leads to better self-esteem, more positive attitudes toward school, and less self-destructive behavior. It lifts them out of passivity. "I discovered how much happier I was when I stopped picking up those fashion magazines and stopped watching TV," says Nicole Zaharko, a world champion in freestyle kayaking, recalling the changes she experienced when she first became interested in sports in high school. "I got outside more, read more, and realized that who I become as a person is far more important than fitting into a size six."

A 1994 study of girls found significant correlations between participation in competitive high school sports and higher grades, higher self-concept, higher educational aspirations, and fewer disciplinary problems. Girls in sports are less likely to smoke and drink. They show more confidence, more positive attitudes toward school, and less self-destructive behavior. A 1996 study by the U.S. Department of Health and Human Services found that the more days adolescent females exercised per week, the more likely they were to postpone their first experience with sexual intercourse. In western New York State (an area with one of the highest rates of adolescent pregnancy in the United States) a study indicated that higher rates of athletic participation among adolescent females were *significantly* associated with lower rates of both sexual activity and pregnancy.

High school girls who participate in team sports are 40 percent less likely to drop out of school and 33 percent less likely to become pregnant. Yet the 1996 *Surgeon General's Report on Physical Activity and Health* found almost half of young people between twelve and twenty-one to be physically inactive—with young females twice as likely to be sedentary as young males.

Children need vigorous physical activity if they're going to resist chronic disease. Girls jeopardize their immune systems when they stop using their bodies. Research shows that low- to moderate-intensity training increases levels of interleukin-1, interferon, and "natural killer cells." "Thus it appears that moderate-intensity exercise may have a positive effect in retarding diseases such as cancer or those caused by viruses and influenza," Patty Freedson and Linda K. Bunker told the President's Council on Physical Fitness and Sports, in a special report, "Physical Activity and Sport in the Lives of Girls." Chronic diseases, some of which often begin in childhood and adolescence and may later manifest themselves in adulthood, such as cancer, diabetes, osteoporosis, and heart disease, are all affected by exercise.

Physical movement is important in weight control for high school girls—and certainly it's safer than dieting, which puts them at risk of developing eating disorders. Obesity is the most prevalent chronic illness among children in North America, according to Bunker and Freedson. Approximately twice as many children are overweight today as were in the 1960s, with girls in cities being particularly at risk. Children who have higher than average levels of body fat have a greater risk of developing elevated blood pressure, total cholesterol, and LDL cholesterol. This is especially important, since children who have high cholesterol levels are almost three times more likely to have high cholesterol in adulthood.

Girls who don't exercise have more physical distress associated with their menstrual cycles and less regularity. (This is interesting when you recall that nineteenth-century physicians believed just the opposite: that exercise would harm menstrual function.) However, girls who *over*exercise—such as elite-level athletes or girls who suffer from a compulsive exercise disorder—can interfere with their menstrual cycles. The body needs a certain amount of fat to produce estrogen, and menstruation doesn't occur if estrogen isn't present. The overexercised body loses not only fat but precious estrogen, putting girls and women at risk of loss of bone density. "Female athlete triad" is a term for the threesome of eating disorders, amenorrhea, and bone loss, which often go together. In one study of gymnasts, 100 percent were dieting, 62 percent were using a method of weight control that was extreme, and yet 75 percent were still being urged by their coaches to lose weight. Ballet dancers are similarly vulnerable to extreme methods of weight control and to eating disorders. These illnesses aren't "caused" by exercise, however. Rather, they may be triggered by psychological issues and also by appetite-regulating brain chemicals like serotonin that require the presence of estrogen in order to be metabolized. In the latter situation, extreme fat loss is the culprit. Endocrinologists recommend that high-exercising girls have their hormone levels tested periodically to be sure they are not estrogen-deficient.

Boys gain in strength and cardiovascular fitness after puberty. Girls don't. Fourteen is an important year for girls. Up until then, maturation-related strength increases at a linear rate. After that, the rate of increase slows—and for sedentary girls may actually decrease. Without systematic exercise, aerobic power in adolescent girls will *decline steadily into adulthood.* This trend was not observed in males across the same age span. But the decline in endurance reverses with aerobic training, which is why aerobic exercise is *crucial* for adolescent girls. Their cardiovascular strength diminishes without it.

Anaerobic power—the capacity to perform strenuous activity in short bursts of time (for example, the ability to perform a vertical jump)—also increases through early childhood in girls, then *decreases* in adolescence and young adulthood. But anaerobic power, too, can be increased with training. Studies of girls between ten and thirteen have shown they can improve anaerobic power up to 20 percent with exercise.

"In order for bones to grow properly, it is important for children, particularly adolescents, to participate in regular (preferably daily) physical activity," states the President's Council fitness report. The bone density of girls who don't exercise (and remember, *most* don't) falls dramatically. By the age of sixteen, unfit girls have already lost bone density in the spine! In the brief period between fourteen, when most stop exercising, and sixteen, girls turn themselves into prime candidates for osteoporosis. At a time when they're supposed to be *gaining* bone, they're losing it—and why? Because they're afraid to make themselves big. Because they loathe weight gain, muscle bulk, appearing unfeminine. And unless something or someone intervenes in this fear and loathing, they may never reach peak bone mass.

The effect of exercise training on attaining peak bone mass is a monumental issue in terms of bone health across the life span, according to experts in reproductive endocrinology. Those who reach peak bone mass during adolescence may be at lower risk of fracture and osteopenia later in life. A study published in the *Journal of Bone Mineral Research* found that in two groups, one with high and one with low bone density, the group whose bone mass had reached a lower peak by the time they arrived at physical maturity had a higher incidence of fractures when they got older. "These findings suggest that the attainment of a high peak bone mass during the first two decades of life is important to minimizing fracture risk later in life," according to endocrinologists writing on exercise and bone health.

Avery Faigenbaum, a professor of exercise physiology at the University of Massachusetts in Boston, says bones are *most responsive* to the stimulus of resistance training during childhood and adolescence. This is the "ideal time to increase bone mineral density and build up the so-called bone bank."

The incredible shrinking girl has a high risk of becoming the incredible shrinking woman. Studies show that nonexercising girls are likely to become nonexercising women. This may well be the reason that women are so vulnerable to osteoporosis: over the course of the life span they simply are not physically active enough. In the interests of "femininity" they keep themselves underdeveloped and physically vulnerable. Their bones are more porous than they should be.

By age sixteen girls are already on the road to fracture, crushed vertebrae, and the dreaded "hump" of the upper back that signifies not normal aging (as has long been thought) but skeletal deformity. Girls are on this track by sixteen not because they are inherently frailer than boys, but because they *make* themselves that way. Female college athletes have a five times greater chance than men of suffering serious knee injuries in soccer, volleyball, and basketball. They are also at greater risk of stress fractures and rotator cuff injuries. Dr. Jo Hannafin, orthopedic director of the Women's Sport Medicine Clinic at the Hospital for Special Surgery in New York, says girls need strength training to prevent such injuries. Basically, they need more athletic opportunity at a younger age, better training, better coaching, and better equipment.

Girls who stop exercising in adolescence may also be taking the edge off their intellectual functioning. New research is uncovering dramatic changes in the cognitive functioning of the brain that occur with exercise. A 1997 "meta-analysis" assessing the results of 134 studies suggests that both single exercise sessions and chronic training programs benefit cognitive performance.

Jean Piaget was one of the first psychologists to suggest that motor development is an important determinant of intellectual development. Since his research in the 1930s, many theories have been proposed suggesting that the body influences the mind, but until recently actual mechanisms that might support a causal link were not known. With advances in the field of neuropsychology, contemporary researchers are now on their way to establishing the mechanisms that could explain such a link. One has to do with cerebral blood flow. Research on humans has found that moderate- to high-intensity exercise produces large increases in cerebral blood flow. These blood flow increases may benefit cognitive functioning by increasing the supply of nutrients to the brain.

Brain neurotransmitters also affect the brain-body link. Mood-enhancing endorphins increase after an acute bout of exercise. Frequent, or so-called chronic, exercise has been shown to raise levels of norepinephrine, a neurotransmitter chemical associated with better memory.

Yet another striking finding is that exercise may result in *permanent structural changes in the brain*. Studies of exercising rats show an increase in the density of veins in the cerebral cortex. The cost of doing this neuropsychological research is high, and more work is needed, but the initial results indicate that exercise may result in changes in either the brain itself or the brain environment and that these changes may well have a positive influence on brain performance. Other studies show that exercise programs lasting several years or more produce the biggest gains in cognitive performance.

Contrary to the stereotype of the "dumb jock," most studies over the years have shown a correlation between athletic success and academic success. There have been numerous studies finding that girls who do sports stay in school longer and do better than girls who are physically inactive. Many female high school athletes report higher grades on standardized test scores and lower dropout rates and are more likely to go on to college than their nonathletic counterparts. Given what learned weakness is doing to girls' brain and bone development alone, the inactivity of adolescent girls is little less than a national health crisis. Gender bias is the cause of this crisis.

What I'm getting at in this chapter isn't just girls' ability to do sports, but their ability to *do,* period. I'm talking about the development of bone, and muscle, and the ligaments that bind them. I'm talking about the brain's ability to communicate with the body's parts, to get them to function smoothly in conjunction with one another. And last, I'm talking about the losses that occur physically, mentally, and emotionally, when body and brain are never asked to perform the complex dance that produces physical intelligence.

Something about the notion of "girl play" and "boy play" has been overemphasized. Boys learn to be tough, to gangsta-rap, to build muscle, to confuse sex with violence. By the time they reach puberty, body size is their biggest image concern. They want to be *big.* Girls learn to be passive, to daydream about the time they'll be able to be mothers with babies or Barbies with dates. They want to be *small.* To ensure this, girls start dieting when they're seven and eight. (One study found 50 percent of nine-year-old girls and 80 percent of eleven-year-old girls dieting to lose weight.)

Parents will swear to you that all this is natural and inevitable, that their boys were interested in driving semis when they were eighteen months old and that their girls wanted nothing more than to spend their time with doll babies that wet. But these gender extremes in young kids are culturally caused. It's hard for parents to conceive of how important our gender fixations are to us and how we perpetrate them so that they infiltrate our children's very dreams. The idea that to be feminine girls have to be small and dainty is harming them—physically, emotionally, and mentally.

THREE

Getting Them Out of the Doll Corner

The child is barely past toddlerhood. She approaches a nine-foot-high chain-link fence surrounding the playground, sticks a sneakered toe into the fencing, and begins to climb, hand above hand, until she is above her mother's head, then out of her mother's reach, then close to the sky itself. There is something odd about the scene, even to the child's mother. She has never seen a girl this age do this. She has never seen a boy this age do it. She stands beneath her child, her head cocked back, trying to be sure the girl is safe. She calculates that if the child should slip, there would be nothing but herself to break the fall. "Look, Ma! Look!" The little girl is exhilarated by her climb, and her mother doesn't want to show anxiety or doubt. She wants to support her child's adventure, but she doesn't want to be stupid about it. What should she do? She calculates that if her daughter should fall, she would be able to catch her. All she needs is the courage not to panic.

The week wasn't out before the girl was climbing to the top of the fence and wanting to climb down the other side. No inhibition of intentionality here. The fence climber was Rachel. I would let her do things I'd never have been permitted as a child, as much from the particular ambivalence about child rearing that afflicted young parents in the 1970s as from feminist conviction of a girl's right to equal strength. We didn't want to restrict and control our children the way our parents had done to us, but we weren't sure how far to let them go. Often this left us biting our tongues and digging our nails into our palms as we stood behind the girl's right to grow, to pursue what interested her—to "be her own person," as we said in the jargon of the times.

We were the generation of mothers who worried about whether we should allow our little girls to play with Barbie and whether GI Joe would turn our little boys into macho monsters. The gender difference expressed by these toys was both ludicrous and disturbing. We wanted to encourage a broader range of behaviors in our kids. Girls should be able to play with trucks, boys to cry. Marlo Thomas's popular children's album, *Free to Be You and Me,* and shows like *Sesame Street* reflected the new and looser attitudes toward gender. And these attitudes contributed to an unforeseeable but major change. By the 1990s mothers watched as their girls became interested in their brothers' most strenuous activities: football, ice hockey, and, heavens knows, soccer. By the end of the century these sports no longer belonged to boys. Girls had gone beyond such archaic activities as cheerleading, way beyond. Goal kicking, tackling, and head butting were more fun.

Perceived Physical Competence

Self-esteem, self-confidence, and perceptions of competence—all predict positive achievement in physical activity and sport. The reverse is also true: Physical activity predicts psychological well-being—

in children as well as adults. Recent studies show that physical activity increases self-esteem in girls in both childhood and adolescence. "It appears to be a cyclic relationship," reports the President's Council on Physical Fitness and Sports. "Better perceptions of oneself and one's abilities lead to enhanced effort, persistence and achievement, which in turn further benefit self-perceptions. The role of significant others is critical in positively affecting this cycle."

Today cognitive motivation theories nearly all highlight the importance of *expectations* and the individual's interpretation of things. "That is, what the person thinks is important *is* important. If you expect to do well at volleyball, you will," says Diane Gill, a professor of exercise and sport science. "If you expect to fall off the balance beam, you probably will."

From infancy the child begins to learn a set of appropriate behaviors and starts inhibiting behaviors that are considered out of character with the sex role. Boys as young as four perceive themselves to be stronger than girls, and girls perceive themselves to be weaker than boys, even though no actual strength differences exist. One researcher followed ten groups of children from kindergarten through grade four and found that boys had a higher perception of competence in nine of the ten groups. Another study assessed the performance expectations of third- to seventh-graders when given tasks with a particular gender slant. Girls predicted lower scores on both dance- and football-related tasks, though their actual performances were equal to those of the boys.

More girls than boys expect to do poorly at sports and competition, and more women than men believe they cannot develop sport skills or maintain an exercise program. "Indeed, this gender influence on expectations and confidence is one of the most important considerations for achievement," says Gill, "particularly in the realm of physical activity."

One stunning influence on boys' and girls' expectations is the different criteria used to test their fitness. The standards for boys are higher. One research group wanted to find out if there were actually enough differences in what boys and girls between ten and thirteen could do to warrant such a seemingly discriminatory practice. What they found, in a nutshell, is that there *were* no significant differences. Maximal oxygen consumption, for example, is considered the single best indicator of cardiovascular endurance. When measured with body weight factored in, prepubescent boys' and girls' oxygen consumption was similar. There was also little difference in maximal heart rates and little difference in strength and muscular endurance. The greatest change in strength for boys occurs between thirteen and fourteen and is attributed to the pubertal introduction of testosterone. But the influence of this hormone spurt on boys' physical prowess as compared to girls' may be overstated. It's recently been discovered that girls, too, undergo a major increase in testosterone at puberty, with high levels relative to estrogen levels. A greater factor in girls' typical physical decline in adolescence is the failure to perform aerobic and strength exercise.

Girls do better than boys in flexibility, or range of motion at the joints, across all age groups. What the authors of this study wanted to do, however, was give boys and girls in an Illinois middle school the Physical Best test battery, a fitness assessment tool physical education teachers are trained to administer. Physical Best originally comprised five tests: one-mile walk/run, sit-ups, pull-ups, sit and reach, and body composition. The body composition test was ultimately eliminated because it was shown to be unreliable. For the remaining four tests, the directions state that the "best effort" is expected. Do as many correct sit-ups and pull-ups as possible; walk or run as fast as you can; for the flexibility segment, reach and stretch as far as possible. Since there are boys' criteria and girls' criteria for each of these, the authors decided to tabulate, in addition to individual scores, what percentage of both boys *and* girls met or exceeded the (higher) criteria set for boys.

The results of their test were enlightening, to say the least. In the walk/run, girls consistently demonstrated that they could meet or exceed the criteria set for boys. In sit-ups, ten- and eleven-year-old boys and girls did not differ significantly. At twelve they were the same at the beginning of the school year, but boys pulled ahead at the end of the year and stayed ahead at the age of thirteen. (It's interesting to speculate why girls' progress in abdominal endurance would begin to flatten at age thirteen—at least if they were *using* their abdominals.) With pull-ups, boys were significantly better than girls *except at age eleven,* when they were the same. (The study showed that very few children of either sex were able to complete pull-ups successfully.) In the sit-and-reach flexibility test, girls were way beyond the boys (as previously noted).

But here is the extraordinary bottom line: In the tabulation of percentages of those who met the boys' criteria, the girls came out ahead of the boys! At twelve and thirteen they fell behind in sit-ups, and only a handful could meet the boys' criteria in pull-ups, but their scores overall were so high, they were the fitness winners hands down. So here's the obvious question, as put by the researchers: "If prepubescent girls are physiologically capable and data from several studies have found no significant differences between boys' and girls' performances on fitness test items, *then why are American fitness test standards noticeably different for boys and girls of the same age?*"

Most disturbingly, what do these different standards of fitness tell girls about their capabilities? Even *after* puberty, the differences between boys' and girls' performance levels may be greatly influenced by societal expectations. In 1988 two social scientists issued a call for change: "Many parents, teachers, coaches, and peers continue to behave as if girls should not exercise and participate in sport to the same degree and level that boys should," they noted. "Girls participate, perform, practice, compete, and behave exactly as society expects. The result is reduced levels of physical activity and practice, in turn resulting in lower levels of health-related physical fitness and sport skills."

Yet eight years later, the discriminatory fitness tests were still being plied in the middle school gyms of America. Girls' most decided "perceived cause" of failure in sport is the fact of being a girl and believing they are constitutionally less able than boys. Psychologists tell us that those who attribute failure to lack of ability tend to be low achievers—mainly because they give up too soon. High achievers, who attribute success to effort, are likely to put in extra effort to reach their goals. Girls grow up thinking that physical effort, for them, is futile.

The Coaching Factor

Basketball coach Mariah Burton Nelson has to work hard to push girls and women past their learned restraints. An example is their standoffishness about assuming the defensive stance that requires a basketball player to squat low to the ground, legs wide, knees gaping, hands ready to deflect passes or shots—a stance that allows a player to react quickly to any moves from the offense. Females *hate* the defense stance from the get-go, says Nelson. "It's the leg spread. It's unladylike to yawn one's legs wide open."

Females have trouble "being big." "They don't like to feel tall, to seem wide, to make loud noises. They don't feel comfortable inhabiting a big space." But taking a big space and being aggressive are important in sports—basketball, for example, where you need to be able to "snatch a rebound as if you're starving and it's the last coconut on the tree," as Nelson says. For girls raised to be feminine, brash aggression during play doesn't come easily. "You have to decide where you want to be, then get there, refusing to let anyone push you out of the way. You have to shout, loudly, to let your teammates know who's cutting through the lane or who's open for a shot."

Girls today are at a critical juncture. The way parents and coaches respond to their physical evolution is crucial. Girls still need more adult approval than boys do, and until they evolve out of that need (and sports will help them do it), the kind of coaching they get is all-important. Coaching attitudes affect not only *how* girls develop physically, but even *whether* they develop physically.

In younger girls, the self-esteem that sport produces is due to challenge, achievement, risk-taking experience, and skill development, studies show. Adolescent girls cite these same sources of self-esteem, but they also speak of feeling good as athletes because of the approval of others. Adolescent males, in contrast, show relatively little interest in others' approval but rather rely on competitive outcomes and ease of learning skills as the basis for judging their physical competence. Parents, teachers, and coaches must be aware of the importance of combining praise with skill feedback when teaching girls. And they must be aware of the importance of pushing them to work harder and not coddling them.

The lack of encouragement girls perceive often comes in the form of criticism and even verbal abuse from coaches and parents. In tee ball, a baseball-type game for five- and six-year-old boys and girls, coaches and parents in some communities make it clear that they're not overly interested in the girls who play. And it isn't because they can't throw. Girls who display strength, power, or physicality when interacting with boys run the risk of being marginalized. "I know the boys don't like it that I run faster than they do," said Amanda, the fastest runner in seventh grade. "But I do."

"Our original expectation was that tee ball might provide girls with a nurturing environment in which to develop their athletic skills," said Melissa A. Landers of the University of Georgia, who observed a YMCA tee ball group during the spring 1993 season. "This proved not to be the case." Most of the girls didn't have their own baseball gloves, for example—a sign, the researchers believed, that parents didn't take their daughters' participation seriously. Worse, the coaches didn't take their young charges seriously, not even the female coaches. "None of the girls want to be there," one coach told Landers. "Not one. If I put a coloring station in the corner, every girl would be there. . . . Dads take their sons outside to throw with. Girls stay inside and play dolls."

This was the decade of women's dramatic entrance into basketball, ice hockey, and soccer, and not *one* little girl wanted to play tee ball? They *all* wanted to stay inside and play with dolls? The fact that this was a female coach made it an even sadder testimony to the persistence of stereotypical thinking. "The coaches' views about girls in baseball prevented them from taking an active interest in the girls' athletic development and instead caused them to focus on the attention and behavior deficits that they perceived were displayed by the girls," says Dr. Landers.

In the Georgia tee ball scenario, the coaches reprimanded the girls more frequently and more harshly than they did the boys—and often for the same behavior that was accepted in boys. When they weren't criticizing individual girls, they were projecting global images of girls as incompetent. When one of the male coaches dropped a ball he was trying to throw, he said, "Look, I throw like a girl."

Apparently he felt so embarrassed, he was compelled to turn the scene into farce: "He contorted his arms and awkwardly threw the ball toward Helen, [a child] who was standing in front of him." This grown man deflected attention from his own gaffes by bringing one of the girls onto the scene as "a prop for depicting her own incompetence," Landers wrote in her field notes.

This male coach might have done better to sharpen his own skills, but instead he used the girls to gloss over his clumsiness. After dropping the ball another time, he said to one of the girls, "I'm a little girl. I can't catch the ball." Such mockery obviously sends a powerful message to girls—not only about their abilities, but about their very worth. This coach was telling his girls they were inferior, weak, and not to be confused with strong, powerful boys. The brainwashing worked. The coach's treatment of them and the unwelcoming attitude of the boys on the team contributed to the waning interest of girls during the season.

"As early as nine years old I began to know my own body in ways that only an athlete or a dancer knows it," wrote Michael Oriard, a former Kansas City Chief turned English professor. "Through football I learned . . . how my body could be used as a force, how my shoulders, back, hips, and legs, driven in a straight line against a ball carrier's legs, could topple him easily."

Putting this kind of typical boy's experience into a cultural context, developmental psychologist John Shotter refers to a "political economy of developmental opportunities." Not everyone has access to growth opportunities, is what he means. Both gender and class make a difference. The development of "personal powers," of the sort Oriard thrilled to when he was only nine years old, requires opportunity. It requires coaching, mentoring, other people "recognizing what is skilled and valuable in what a child does and holding it up for a child's own recognition and pleasure." Out of this, Shotter suggests, comes a boy's or girl's desire to develop natural capacities into personal skills.

Consider the effect of positive coaching on an eighth-grade Georgia girl. Tonya Butler, the manager of a junior high football team, was watching practice one afternoon as one after another of the boys failed the seemingly simple task of kicking an extra point. One of the coaches called over to her, "Tonya, you play soccer. Why don't you come out here?"

"I thought he was just joking around," says Tonya. "So, during a water break, I went out to kick it—and I nailed it. And he was like, 'Let's back up.' I finally missed on like the thirty-five. He was like, 'Wow! Go suit up.'" (This took place an all-important five years after the humiliating experiences of the little girls on the tee ball diamond.)

In tenth grade, after making seven of eight field goal attempts and twenty-eight of thirty-one extra points on the Riverdale High football team, Tonya became the first girl ever to make the all-state team. At five feet six inches and 125 pounds, Tonya is "ready to break new ground," says her coach. The all-except-Tonya male team loves her. The quarterback notes proudly that she doesn't get any breaks because she's a girl. "She does what she needs to do," he says. "I wouldn't want to have anyone else kicking for us." Clearly Tonya's acceptance by her male teammates was influenced by the enthusiastic treatment she received from her male coach.

Not all coaches can maintain this gender neutrality in all situations. Tawana Hammond of Union Bridge, Maryland, was one of 109 girls playing high school football in the United States in 1989. After being tackled in a game, she suffered severe internal injuries and her spleen and half of her pancreas had to be removed. While girls who play football are no more likely to get injured than boys who play football, this episode became the occasion for gender bias to raise its ugly head. Tawana received little sympathy from "a lot of people" who thought "she shouldn't have been there anyway," the mayor of Union Bridge said. "A female playing a man's game has created a lot of hard feelings in this community." Even the coach could not refrain from telling Tawana, "You realize that you are at a major biological disadvantage because women are not as strong as men."

Well, not as strong as *some* men, perhaps. No one talks about the "major biological disadvantages" of the smaller, weaker boys and men who are injured in football every day. In the 1992 season 21 percent of the players in the National Football League endured injuries severe enough to keep them from at least one game. Injuries in this sport occur frequently, battering away at the human body, male *or* female. Seventy-eight percent of retired football players suffer from permanent disabilities. The average life expectancy of a pro football player is fifty-six years! "The truth is, *men* are too weak to play football," says Mariah Burton Nelson. But putting aside the question of the sanity of football, the fact that an increasing number of girls are signing on to their school teams is an indication of a breakdown in gender bias.

Aware of the motor deficits girls experience as a result of being held back in sports, some coaches are organizing programs to help close the gender gap. At his training gym in Orlando, Florida, Dave Oliver, the strength and conditioning coach for the U.S. women's soccer team, offers resistance training for girls starting at eight, using exercises like push-ups that rely on their own body weight. For girls between eight and eleven he focuses on neuromuscular activity and speed drills, "teaching them how to cut and turn effectively, developing their balance and agility." Girls interested in athletics should begin working with weights at age twelve, Oliver says. In middle school they should be out on the field doing lunges, squats, and high knee kicks.

In her report to the President's Council, "Physical Activity and Sport in the Lives of Girls," Professor Margaret Carlisle Duncan, of the University of Wisconsin, said it's of primary importance that girls be given opportunities to develop their physical skills. This will happen only when we banish gender bias. Dr. Duncan offered the following guidelines for teachers, parents, physical educators, and coaches.

1) It is essential to eliminate gender-typing whenever possible. Activities should never be labeled as "girls' games" or "boys' games," "feminine" or "masculine."

2) Leaders should avoid using sex as a basis for forming physical-activity groups. Arbitrarily segregating girls and boys may create hostility and perpetuate power imbalances.

3) When adults observe inequities or gender stereotyping on the playing field or in the classroom, it is often best to openly confront issues of sexism, prejudice, or discrimination.

4) Coaches and physical educators should give girls equal access and attention. Both girls and boys should play the important and interesting positions in a game (e.g., pitcher, goalie, forward).

5) All of us must challenge stereotypes whenever possible. When teachers choose games and lead activities, a female teacher might play football, a male teacher might jump rope.

Society continues to fight against the inclusion of girls in sports. From the time Little League was founded in 1939, little girls wanted to join. For decades the Little League organizers said no. In the 1970s, when federal pressure against discrimination against girls in sports grew hot and heavy (owing in part to the Title IX legislation I'll discuss in chapter 5), Little League officials spent almost $2 million fighting to keep girls out. Even more outrageous than the amount of money spent in the attempt to exclude girls were the reasons proffered, among them the daunting possibility of girls being molested. "It wouldn't be proper for coaches to pat girls on the rear end the way they naturally do boys," said Dr. Creighton Hale, the president of Little League. "And suppose a girl gets hurt on the leg? Why, that's just not going to go over—a grown man rubbing a little girl's leg."

Vivid as it apparently was in Dr. Hale's mind, this image was not what motivated resistance in New Jersey, where teams eventually voted to suspend activities rather than allow girl players. Whole families marched on the state capital in protest against the hideous possibility. A petition against the move to integrate girls got fifty thousand signatures. "This issue is as fraught with backlash as any I've seen," said the female attorney who represented the girls. "We're seeing the same hostility and fanaticism on behalf of segregated baseball as from the right-to-lifers."

"The sooner little boys begin to realize that little girls are equal and that there will be many opportunities for a boy to be bested by a girl, the closer they will be to better mental health," announced Sylvia Pressley, the hearing officer who ruled that girls must be allowed to play.

It's hard to imagine what those Little League resisters would make of girls today bashing past boys in soccer, ice hockey, and football. The striking thing is that girls pioneering in contact sports *had* to play with boys. At first there was no one else to play with. In the Ohio Games, for example, only one under-ten girls' soccer team signed up, so the girls played against the boys' teams. It was 1993. The boys resisted—"I'd rather be shot than play against girls," one said—and it soon became clear why: The girls won the title, defeating all four teams they played, three in shutouts.

As one "boys only" sport falls, a new one comes along to temporarily patch crumbling gender barriers. The boys in a skateboarding community in Colorado told sociologist Becky Beal that this sport was a "naturally" male activity, that boys' and girls' abilities were intrinsically different, and that girls lacked what's needed for skateboarding. When Beal pointed out (this was in the 1990s) that females succeed at many sports requiring balance and coordination (she offered gymnastics and figure skating as examples), the boys couldn't get past the idea that skateboarding was different. They dismissed four girls who'd tried entering their group as "just trying to skate around" or "just trying to balance on the board." They called them "skate Betties" and assumed they were mainly there to meet boys.

By the end of the decade girls had definitely proven they were serious skateboarders. The first national all-girls skateboarding competitions in San Diego (1999) demonstrated just how strong, agile, and courageous girl athletes can be. Extreme sports are every bit as girl-doable as they are boy-doable, these skateboarding champions proved.

The Dad Factor

Today a father is often the first coach a girl has. Many fathers delight in encouraging their daughters to take physical risks and learn to trust themselves. When Keven McMurray took his ten-year-old to rock climb in the White Mountains of northern New Hampshire, he hired a good instructor who would teach both of them at the same time. For two hours Joe worked with father and daughter, teaching them about the knots and anchors and techniques and helping young Kelly face her fears. "We were to climb four pitches, or lengths, of the seventy-meter ropes up the mountain and rappel back down," McMurray recalls. Kelly had no problem with the first two pitches, but as the incline slowly approached sharper angles she began to hug the rock, clinging with her hands. Joe told her it was okay to be scared and gently urged her to trust herself and the equipment. Slowly she began to rely on her legs to support her in her toeholds. Three hours later they were sitting on a ledge 370 feet above where they had started. "Kelly beamed as she surveyed the lush mountains, perched high enough to see soaring hawks in search of prey below us."

The next day they took a steeper route, and Kelly froze more than once during the two-and-a-half-hour climb to the top. But the previous day's success had given her confidence, and she made it. "I could say a lot about all the obvious—the bonding of father and daughter in a shared challenge, witnessing a dramatic step in the maturity of one's offspring, and enjoying nature's wonders together," her father says. "But I think it was the sheer fun of it all and the simple pleasure of making it to the summit of a mountain with someone you love that I cherish the most."

Ila Borders, whose photograph is on the cover of this book, was ten when her father, a minor-league pitcher, took her to her first baseball game. "I told him right then I wanted to be a pitcher," Borders says. "He said, 'If you really want to do it, let's go to work.' Every Saturday and Sunday, we threw from six A.M. to noon. I owe him a lot."

The Dad Factor, in action. Phil Borders knew he'd have to build up his daughter's strength, particularly in her shoulders and wrists, just as he would have had to do had she been a boy. Professional sports dads don't blink at the work athletics requires of their girls. They know the skills can be developed, and they know what the payoff will be: dexterity, pride, and fun. For Ila, the payoff was bigger than anyone might have imagined. At age twelve, she faced eighteen batters in one game and struck out every one. By fourteen, she was playing semipro baseball.

It's doubtful, however, that fathers ever fully expect the hostility that will greet their athletically talented daughters. Grade school boys threw rocks at Ila in Little League. In high school, she was the most valuable player on the boys' team, but it wasn't always appreciated. Once, after striking out a male opponent, she was threatened with a knife by his girlfriend.

In 1993, she became the first woman to be awarded a college baseball scholarship to the University of Southern California at Costa Mesa. She played three seasons with the USC men's team. Teammates threw hard at her face during soft-toss drills. The taunting never broke her. She just went on racking up "firsts." When she was picked to play by the Duluth Dukes, a minor-league team in Minnesota, that was a first. Then, at twenty-three, she became the first woman to win a men's pro game. Every time Borders played, the team's attendance jumped eight hundred fans. People loved her, even if some male competitors found playing against her hard to take. At five feet nine inches she had bigger hands than a six-foot-six male teammate. The Dukes called her "Paws." "My hands are bigger than my dad's," she says, "and I can throw all day." Yet the rest of her isn't particularly big. "People are surprised by that."

Two years ago she was throwing the ball eighty-three miles an hour, "but it came in straight," she says. "Now my fastball's down to seventy-seven, but it's moving. Over the off-season I want to try to pick up four miles an hour but keep it moving." Her goal is to make it onto a major-league team. In the majors, pitchers throw ninety miles an hour. Will she be able to do it? It's never been done by a woman, so who knows? *Can* a woman pitch ninety miles an hour?

Borders has already developed her pitching prowess so much, my bets are on her for getting her speed up there even further. She's only twenty-four and has come a long way since her father took her to her first ball game. She's steady-eyed, focused on building skills and winning, and she just keeps working at it. In the meantime, her jersey is hanging in the Baseball Hall of Fame in Cooperstown, New York, a tribute to her achievement as the first woman to play men's pro baseball.

Some dads start training their daughters when they're much younger than Ila was. Allison Jaime Mleczko, one of America's first female ice hockey stars (known as A.J.), was only two when her father, a hockey coach, took her to the center of a frozen pond, put skates on her, and then walked off the ice, leaving her there. She cried, but she managed to work her way back to the pond's edge. It was a tough initiation, but it took. By the time she was four, A.J. wanted her father to file the picks from the front of her figure skates so she could play hockey.

When A.J. announced she was ready for a team, her father went to a meeting of the organization that ran the local boys' hockey leagues and said his daughter wanted to play. The league heads decided she could. From the beginning A.J. would play with boys, since women's and girls' hockey didn't yet exist as an organized sport. For years she was the only girl on the team, or even in the league. At nine, when she had to try out for the Squirt team in suburban Connecticut, where they lived, she was nervous. No girl had ever tried out before. When she made the team the coach asked her mother, "Are you sure you want her to do this?"

"Is she good enough?" her mother asked.

"Ability-wise, she's right up there," he replied. "But it *is* a boys' game."

"Well, if she's good enough and she wants to play on the team, we want her to play on the team," said A.J.'s mother. There was no body checking allowed in the lower leagues, but when A.J. entered the higher ones some adults were worried about how she'd manage. In her last prechecking game, a boy on the opponent team skated over and gave her a hard, gratuitous whack. She wheeled, hit him as hard as she could, and knocked him on the ice.

When A.J. was fourteen she saw the boys her age becoming stronger than she, but she recognized it as a sign not of their physical superiority, but that she needed more work. She began taking lessons to improve her strength and speed. When she went to a private high school and played other girls, she was a standout, but a few years later, when she decided to start training for the 1996 Winter Games in Nagano, A.J. had a shocker: she was far weaker than she'd thought. She could bench-press only sixty-five pounds, and squats and pull-ups were beyond her. It would take torturous training to get to the next strength level, but A.J. decided to go for it.

She took leave from her senior year at Harvard. Four times a week she went to the Boston University varsity weight room to train under the supervision of Michael Boyle, a BU strength and conditioning coach, along with a dozen other talented women who hoped to become members of the first U.S. Olympic women's hockey team. The three-hour workouts were thrilling, if exhausting, for the women, whose access to the weight rooms at their own colleges, where they'd been more tolerated than challenged, had always been limited. They had to leave jobs and schools to pursue the rugged program. Workouts left them so out of it, they couldn't even manage part-time jobs. But at BU they got to work out side by side with the best—not just college athletes, but in the spring and summer a group of NHL and NFL players who were training with Boyle to get in shape for their upcoming seasons. These women were pursuing their dream against all sorts of odds that weren't there for male athletes; for years they'd been challenged by male officials who didn't want them on teams and by boys who taunted them on the ice.

Full-body pull-ups were especially hard for A.J., who at five-eleven was a big woman. By the third month she'd begun to see some improvement. By summer she could do three sets of eight reps on the bench at 105 pounds and three sets of five pull-ups. What kept her going was her dream of becoming an Olympic hockey player. "What also kept her going," said David Halberstam, who profiled her for *Condé Nast Sports for Women*, "was the attention of Boyle, a coach who could easily have been using his time in other ways but who seemed gender-blind. Boyle took the female athletes as seriously as he did some of his most celebrated male athletes."

It was new for Boyle, working with women at this level, elite players who weren't spoiled, who had no attitude problem, who were as dedicated as any male player, if not more so. "Coaches who haven't coached women before don't know what they're missing," he says. These women had worked hard and long, but always with the knowledge that there were limits to their expectations that wouldn't have been there if they were men. They were a pioneer generation. And it was undoubtedly under the aegis of men like Boyle who were "gender-blind" that they broke through. His expectations of A.J. were no less than what her father's had been that long-ago day when she had first been put on the frozen pond to fend for herself.

———

Today, younger girls are getting tough coaching. In 1998 soccer coach Ashley Hammond committed himself to training an under-eight girls' team just as rigorously as he trained the boys. He wanted to see what would happen to them with more practice, harder practice, practice when the weather was lousy. He felt they hadn't yet been pushed to their limits.

Even their parents were skeptical. But after a season of perfect attendance and hard play on the part of his girls, Hammond saw big changes. His recommendation to other coaches was "Don't set limits. If you treat [girls] as soccer players, they will go out and work as hard as, if not harder than, any of the boys' teams."

It's extraordinary that 42 percent of the kids playing soccer nationally are girls, sportswriter Harvey Araton has observed in his weekly column in *The New York Times.* A grassroots movement, girls' soccer presents an important opportunity for parents to "help repattern the way boys view girls and, by extension, the way boys view boys." Moms are contributing to this repatterning by becoming players themselves. Araton is proud of his own wife for taking up soccer at forty, and in his column he contemplated the possible benefit to the young male of having a mom who plays: "Junior may not be as likely to bask in his athletic and physical superiority if he is told enough times that he can't have the field this afternoon because his sister's playing at two, and then, if he's really lucky, his mother's on at four."

Crossing the Swinging Rope Bridge: Programs for Change

"There is still a tremendous amount of ambivalence about girls being competitive in our society," M. Burche Tracy Ford, the headmistress of Miss Porter's School in Farmington, Connecticut, told a reporter. "But I think for girls to be really successful, in their personal lives, in a business or political context, or any other venue, they have to learn from boys and men about exercising their strength and power, and sports are perfect vehicles for teaching that."

One of the oldest girls' schools in the country (it dates back to the 1800s), Miss Porter's recently reviewed its long history of using sport to instill its students with "grace" and "form" and decided to ditch the agenda. Grace and form, it had become quite plain, were no longer enough. In the late 1990s it seemed more important to help girls gain an equal chance at getting power in the world. If they were ever going to have a shot at this, they'd have to stop holding back their aggression and learn to compete.

Like most private girls' schools, Miss Porter's had offered sports for years, but mainly for nineteenth-century reasons: to straighten their students' spines and put roses in their cheeks. In a word, to make them marriageable. Its sports teams were so bad, the school eventually dropped its membership in the prestigious Founders League, tired of always being at the bottom. But by 1997, only the second year after a new athletic director had been hired to fulfill the headmistress's new vision for her girls, Miss Porter's was back in the Founders League and looking good. It had taken more rigorous practice schedules and the firm countering of resistance from the old guard among the faculty. At an early meeting, Kathy Noble, the new athletic director, was told by a top administrator, "Kathy, we are a girls' school. That's not how we do things." Noble was confused. Hadn't she been hired to make physical literacy part of the program? The assistant head of the school explained to Noble that even though Miss Porter's was "very pro-girl," many faculty still thought there were some things girls should not do, things they needed to be protected from.

Controversy had begun to roil with the beefing up of the girls' rowing team, which had gotten so good that it actually won the New England championship. That doesn't happen with mere grace and form. It takes aggression, strength, and endurance. The rowing coach who'd brought the team to victory also coaches boys at another school. He said he coaches girls the same way he coaches boys—he coaches them to win. This was a rocking concept for Miss Porter's old guard, whose influence was fast disappearing. The school's new coaches found teaching the girls to throw themselves into competition no less challenging than teaching them to get over their fear of calculus. The new goal was to level the notion of "gender appropriateness" and get them into the real world. "You have to teach them to do what they need to do to win," one of the school's tennis coaches told *The New York Times*, "or they will be at a serious disadvantage in their professional lives."

Elite progressive schools may be changing their approach to girls' physicality, but what happens to girls who go to public schools that are still likely to be dumbing down the PE courses for their female students? Fortunately there are programs springing up around the country that are helping these girls get strong too.

When I first met Elizabeth McLeod, she was on her way to San Francisco to start up a center for early-adolescent girls. She had been at Harvard, studying in a graduate program about the drop-off in motivation and self-confidence that occurs in girls at about the time they enter puberty, and she had a plan. Her idea was that instilling girls with physical competence would head off the psychological difficulties that hit so many as they approach womanhood.

When she sat in my living room, the cool winter sun shining on her blond hair and smooth, stylish boots, it was hard to imagine that

Elizabeth had ever been anything but self-confident. Not so, she assured me. Not so at all. In junior high school she had begun the painful splitting off from her self that has become so commonplace among girls. She and several close friends had found themselves, in seventh grade, shocked to discover that with their creativity and brains they stood out in a way that disturbed others and made them the objects of derision. The girls backtracked, *fast*—and constructed what would become an elaborate alter-world for pursuing their individuality and bridging them gently into the sexual world to come. The alter-world, Elizabeth told me, allowed them to be "normal" bland, passive girls at school, disguising what they actually *were*: feisty, wildly original, risk-taking, funny. They called themselves the PRA (for Popular Recreation Association), adopted personae and alter-names, dressed a certain way, drew a certain way, made up a secret language, and spent all their free time together. Three years later they gave up their after-school fantasy world. Having protected themselves and still grown stronger in the interim, they could now get involved with the rest of their classmates and still remain true to their aspirations. They had found a way to keep themselves from shrinking into dull conventionality.

It was to girls in such pubertal crisis that Elizabeth McLeod would dedicate her career. At the stage of her life when I met her, she was physically as well as intellectually sophisticated. She could sail, rock climb, fend for herself in the wilderness. At Harvard she had met the founder of a special Outward Bound program for twelve- and thirteen-year-old girls that teaches them not only how to get about in the wilderness but how to mediate altercations and be true to themselves while developing intimacy with others. The program, Connecting with Courage, combined rock climbing, ropes courses, sailing, and other physical challenges with expressive arts activities. "The model was designed to encourage leadership and self-discovery by engaging in challenging outdoor activities and group dynamics," Elizabeth explained.

When she was in graduate school, Elizabeth worked one summer as an assistant instructor for one of the Connecting with Courage courses. Her first group consisted of ten Caucasian girls, twelve to thirteen years old, most of whom had had some experience with camping, sailing, or hiking but felt they wanted more self-confidence. At the graduation ceremony the girls reported new courage, the willingness to take risks both physically and expressively, and a greater sense of their capabilities. On wilderness expeditions the instructors had given them the responsibility of organizing themselves and of working up a contract, a process of norm setting in which the girls themselves figured out what needed to take place to create a safe learning environment. One girl said, "It was the first time in my life that somebody who was supposed to be in charge asked me, Do you want to do it this way or that way?"

Barely out of childhood, girls this age are zooming toward adulthood and a different relationship with their bodies. "We want them to see that their bodies serve a purpose," said one Outward Bound instructor. "But it's not to be squeezed into clothes and to be looked at." Another noted the importance of challenging them without the presence of boys. "If you put girls in with the boys," she said, "the boys would end up carrying all the heavy stuff and the girls would sit back and let them do it."

The object is unlearning the self-crippling attitudes of princesshood. "Belay school" teaches girls responsibility for themselves, as well as how to trust one another, Elizabeth McLeod told me. Belaying is an important skill needed in rock climbing. The climber wears a harness attached to a rope that passes through a metal divide at the top of a rock tower (a sixty-foot structure for practicing climbing) and is held by a person, the belayer, on the ground. If the climber falls, the rope and the belayer prevent her from falling more than a few inches. "In my group I stressed the commands and talked about the importance of the verbal contract entered into between climber and belayer," Elizabeth recalled. "Since one person is literally holding the other's life in her hands, trust and communication are essential. The *realness* of this situation is a valuable teaching tool."

The realness is what puts girls back in touch with their essential selves. "When you get out into the wilderness, you know what you really do need," one girl recalled. "Put aside the makeup and good-looking clothes. You'd rather have toilet paper! You would trade your makeup for that!"

Crossing a swinging rope bridge was at least as challenging as doing without makeup. One girl was so scared, she almost convinced the instructors she couldn't do it. But then one of the other girls in the group got the idea of coming and taking the frightened girl's backpack and helping her across the bridge. "Without any input from the instructors they came up with a solution that involved helping each other and keeping the group together," McLeod says.

Boys are systematically taught to cope with the anxiety of taking physical risks. They grow up to be men who actually court fear—with the goal of conquering it—over and over again. Girls are systematically taught to *avoid* risk and its accompanying anxiety.

The delicate question of how to prod girls to take risks for the right reasons (to gain self-confidence, not social approval) is, for psychologically oriented educators like McLeod, crucial in helping girls get the most out of physical challenge. To goad a timorous girl named Alicia, McLeod told her about the existence of a journal that had been placed halfway up the sixty-foot tower in a plastic container on a platform. Alicia struggled and eventually made it up that far, if only so she could get to write in the journal. What did she write? "I feel sick." But of all the girls that day who were excited and proud, Alicia was the proudest.

Before taking one of Elizabeth's courses at the Bay Area Center for Girls in San Francisco, sixteen-year-old Helena had had difficulty, she says, in trusting people, even her beloved dad. While he reassured her he had the rope, she wondered, "What would happen if the second he needs to scratch his nose is the second I fall to a place where he can never physically comfort me again?" Speaking metaphorically, Helena was describing precisely the transitional psychological task of adolescence. But in Project Courage she had physical experience to push her to the next level of maturity, which was trusting in herself. "I had to realize that the only way you can climb the ladder of life is by taking the risk and finding out that the rope will always be there to catch your falls when someone else isn't."

Sportsbridge ("Empowering Girls Through Sports") is a San Francisco mentoring program that matches area athletes with young girls in sports. "We know you have to start at age eight or nine," says the founder, Ann Kletz. "At that age, all of their notions about themselves are already happening." Most boys start developing their sports skills when they're four or five, she says. The girls don't.

There is a real social movement under way to help girls develop strength and trust in their bodies. In Chicago, A Sporting Chance Foundation is a nonprofit group dedicated to empowering girls through athletics. StartSmart, a nationwide program pioneered by the National Alliance for Youth Sports, features a basic skills curriculum aimed at three- to six-year-olds that engages parents in the coaching of both boys and girls. Even the Girl Scouts has jumped on board, with its GirlSports program.

A remarkable program is Eureka!, brainstorm of its deceased founder, Alice Miller, which combines sports training with science and math education for girls. Founded in 1987, Eureka! is a three-year protocol that begins in the summer after eighth grade. Its goal is countering prevailing attitudes about girls in both science and sports. One grad said that what was most eye-opening for her was learning. "Anybody can do it. It's not a question of how you look. All the girls in Eureka! learn how to play basketball or volleyball or run track or do something else." Their size doesn't matter. That is an important lesson reiterated in Eureka!: It doesn't matter how you're shaped; you can do any sport you want to do.

Physical girl power is a grassroots phenomenon, with small but potent organizations fighting discrimination against girls. Cindy Peterson, who directs the sports program for five hundred girls three to ten years old at Atlanta Northside Methodist Church, tells her kids' parents: "These days our girls are learning to throw like boys. There's no reason for a girl not to learn the correct technique. If a boy can learn it, I know a girl can learn it. We're going to get rid of this myth. In six or eight weeks the girls are gonna leave here knowing the correct technique."

Two months before the millennium turned, a report on schoolchildren in *The Boston Globe* gave reason for hope. Boys and girls who play school sports together—rather than being segregated—are transforming their ideas about one another. It all started two years ago, when Dan Cullen, then a fifth-grader, made the unprecedented move of inviting girls to play kickball with the boys. "We didn't have enough players," he recalls, "and nobody else wanted to play."

"Dan invited Emily to play, and we just followed," remembers Jamie Connor, who today is twelve and at five feet four towers over Dan.

A year later, in sixth grade, boys and girls playing kickball together had become routine. At recess one day, writes reporter Anne Driscoll, "about 20 boys and girls were playing kickball in mixed teams on the sloping land near the school's side entrance. As one girl walloped the ball, sending it sailing through the air, several of her teammates—boys and girls—screamed in the excitement of the moment."

Recess a generation ago, recalls Driscoll, was that brief period during the day when girls played jump rope, if they did anything physical at all, and boys wrestled, and raced, and hurled footballs at one another. But today, "sex-segregated recess would seem totally weird" to the sixth-graders, she observes. Boys have actually begun looking up to girls who are strong and athletic. Ryan Spinney, a senior at Newburyport High, and captain of the boys' cross-country, indoor track, and outdoor track teams, says, "All the girls have determination; I admire that. They're not different than the guys—anybody who is an athlete is an athlete. . . . I don't really understand the concept of girls being inferior to men."

More and more girls are daring to cross the "gender divide," insisting on their right to play baseball, softball, basketball, football, and soccer. A survey of seven thousand women found that the most physically active were those who'd played primarily with boys or mixed-gender groups as children, rather than mostly with girls.

It's the trickle-down effect of a change in the law that requires schools to place as much emphasis—and money—on girls' sports as on boys' that has created the fledgling sense of equality some schoolgirls are beginning to experience. Those changes, as I'll discuss in chapter 5, didn't take place smoothly. And as the following chapter shows, *most* girls in this country are still physically discriminated against, and dominated in ways that are very harmful to them. But this much seems clear: the *only* thing that will finally break down the domination boys have held over girls is girls getting stronger. "I think the boys have gotten good about our playing with them because we can beat them at stuff and they can beat us at stuff—it goes two ways," one twelve-year-old girl, a competitive swimmer, soccer player, and basketball player, has noticed.

It does go two ways. "The girls look at us in a different perspective," says Dan from the pinnacle, now, of his seventh-grade wisdom, "and we also look at them in a different perspective. They know what happens to us and why we get so competitive, and we know how they can get competitive, too. I kind of think that's broken down the walls, so to speak, between the boys and girls."

The tide is definitely turning. "Girls seem to have more of a sense of confidence," says Carol Snow, who's been a sixth-grade social studies teacher at Newburyport High School since the 1970s, when she played field hockey there in a raggedy uniform and without protective equipment. These days girls are more willing to speak up in class, she says. "They are more confident, more willing to express ideas, and more comfortable with themselves. They move more freely in the world."

These girls are in the vanguard of a physical revolution, one that is long overdue and that ultimately will change the experience of all women. As strong girls, they will grow into women who will no longer allow themselves to be physically victimized. Women's endangered bodies are the last obstacle to their gaining psychological freedom. Historically, as we'll see in the next chapter, their chronic sense of endangerment begins very early in childhood. This is a life-shaping legacy of fear no girl has escaped.

FOUR

Endangered Bodies

A mere hundred years ago doctors still didn't understand a great deal about women's reproductive cycles. Dr. G. Stanley Hall, whose eugenic theories of women's role I talked about in the first chapter, admitted in 1904, "Precisely what menstruation is, is not very well known." Dr. Albert F. King, a professor of medicine at Columbian University in Washington, D.C., claimed that menstrual bleeding was "new," the result, he suspected, of such modern forces as higher education for women, later marriage, and deliberate family limitation, none of which he thought healthy or conducive to breeding. (When women had more children, started having them younger, and breast-fed them forever, they had fewer periods—*so* few as to apparently be invisible to some doctors.)

During the Victorian era, a movement historian Joan Jacobs Brumberg refers to as "ovarian determinism" was building. A major proponent was the popular and highly regarded Dr. Edward Clarke, a Harvard Medical School professor who argued against higher education for women because, he said, their bodies were more "complicated" than men's. Clarke thought developing girls were physically and emotionally jeopardized by intellectual challenges that "drew energy to the brain and away from the ovaries." In a revealing bit of history, Brumberg explains, "In the Victorian mind, age at menarche came to be regarded as a marker of the moral quality of civilization rather than as a sign of economic conditions." Instead of relating onset of menarche to material well-being, as reflected in diet and general good health (as we now know it to be), nineteenth-century Americans had a very different idea: "[T]he lower the age, the more libidinous or sexually licentious the society, nation, or race; the higher the age, the more 'civilized.' "

Worried that their daughters might be too young when they started menstruating, Victorian parents and physicians sometimes restricted girls from eating foods considered sexually "stimulating" and thus liable to bring on the dread menarche. Cloves, pickles, and meat were among the talismans thought to interfere with the desired stasis. Girls had to be kept from maturing until the time was right.

Part of this concern was about keeping them virgins until they married. As menarche started arriving earlier and marriages happened later (both trends products of economic progress), the question of how to prevent unmarried girls from becoming pregnant was a real one. But instead of strengthening girls by teaching them what to expect and how to look after themselves, society opted for keeping them children until they could be delivered into the protective embrace of their adoring husbands. Certainly girls weren't given much information—about their bodies or about sex. That job was left to their husbands, into whose hands their entire well-being was placed, whether or not such trust was warranted.

I can't help thinking that if it were men whose reproductive capacity required menstruation, medicine wouldn't have taken quite so long figuring it all out. The twentieth century was well under way before estrogen was identified (in 1920). It took another decade and a half before the hormone's role in reproduction was understood. That means I was riding around in my mother's belly at about the time people were just beginning to get the full picture on how it was I'd got there! No wonder, then, that barely a decade later my mother was having trouble figuring out what to tell me about my own up-coming menses. It wasn't prudishness that had silenced my mother, as I'd always imagined, so much as sheer lack of information.

A century ago menarche began at fifteen or sixteen, and most girls remained virgins until they married in their early twenties. Today, as we know, they may be as young as ten—and on average are eleven, twelve, or thirteen—when they start menstruating, at which point they begin getting the message that society is interested in them mostly because they're sexually "ready." Who they are in any other way seems, to them, to have become irrelevant overnight.

I'm not advocating a return to the Victorian prison of early mar-riage, but most girls today are too young when they find themselves thrust into the precarious world of adult sexuality. Though they are not supposed to *be* sexual, girls learn everywhere—from movies, from magazines, from music videos, and, yes, from their parents—that to be "sexy" is socially valuable. And the rules on sexuality and virginity have gotten a lot looser. While Victorians were overweening in their attempt to exert control over girls' lives, contemporary adults, fright-ened by their own inability to comprehend the world their daughters are entering, sometimes abandon them altogether.

Wittingly or not, parents today often encourage premature sexual behavior on the part of their young girls. They think dressing sexy is cute. Sexy dresser to the max was a tenth-grader at Manhattan's Con-vent of the Sacred Heart when she made her grand entrance to a birth-day party at midnight dressed in black opera gloves, high heels, and a low-cut pink dress notched in the front to show her slip. Seduction was the goal—visual seduction, if not actual seduction. Nor was this charmer's Hollywood style of dress atypical for a New York private school girl celebrating her sweet sixteenth. Photographs of such parties are run regularly in *The New York Times*. The girls dance sexily with one another, showing off their bodies for the boys. Mom helps, pouring champagne ("bottles and bottles" at this particular party, according to a newspaper feature). Soon any ambivalence about behaving sexually dissipates in a blear of booze. "The rule in the whole entire thing is that the adults totally don't care, and they can't stop anything that's happening," one of the boys attending the girl's party told a reporter.

By the time they are eleven, twelve, and thirteen, female children in our society are plucked from the world of childhood in a way that is harsh and abrupt. They feel flung out of safety, dangerously unmoored. Society's focus on female sexual characteristics—a glaring, virtually voyeuristic focus—has made girls excruciatingly self-conscious. Internalizing the view of them presented by a male-biased culture, they learn to overvalue their external selves. The body becomes a fetish, one they are obsessed with in the same objectifying way the culture is. But of course girls can't measure up to what they think is required of them.

Shrinking Self-Image

What we *do* with our bodies or don't do—how we live in them—tells a great deal about the state of our ego. Whether we hoist our breasts into view or hide them, or reshape them with the aid of WonderBras and silicone or militarize them à la Madonna's atavistic metal cones relates directly to body image. Generally speaking, when one body part is given importance above the others, the image of the body as a whole is distorted. When legs are bared under shortened skirts for the frank purpose of manipulating someone else's response, body image suffers loss of integrity or wholeness.

"The ego is first and foremost a bodily ego," Freud wrote. Being in touch with one's body, he believed, was central to having a healthy ego. Teenage girls are often disconnected from their bodies (their showy dress notwithstanding). Inwardly they may shrink from the observation of others. Too much of the wrong type of attention put on their bodies makes them uncomfortable. I remember how furious I felt on the day of my high school graduation, not wanting my mother's camera pointed at me in my long white organdy gown. I was sixteen, and my mother seemed implicated in the loss of my girlhood. I hated my body, and she seemed implicated in that as well. She wanted to photograph it? I would make her pay. I refused to smile. To send to her sisters out west she would have only the image of a thin, awkward girl with a preposterously huge bouquet and anger in her eyes.

It's important to recognize the extent to which our psychic map of our bodies is influenced by others. The "imaginary anatomy," as French philosopher Jacques Lacan calls it, "varies with the ideas (clear or confused) about bodily functions which are prevalent in a given culture." "Confused" seems to be the operative word when it comes to women's "bodily functions." Society foists its ambivalence about females onto girls before they have any idea of what's happening. They are overprotected in one way, underprotected in another.

My mother tried hard to understand me during those years. She even took a course in adolescent psychology, but to little avail. There wasn't much on adolescent girls to guide her. Why, for example, was her teenage daughter so upset with her body? Was this normal? My mother saw my misery, saw me scrutinizing my face in the mirror, heard me complaining that my rod-thin body was shapeless and thus unacceptable. (In those days it was thinness that was verboten.)

Yet as a child I was active and eager. I never thought about my body. My body carried the day. Then, as if overnight, the little nubbins of breasts appeared. I hadn't noticed them, but someone else had. It was a neighbor woman who'd seen me tearing around on my broomstick horse in my thin little blouse who was the first to inform me I was too old to be going without an undershirt.

I was only eleven, but that day was the beginning of my adolescence. It wasn't puberty that sent me there (I wouldn't even menstruate for another three years), it was "the look." The look separated me from my body. The look took me away from myself—and triggered my entry into the war zone. It is unspeakable, this phenomenon, because it is incomprehensible. A publicist I know told me her fourteen-year-old daughter, painfully thin, goes to bed at night wearing a bra under her nightgown. She even wears a bra in the shower. She doesn't want to have to see her own breasts. Her mother tries talking to her about it. The girl doesn't want to talk. The subject of her body is painful and confusing, something she can't share with her mother, something she feels her mother wouldn't understand.

Few boys agonize about their bodies the way girls do. They're more likely to throw on a shirt and jeans before school, unmindful of the girl down the street frantically trying on "outfits" behind her bedroom door. Of if they see their sisters going through their morning agonies, they're contemptuous. It's a girls' ritual, singular, obsessive, stupid. They thank God they're not girls.

Boys are as aware of the duplicity being played out as girls are. They see the primping, panicking, and pandering as beneath their dignity, and they don't know why girls do it. Everything about being a girl seems, to boys, to be hyped in some way or made precious. When Rachel brought home from a fourth-grade health class a manila folder with "My Menstruation" printed on the cover and strewn with hearts and flowers she'd drawn, her sixth-grade brother hooted. "God, Rachel," he said, "don't you see how stupid it is?" She didn't, at first.

"Well, imagine if I came home from school with a folder marked 'My Ejaculation' that had little footballs and helmets drawn all over it."

"The teacher made us," Rachel said in a voice deprived of conviction.

I can remember that episode to this day. I can remember the slant of the late afternoon light coming through the kitchen window. Of course, her brother had a point. The teacher, in a semienlightened attempt to bring female reproductive health into the fourth-grade classroom, had sentimentalized it beyond all recognition. The subject of boys' reproductive health wasn't treated in that way. Rachel had suddenly found herself on the receiving end of the culture's confusing messages about the way her body functioned. As her mother, I could see what was happening to Rachel but felt speechless in the face of it: the trapdoor was closing.

The contemporary idea of body image is one-dimensional. "She has poor body image," in popular lingo, means a woman's internal image of the way she looks is distorted enough to lower her self-esteem. But body image has a more complex psychological function. Among other things, it serves as an inner model for the execution of motor activity, according to Alexander Lowen, a psychiatrist known for his emphasis on the relationship between the body and mental health. We unconsciously "rehearse" motor activity before performing, visualizing the upcoming sequence of movements and using our internal image of our bodies as a guide. When that image is distorted, our ability to perform movement will be handicapped. Think of getting ready to swing a bat during a softball game. If you stand up to the plate with a disconnected inner picture of yourself, you likely won't do a great job of connecting with the ball. You will also probably assess yourself as weak.

That girls' problems with their bodies devolve from magazine presentations of skinny fashion models is a simplistic idea about body image that caught on in the seventies and eighties and continued into the nineties. The Twiggy effect, you could call it. Our body image is said to be "good" or "bad" according to whether or not we think our bodies are acceptable by some idealized media standard. But used in this limited way, the concept of "body image" is robbed of its real richness and descriptive meaning. To say of a despairing adolescent girl, "Her body image isn't good," and mean only that she doesn't like her body is to miss the extent of her confusion. When you watch a girl running back to her closet three, four, and five times to change her clothes before going to school in the morning, shoving shirt in waistband, turning sideways to look at sweater in mirror, tugging miserably on hemline and neckline, all in an effort to create some relationship between what she sees in the mirror and what she sees in her mind—then you know that something profound and terrible is going on: your daughter is fighting for her psychic integrity.

A healthy relationship to our bodies used to be thought of as beginning, and ending, with Mom—with how she looked at and handled her infant, whether she was under stress, whether she found her baby demanding or irritating, whether she was disgusted by its bodily functions. Presumably, if the perfect, unneurotic, madly-in-love-with-her-husband young mother were tweaking your toes and tenderly cleaning your little rump, you'd go forth into the world feeling strong and positive about your body. If you had a paragon of maternal empathy for a mother, you'd be able to fly out of the nest and into the world, protected as by an amulet against anything hostile or demeaning you might find there. When a person's body image is "defective," wrote Alexander Lowen in the fifties, "it *always* denotes a disturbance in the mother-child relationship." That's how one-dimensionally it was seen then. Body image was thought to be more or less fixed by the time you started to toddle. Aside from extreme physical trauma like burns or accidents, the events of later life weren't expected to greatly influence one's internal picture of one's body.

But they do. Today psychologists recognize that it isn't only the "nonempathic" mother who has the power to destroy a young female's inner self-image. The culture's conflicted, and often hostile, attitude toward girls, especially as they enter into their sexuality, is every bit as damaging. Adding to girls' psychological vulnerability is the frailty myth. Not only are they endangered by the environment they live in, they are straitjacketed by their belief that they have no way to confront the danger. This victim position is deeply supported by the system. Even in spite of the public's new interest in strong, aggressive female athletes, girls are still taught that physical frailty and passivity are appropriate for their gender. It's all right for female athletes to be powerful, as athletes are in a separate category. They're meant to be heroic and larger than life because they're considered entertainers. But ordinary girls? They are still supposed to be "feminine"—and that means anything *but* physically powerful. Feminine means weak. Feminine means victim.

Adolescence: The Crisis Years

At the time of life when boys start becoming proud of their bodies— their muscles, their penises, the expressive arc of their urine—girls begin retreating in shame. They have an idea of a perfect, feminine, all-appealing body that can never be realized. Unconsciously girls have an emotional investment in this goal of perfection: it keeps them from having to move and strike out on their own. It allows them to remain passive. It allows them to persist with a rigid illusion about boys and girls, men and women, beauty and nonbeauty. The illusion is so compelling that it captures them, allows them for the longest time to do little more than tread water. Maintaining the illusion of perfection is how girls defend themselves against taking the huge, impossible-seeming risk of *doing,* of *being.*

It is a sad legacy, the legacy of the frailty myth. Psychologists today see girls' self-esteem *peaking* at nine. This is when they are the feistiest, the most self-accepting they may ever be. At nine most girls still have an integrated sense of their bodies. Then, at ten and eleven, their connection to the body becomes more tenuous and self-esteem starts its precipitous fall. Suddenly they're not talking anymore about what they really think and feel. They've become pre-occupied with *size* and with looking too big. They begin dieting frantically. Dieting girls of twelve and thirteen are setting themselves up for uncontrollable eating disorders by the time they're fifteen and sixteen. Scientists now know that restricted eating is the trigger of these illnesses, if not precisely their cause.

Up to 25 percent of adolescents—90 percent of them girls—regularly purge to control their weight, according to a survey conducted by the Commonwealth Fund. Nearly one girl in five in ninth grade admitted to having binged and purged. (Bulimia is related to obsessive-compulsive disorder, according to psychiatry's *Diagnostic and Statistical Manual of Mental Disorders.* Anorexia is the perilous self-starvation disease connected with extreme distortion in body image.) Unfortunately, eating disorders are more prevalent than they've ever been. An estimated 5 to 7 percent of America's twelve million undergraduates are afflicted with anorexia, bulimia, or binge eating, according to a Seattle organization that promotes awareness and prevention of eating disorders. Anorexics have a mortality rate of 20 percent, the highest of any mental disorder. What could possibly be the matter here? Surely this epidemic can no longer be attributed to Twiggy and all the skinny models who came down the pike after her. Psychologists will tell you that eating disorders are "biopsy-chosocial" in cause. That's the sophisticated catch-all phrase many psychiatric illnesses are assigned these days. And who would take issue with a term so broadly comprehensive? But its very broadness ends up obscuring, because it doesn't say enough. *What* bio? *What* psycho? *What* social? Intelligent discussion gets foreshortened by a convenient buzzword.

Extreme dieting produces dangerous hormonal drops, which in turn affect brain serotonin. When girls, or women, strip too much fat off their bodies (which they can do through extreme dieting or extreme exercise), their lowered estrogen knocks hell out of their serotonin levels. Lowered brain serotonin is related to both compulsive behavior and obsessional ideas. So here we begin to see the biochemical underpinnings of what happens to girls who diet, who then can't stop thinking about food and weight (because lowered brain serotonin has caused the obsessive component of the illness to kick in), and who ultimately find themselves caught in a trap of uncontrollable, self-destructive behavior that is highly influenced by destabilized brain metabolism. The food restriction has to be pretty severe to trigger such a cascade of biochemical events. Minor dieting won't do it. But many girls *do* go off the charts in restricting food intake and often exercise compulsively as well. Yet with all of this we are still left with the question of what, possibly, could be causing girls' overwhelming need to be small. I believe there's a connection between the diet-triggered epidemic of eating disorders in girls and their anxiety about living in a world that, clearly, becomes more and more dangerous for them the older they get.

The sense of danger heightens when girls reach puberty. Even before adolescence, many are the victims of incest and other forms of sexual abuse. By adolescence the likelihood that they will be molested skyrockets. Two studies have found that one in four adolescent girls has been sexually or physically abused or forced by a date to have sex against her will. "Although these rates are stunningly high, they're very consistent with what's been seen in earlier studies," according to Dr. Robert Blum, chairman of the adolescent health department of the University of Minnesota. "The association between abuse and other problems is so striking that all of us in the education and health systems must have our antennae up about abuse whenever we see a kid who isn't functioning well, whether it shows up as emotional distress or suicidal thoughts or school failure."

One important survey of almost seven thousand students in grades five though twelve found that *most* abuse is perpetrated by a family member or family friend, takes place at home, and involves more than a single incident. The same study—published by the Commonwealth Fund—found that one out of four girls is depressed. When it was first published in 1998, this study received a great deal of attention. Everybody knew teenage girls were a mopey lot, but the epidemic of depression revealed by this government-sponsored research was appalling—beyond what anyone had imagined was happening to girls. An alarming 29 percent "reported suicidal thoughts, 27 percent said they were sad 'many times' or 'all the time,' and one-third of older girls said they felt like crying 'many days' or 'every day.'" A quarter of the girls said they had at some point wanted to leave home because of the violence. One in three of the girls in high school had thought about suicide in the two weeks prior to the survey!

But somehow the connection between girls' depression and their sexual endangerment is often overlooked. What happens to most girls, if not actual rape or incest, is subtler though sometimes only marginally less harmful experiences (especially when taken in the aggregate) of sexual domination. What it's like to live in such an environment is left to artists and writers to convey. Evoking the endless sexual transgressions a female child must endure, Simone de Beauvoir wrote, "[T]here is that knee pressed against the little girl's in the moving picture theater, the hand which at night in the train glides along her leg, those young fellows who titter as she goes by, those furtive touches."

The humiliating gestures de Beauvoir wrote of in the 1940s in *The Second Sex* seem almost delicate by current standards. Today girls are more likely to have semen squirted on them in a crowded elevator or to witness the naked, hairy genitals of some stranger on a bus. Such behavior is not simply an extreme expression of the male sex drive, as some would have it. Harassment is intended to disturb the targeted recipient, and it does. Sexual intimidation rings an alarm bell in the brain, triggering rapid heartbeat, rising blood pressure, and floods of adrenaline and other stress hormones. Memories of earlier assaults may be triggered. Even "low-level" aggression can initiate intense fear. And girls are bombarded with aggression, low level and high. Their endangered bodies are making them psychically vulnerable. The "crisis years," as *New York Times* writer Jane Brody referred to them in an article on girls' pandemic decline at puberty, are not years of so-called normal adolescent turmoil; they are the years when the likelihood of sexual assault is greatest.

Carol Gilligan was the first to publish observations of "splitting" in teenage girls, by which she means a disconnection between mind and body, thoughts and feelings. In a famous series of studies that led to her becoming the first director of Gender Studies at Harvard, Gilligan announced that splitting had become so pervasive, and so potentially impairing of girls' identity, it signified nothing less than a "developmental crisis." Others, of course, were also aware of the mental health problems of teenage girls—that they are more disparaging of themselves and more disturbed in body image than boys. Starting with puberty, girls become more than twice as likely as boys to experience depression. Since Freud, the so-called flight from self has been considered predictable—and even inevitable—for female adolescents. Yet no one until Gilligan had ever attempted to study what actually *happens* to girls, psychologically, as they go from prepubescence into their teenage years. What had so long been recognized as a "falling apart" time for girls was glanced at, taken note of, and dismissed as part of normal development in young females.

Girls, once happy, energetic, and self-confident, "lose their vitality, their resilience, their immunity to depression, their sense of themselves and their character" once puberty hits, Gilligan and her colleague, Lyn Mikel Brown, wrote in *Meeting at the Crossroads.* But while they drew important attention to the critical downspiraling of girls in adolescence, these researchers and other colleagues in the new field of female developmental psychology never quite zeroed in on the connection between the hostile sexual environment girls enter at the time of reproductive maturity and the striking deterioration that simultaneously sets in.

Entering the War Zone

By the 1990s the story had come out about the vast numbers of girls being sexually assaulted and harassed—often in their schools. The American Association of University Women (AAUW), in *How Schools Shortchange Girls,* reported sexual abuse of girls to be four times higher than that of boys. Even places where they might expect to be safe weren't. "Sexual harassment occurs in the mundane, daily matters of school life: in the chemistry lab as well as in the carpentry shop, in the driver's ed car and on the practice fields of extracurricular sports," Dr. Nan Stein of the Massachusetts Department of Education told the AAUW researchers. "Yet despite its frequency, sexual harassment is rarely reported, tallied, investigated or systematically documented."

To do some of its own tallying on sexual violence in America's schools, the AAUW conducted another study, whose disturbing results prompted the report's title, *Hostile Hallways*. Seventy percent of girls in public schools experience harassment, the AAUW found. Fifty percent experience unwanted sexual touching. One-fourth report being cornered and molested. "It made me confused, whether I should tell or not," said one girl thirteen years old. "I didn't know if I was overreacting since this was a teacher I trusted and looked up to."

"In school, a girl doesn't get called on by her teacher, but she is the subject of catcalls; she doesn't hear stories about women of achievement, but she hears rumors about her sexual behavior," says Anne Bryant, executive director of the AAUW Educational Foundation. "Sexual harassment takes a toll on all students, but the impact on girls is devastating."

Five times as many girls as boys who've been harassed end up feeling afraid in school. One in three girls who've faced harassment no longer want to attend school—not surprising when you consider how utterly undefended these girls have been and how pervasive the violence is. In 1998 alone, in New York City, the Board of Education paid out almost $3 million to settle sex attack suits. Yet the schools are still trying to cover up. "There are some schools that tell parents and the child straight out that they're liars and nothing can be done," says Eileen Treacy, a psychologist who interviews student attack victims for the city's district attorneys.

The *New York Post* ran a three-article exposé of student-on-student sex attacks in the city schools. "The public rarely hears about them unless parents call police or sue," *Post* investigator Maria Alvarez found. She reported the case (among a number of others) of a tenth-grade Brooklyn girl who was grabbed by three male students in the middle of the school day and dragged to an isolated area in the basement of Lafayette High School, where she was raped. "These cases are terrible—there seems to be a constant flow of them," said the girl's attorney. "The Board of Ed should do something." But the board's former safety chief says, "Parents should tell their kids not to walk in hallways alone or even go to the bathroom alone."

These are cases you'd expect to find only in a city like New York, right? Not right. In Duluth, Minnesota, in the spring of 1999, the Board of Education felt it necessary to create a new job that it called "school system harassment specialist." There was trouble in the Duluth schools. There had been trouble in the Duluth schools for a long time. But a system for dealing with the trouble wasn't created until the groundbreaking Supreme Court decision that found an elementary school in Forsyth, Georgia, guilty of failing to stop a student from subjecting another student to "severe and pervasive sexual harassment." This decision was a first, and it had tremendous ramifications. We're still feeling the shock tremors and will for some time. Schools are no longer permitted to look away, or outright ignore parental complaints, when schoolkids—even quite young ones—behave in a sexually predatory way.

The groundbreaking case in Georgia was brought by LaShonda Davis, whose mother, Aurelia, went all the way in fighting for her daughter's right to be in school without being harassed. But the fight was far from easy.

The harassment of young LaShonda (she had been ten, the boy eleven) began in December of 1992 and went on almost every day for five months. It included direct and explicit pressuring on his part for her to have sex with him. From the Davis plaintiffs' brief to the Court:

the boy "repeatedly attempted to touch LaShonda's breasts and vaginal area . . . told her in vulgar terms that he want[ed] . . . to get in bed with her . . . placed a doorstop in his pants and behaved in a sexually harassing manner." LaShonda had asked to have her seat changed. The teachers ignored her. No one at the school helped her. Unable to concentrate, the girl saw her grades drop. Eventually she wrote a suicide note.

The whole point of the Supreme Court case was to determine whether or not harassment charges could be brought under Title IX of the Educational Amendment Act, which prohibits discrimination against girls and women. The Court ruled five to four that such charges *could* be brought. The decision, which appeared on the front page of *The New York Times,* opened school districts to liability for sexual harassment by students on essentially the same grounds a Supreme Court decision a year earlier had set for liability when teachers harass students. But *students* harassing students? That was just too much. The heaviest-hitting dissenter was Chief Justice Anthony M. Kennedy, who angrily derided the decision as a federal intrusion into the classroom. The dissent maintained that the ruling would "teach little Johnny a perverse lesson in federalism." Justice Sandra Day O'Connor, in an unusually direct rejoinder from the bench, told the dissenters that the decision, rather, "assures that little Mary may attend class." Justice Kennedy insisted that "a teenager's romantic overtures to a classmate (even when they are persistent and unwelcome) are an inescapable part of adolescence."

Inescapable yes, romantic no. And these weren't even teenagers to begin with. The antediluvian thinking that confuses "romance" with hostility continues to exist in spite of an explosion of research showing that girls in this country are being seriously harmed in schools. They are required by law to spend roughly forty hours a week in what is all too often a hostile, denigrating environment, and until this court decision they had little possibility of legal recourse when schools refused to protect them.

But the tides are slowly turning. The Duluth school system harassment specialist, Judy Gillen, says that today boys can no longer expect to just get away with passing around annotated lists of the school's "25 Most Fucked Females" (an actual case brought before the Minnesota Department of Human Rights, in which the school district paid a $40,000 settlement to the senior class girl who brought the complaint). Today schools are more likely to snap to attention when parents complain. The particular case that helped inspire the creation of Gillen's job was the famous bathroom graffiti story, fictionalized as an ABC movie for television, *Boys Will Be Boys*. The real-life protagonist, ten years ago, was Katy Lyle, a fifteen-year-old sophomore at Duluth Central High. When she began hearing that someone had written obscene graffiti about her in the boys' bathroom and noticing girls as well as boys avoiding her in the halls, she became upset and told her parents. Her parents immediately complained to the school. The school did nothing. Her parents didn't let up. Katy's mother entered the bathroom on a day when school was out so that she could see for herself the writing that covered a substantial portion of one stall's inside wall. As reporter Cynthia Gorney put it, " 'Slut' was the mildest, most old-fashioned of the slurs; there were pornographic references to dogs, to farm animals, to Katy engaging in sexual relations with her brother. 'It took my breath away,' Carol Lyle says. 'I just burst into tears.' "

Legible portions of the graffiti stayed up for sixteen months. "What infuriated Katy's parents most," says Gorney, "was the school official who, in a district that actually had a written public school sex harassment policy in place, could not seem to *do* anything—who for nearly a year and a half could not manage what seemed to the Lyles the simple act of cleaning graffiti off a bathroom wall." One of Katy's older brothers finally went in with a bucket and washed down the wall. The scratched-in graffiti remained.

Katie Roiphe and other so-called power feminists are against including *words* in the concept of sexual harassment (if they're not against the concept of sexual harassment itself). Words, Roiphe claims, "have no special power to harm, humiliate, or invade." Rather, she says, "it is the political context that twists them and gives them resonance." The power presumably comes in the *naming* of the behavior. Call it harassment, and it's hurtful. Call it nothing, and it's nothing. But Roiphe's theory about the powerlessness of words contradicts itself. "In teaching children to 'recognize' sexual harassment," she says, "we are training them in victimhood." The tossing of insults among kids is historic and therefore harmless: "Your mother's a ————." "So's yours." One can only assume that Roiphe hasn't spent much time in schoolrooms lately or she'd know that taunting today goes far beyond what she nostalgically refers to as "the push and pull of childhood banter."

The resistance of institutions and individuals to acknowledging the massive abuse of girls' bodies is part of a virulent backlash—today's version of the same frailty myth that has been holding sway since the nineteenth century. Girls are not meant to stand up for themselves—to set physical boundaries, to say, "Hands off!," to demand freedom and respect. Conservatives' response to the AAUW's ongoing reports—four in a decade—is clear indication that the frailty myth is far from dead. "The AAUW is at it again, issuing another overwrought victim report," railed John Leo in *U.S. News & World Report*. He took the 1998 publication of *Gender Gaps: Where Schools Fail Our Children* as the occasion to lash out at the organization for its influential 1992 report, *How Schools Shortchange Girls,* which annoyingly (to him) "led to girls-only financial plums in the Gender Equity in Education Act." He accused the AAUW of basing its reports on "politicized research"—the politics being those of "radical feminism." John Leo's final pronunciamento? "The truth is that our schools have many flaws, but the oppression of females isn't one of them."

It is not only male writers who look at the oppression of girls in this way. Christina Hoff Sommers, a scholar at the American Enterprise Institute for Public Policy and Research in Washington, raised a similar protest on the op-ed page of *The New York Times.* In an article in which she sniffed over the absurdity of "preteen" sexual harassment, Sommers lit into cases like that of LaShonda Davis. These "children" need moral guidance, not legal intervention or protection, Sommers said in her op-ed piece. She complained that women's groups had "injected themselves" into the Davis case, along with the American Jewish Congress, the National Education Association, and "dozens" of other buttinskies. Among those dozens was the National Organization for Women (NOW). Sommers accused NOW of going so far as to claim that "sexual harassment is a form of violence used against women to keep women 'in their place.' "

NOW had protested that schools had become virtual "training grounds for sexual harassment," noting, "[B]oys are rarely punished—while girls are taught that it is their role to tolerate humiliating conduct." Such combining of "moral fervor and misinformation," Sommers insisted, is "dangerous." She is quite unyielding on the point that schoolboys in this country are *not* using sex to intimidate girls. Whatever "crude sexual behavior" may go on in schoolrooms, the "intimidation is nonsexual," she wrote in the *Times.* Good old-fashioned discipline is what she prescribed. Kids like LaShonda simply don't require the protective intervention of law. That's intrusive "federalism" again, something to be feared far more than the physical oppression of half the species.

After reading what happens to girls in the same "radical" report that so outraged John Leo, Pulitzer Prize–winning journalist Peggy Orenstein wanted to observe things firsthand. She set off to spend a year in two eighth-grade classrooms in California, one in an inner-city school, the other in a "nice" suburban school. The picture, which she drew so vividly in her book *Schoolgirls,* wasn't pretty. Andrea Murray, the principal of Weston Middle School, told Orenstein of "boys insulting girls; boys restraining girls; boys grabbing girls' breasts, buttocks, and crotches." It mystified Ms. Murray, who couldn't understand why, when they're treated this way, the girls don't speak up. They even defer to their harassers if the boys are popular. "They don't see this as something boys do to girls as one group to another, like racism," Ms. Murray says. "If they could just see themselves as a group, as powerful, if they just agreed to look at those boys as if they had leprosy, the boys would correct their behavior immediately."

Andrea Murray had been at the school only a year when Orenstein began her reporting, and she was amazed by the level of harassment going on, but she would soon get some backing for dealing with the problem. On January 1, 1993, a new law in California required every school in the state to develop a written sexual harassment policy for staff and students, to display it prominently on campus, and to distribute a copy to each teacher and parent. The law also allowed a principal to suspend or even expel students as young as fourth-graders who engage in sexual harassment. So Andrea Murray had something with which to back up her decision to take action. She wanted not just punishment of harassing boys, however; she wanted the girls to begin to stand up for themselves. In the interests of raising girls' consciousness, she asked Edie Deloria, a half-time counselor at the Weston school, to convene a discussion group of girls who'd witnessed or experienced harassment.

"We want to make the school safe," Deloria told the girls. "We want you to be free from remarks and other things that keep you from feeling comfortable learning here." Finally one girl said there are guys who call "other people" sluts.

"That happened today in another class," a second girl reported. "This guy called this girl a slut and . . . things like that. . . ." Her voice trailed off.

Another complained that guys say to girls that "they're half guy" if they like sports.

"Today, when we were playing hockey, they'd take the stick and make this motion." She held her hand near her crotch and pumped it up and down.

"Like masturbating?" the counselor asks.

The girls nodded.

"Who does that?"

The girls gave a few names but said that, in fact, lots of boys did that. Now the subject has opened up. A girl says that one boy, whom she names, says he had sex with her mom, that "my mom gave him a blow job." Now they begin talking about boys' remarks in detail. "They talk about boys who say, 'Suck my fat peter, you slut,' who call them 'skank' and 'ho' [a variation of "whore" popularized by male rap artists]," reports Orenstein. "And it isn't just 'bad' boys who harass them. It's boys with good grades, boys who are athletes."

The counselor tries to help them to reframe the way they look at the situation. "Girls think that guys 'just say these things,'" she tells them. "And after a while you think that this is the way that guys are supposed to talk to girls. But it doesn't have to be that way. If you girls want them to stop, you have to tell them what's going to happen if they do it; and then you have to follow through."

With this, a girl name Jeanie lowered her head and said, "Jeff Bellamy grabbed my breasts. . . ."

Later, in her office, Ms. Deloria told Orenstein, "A lot of girls think they have to take this. They're taking it now, and by sixteen years old it will be so ingrained in them that they'll just accept it."

The principal, Andrea Murray, was trying to get a message across at Weston Middle School. During the next several weeks she suspended five boys for sexual harassment, including the boy who'd grabbed Jeanie's breasts. It buoyed the girls' spirits, Orenstein observed. But not the boys'.

Some of the boys said they weren't sure what inappropriate behavior was. Sexual harassment was too subtle to define, said others. One, who'd been suspended for making masturbatory motions toward one of the girls and telling others that they "suck dick," complained to the reporter that you couldn't even compliment a girl anymore.

Even Jeffrey Bellamy, the boy who'd grabbed Jeanie's breasts, had trouble understanding the charges against him. It wasn't that he didn't know his behavior was wrong, it was that girls had always put up with it. "The girls don't mind," he told Orenstein. "I mean, they don't do anything about it. I'd beat the crap out of someone if they touched me like that."

You might think assaultive and denigrating sexual behavior happens only in inner-city schools, schools filled with poor, deprived, ignorant kids. But this is not a phenomenon of social class. If anything, the more privileged the boys, the more outrageous the behavior they're permitted. In his careful investigation of the famous case of the Glen Ridge High School athletes who bat and broomstick raped a retarded girl, Bernard Lefkowitz, a Columbia University journalism professor, learned that these boys had not simply gone momentarily berserk that afternoon in someone's club basement. Their atrocious behavior had been building ominously—and just as ominously overlooked— for a long time. The boys in well-to-do Glen Ridge were far more out-of-bounds than the kids Orenstein witnessed in California. One of the criminals, Kevin Scherzer, had been known for his proclivity to unzip his pants and masturbate while teachers looked the other way. "This rape was not a surprise if you look at the history of these guys and the town," Mr. Lefkowitz said in an interview. "It was almost a logical outcome of their behavior."

These boys were not committing rape for kicks. They were not doing it for sex. How sexy could it have been, shoving the wide end of a bat into a girl's vagina? They were doing it for the sense of power that humiliation of another can produce. They believed they were born to power. Power was their silver spoon.

In the aftermath of this case, a great deal was made of the victim's having been retarded. She encouraged the boys because she wanted the attention, some said. It wasn't exactly her fault, but it wasn't exactly *theirs,* either. The problem had to do with the girl's "disability." But the same equivocation could be made about any girl: that she wasn't sure what was going on. That the benighted boy "misread" her signals. Et cetera, et cetera. To this day, the head of the Sexual Assault and Rape Analysis Unit in Newark, which handled the case, views it chiefly as an example of how people with mental disabilities are "routinely sexually abused." But while the fact that the girl had an IQ of 64 made the gang-raping of her all the more disturbing, to regard *her* mind as the focus of the incident is utterly misguided. It implies that had she been better able to establish boundaries, these boys would not have assaulted her. That is entirely wrongheaded. These boys felt entitled to do whatever they wanted to do, to humiliate and criminally molest whomever they wanted to. Other girls in this upscale New Jersey town knew it. They knew it perfectly well. They told Bernard Lefkowitz, "It could have been me."

And so it could have. Little social support of the girls' safety was evident. The town had backed the boys all the way to the indictment. There is still, in the country as a whole, the sentiment that boys' burgeoning entitlement should not be interfered with, regardless of who gets hurt while they're exercising it. Recall the famous "Spur Posse" case in California. The "posse" was a group of popular white high school boys—athletes, again—who competed with one another using a point system for their sexual "conquests." When girls finally complained, several of the posse were charged with crimes ranging from sexual molestation to rape. Some parents excused, and even defended, their son's behavior. "Nothing my boy did was anything any red-blooded American boy wouldn't do at his age," one father said.

Fascinatingly, in boys (and in boys only), athletic team participation has been linked with "identity foreclosure," or stunted identity—that is, psychological development that comes to a premature halt. Society views male athletic prowess as the ultimate triumph, giving athletes even more attention and glory than it does figures of state. "The high status afforded male athletes is detrimental to their overall psychological development," the study's authors concluded.

Too much too soon. Or maybe just too much, period. Even adult celebrities have trouble *not* becoming self-involved, arrogant, and antisocial. Imagine how the celebratory worship of adolescent athletes might infect the boys' mental and emotional processes.

The power girls have always had is the power to attract sexually. Boys don't want girls exhibiting real sexual power (which of course is what emerges at adolescence) and so humiliate them sexually, which cuts off their power at the pass. What girls feel, instead of joyful excitement about their emerging sexuality, is shame. Victim shame.

Slut shame. And, perhaps most devastating of all, complete confusion about what's happening to them.

"It freaks me out that I'm being portrayed as just my body like that," a thirteen-year-old named Becca told Peggy Orenstein. When she was younger, the girl said, if a man commented on her, she would just "diss him as a pervert." But at thirteen, sexual humiliation wasn't so easy to pass off. Inside her thirteen-year-old body, it felt dangerous. When a bunch of older boys hanging out on a street corner started making sucking noises at her, Becca told Orenstein, she was unable to say anything. Suddenly it felt like open season.

Welcome to the world of womanhood. There are still "experts" who believe that learning to tolerate sexual denigration is part and parcel of maturity—for females. Wardell Pomeroy, coauthor of the famous *Kinsey Report,* is such an expert. Girls have turned to him for guidance. To get help in figuring out why, barely a teenager, she was suddenly being treated like a hunk of steer in a meat market, Becca consulted Pomeroy's 1991 book, *Girls and Sex.* There was little in its message to reassure her. "Much as feminists may deplore it, appreciative whistles from strangers on the street or from passing truck drivers are trivial," Pomeroy offered. "The feminists argue that such behavior degrades women by making them sex objects, but this has been so through recorded history."

The old down-through-the-aeons argument again: if it's happened forever, it must be normal. Becca, at least, grasped the author's unfairness in *Girls and Sex.* Denigration is "different from if a cute guy says hi to you—then your stomach drops straight down, but it's a kind of good feeling," she says. "The other feeling is mortifying. It makes me feel like I don't want to grow up."

Listen to enough of these stories and you begin to understand *why* girls don't want to grow up. You begin to understand why they want to remain small. On her first day of junior high, Geena, a girl who plays clarinet and chess and is more interested in computers than makeup and designer clothes, is standing at her locker when a boy flinging open the locker next to hers crashes into her and says, "Move your fat ass." After school Geena goes home and tells her mother, "I hate my looks. I need to go on a diet."

Sociologists use the term *gender harassment* to distinguish incidents related to domination that aren't particularly sexual in tone. "Move your fat ass," presumably, would be an example. Such verbalizations of contempt are damaging—particularly since they're likely to be glossed over as unimportant, something the girl should be able to "put up with." Note the silence of the Weston girls in the face of boys' harassment of them. They were afraid to complain because they so desperately wanted the boys to like them. The double message that girls are being treated contemptibly *because* they're girls, but that they might prove themselves a little *less* contemptible by taking it in stride only adds to the destructiveness of the experience.

Boys, having set off on their own search for the elusive "masculinity," separate emotionally from girls, ridiculing them to create distance as they struggle with their conflicted feelings about females and sexual power. The whole arrangement is painfully destructive, more so than when I was an adolescent. Listening to the histories of her girl patients, psychologist Mary Pipher had no personal point of reference for what they were going through, she wrote in *Reviving Ophelia*. Harassment is in another league compared to her own experiences coming of age. Today "girls are taunted about everything from oral sex to pubic hair, from periods to the imagined appearance of their genitals."

Pipher used the word *trauma* in talking about what girls' social experiences do to them. She told of girls' crying spells, of their eating disorders, of terrifying nightmares. "They dream of drowning, of being paralyzed, and of being stuck in quick sand. A common dream is of being attacked, and of being unable to scream or fight back in any way," she says. The most compelling elements of the girls' nightmares are "the attack, the paralysis, and the imminent destruction of the self."

Double Bind

Women don't forget the humiliating incidents they experienced as girls. "Theresa," a woman in her forties, still remembers the searing shame she experienced one day shortly after starting sixth grade in a new school. She'd gone into the coatroom at lunchtime and found her head scarf filled with mucus, having been used as a handkerchief by a boy who smirked in the corner, waiting to see her reaction. She stuck the awful thing in her coat pocket and ran home. "My mother marched the scarf back to school in a brown paper bag, presented it to the school principal, and said, 'Can't you control these kids?'"

Though she knows it's mild by comparison, Theresa thinks of this episode when searching for a way to understand the humiliating school experiences of her seventh-grade daughter. "When I consider how long it took to recoup from finding that scarf, I wonder how it's possible for girls today."

How it's possible, that is, for them to process the hour-by-hour assaults they are subjected to in classrooms and on the street. What does it do to them to have to respond so continually to threat, and danger, and mortification?

In the 1990s over half the sexual harassment cases investigated by the U.S. Department of Education's Office of Civil Rights involved occurrences in elementary and secondary schools. "We now know that sexual harassment in the classrooms and hallways of America's schools is a major problem—one we can no longer afford to ignore," wrote Alice McKee, president of the AAUW Educational Foundation, in *Hostile Hallways*. "Unchecked, it will continue to deny millions of children the educational environment they need to grow into healthy, educated adults."

Hostile Hallways was the report of the first survey to assess how sexual harassment in the schools was affecting girls—educationally and emotionally. Girls told researchers of not wanting to speak in class after they'd been mocked or assaulted and of finding it hard to pay attention. Some considered changing schools. Most said they felt self-conscious, less sure, and less confident about themselves. Nearly one in four felt afraid or scared. Sadly, a third doubted whether, as scared as they feel, they would ever be able to have a trusting relationship with a member of the opposite sex.

Hostile hallways don't vanish into the distance like the yellow brick road once girls get out of high school and go off to college. This is a continuing story. On college campuses hostility toward females gathers roller-coaster momentum.

Girls who are athletes, it turns out, have yet one more source of danger to worry about: good old coach. In 1998 the lid finally flew off the top of the pot as young female athletes began filing complaints. A $762 million lawsuit was brought by two student tennis players against Syracuse University and the school's tennis coach, Jesse Dwire. The suit alleged that Dwire massaged, fondled, and propositioned two scholarship tennis players and that both Dwire and the university retaliated against the players after they pursued a complaint through the school's grievance system. A university panel, finding he had violated sexual harassment and discrimination policies, had recommended that Dwire be banned from his job for two years, but his punishment was reduced to a three-month suspension. A year later, three days before the trial was to begin, the university settled for an undisclosed sum.

Anson Dorrance, forty-seven, coach of the U.S. women's national soccer team in the mid-1980s and currently coach at the University of North Carolina, has had a suit filed against him by two players. Debbie Keller, a leading scorer on the U.S. national team, accused Dorrance of inappropriate behavior that included uninvited sexual comments. Melissa Jennings accused him of creating a hostile environment for her before he cut her from the team. Dorrance denies harassing his players or abusing his authority. He says he plans to defend himself vigorously and so far has succeeded in getting the venue for the court case changed from Chicago to Greensboro, where he is a local hero. A dismissal motion by the University of North Carolina attorneys was denied.

In the meantime, it's clear Dorrance has "boundary issues" if nothing else. He acknowledged that he "participated in group discussions of a jesting or teasing nature" that were "inappropriate." He also apologized for borrowing four hundred dollars from the student, and repaid the loan.

Deborah Keller alleges that Dorrance twice made an "uninvited sexual advance" toward her; that on other occasions he made "inappropriate and uninvited physical contact" by placing "his hands and arms on her body"; and that he would "constantly interrogate" members of his team about their personal lives and sexual activities. The suit alleges that Dorrance began placing "unwanted and uninvited" telephone calls to her for the purpose of monitoring her personal activities. In October 1996, she alleges, Dorrance "coerced" her into meeting him in "a secluded area" and "made an uninvited sexual advance."

A series of letters from Dorrance to Keller, published in *Sports Illustrated,* shows the coach expressing increasing intimacy toward his player over time, from "just in case you couldn't tell, I have great affection for you" in January 1994 to "I never dreamed I would end up with someone like you. . . . My respect for you runs deep, and like your sweet note showed, it goes beyond your soccer prowess into the core of who you are. I am trying hard not to lace these thoughts with affection but as you can tell I care for you Debbie, and all that you do" the following October.

Into the core of who you are. "Anson cultivates an environment where the players become dependent on him," another former player, April Heinrichs, explained to a reporter. "I was the epitome of that when I was at Carolina. I got convinced that he was the only one who could coach me. It's a drug that you're on. Anson is a very powerful man, and charismatic—and you're under his spell."

Debbie Keller subsequently got bounced from the U.S. national soccer team. In 1998, she had played in twenty-three of the United States' twenty-five games, scoring fourteen goals. Yet the U.S. coach, Tony DiCicco, dropped her at the start of the year, saying she had not distinguished herself as a starter. Keller, clearly a fighter, tried to get reinstated on the team by pursuing an arbitration hearing against the U.S. Soccer Federation. The arbitration panel took testimony for three and a half days before deciding to reject her request. Coach DiCicco, a friend of Anson Dorrance, had given eight hours of testimony against Keller.

"I've had to sit down with my coaches and make them aware that what previously may have been acceptable, like patting a player on the bottom, is not acceptable now," said Christine Grant, athletic director at the University of Iowa. Males in the coaching business will speak of the "fine line" between friendliness and unacceptable intimacy. But these "confusions" about what's appropriate behavior with their female students is sheer equivocation. "I don't think there's a fine line at all," says Keller and Jennings's lawyer. "Conduct that would not be approved of in the classroom shouldn't go on in the gym, either."

The problem exceeds butt patting and sexual innuendo. A young New Jersey tennis player finally broke down and told her parents that her coach had begun fondling her when she was twelve and had coerced her into having intercourse when she was thirteen. The girl was a county champion and a junior in high school when she finally went to her parents. "She was shaking and crying," her mother said later, "and she didn't want anyone to know because she felt so terrible about it." They went to the police immediately. Stuart Gerechoff was arrested three days later and pleaded guilty to aggravated sexual assault in March 1998. In June 1999 he was sentenced to eight years at a facility for sex offenders.

The girl's mother worries that she "should have seen the signals." Well, in fact she did see the signals; she just didn't believe in herself enough. "He didn't want me around the courts at all," she said of Gerechoff. "When I told him I didn't like all the hugging that went on after practices, he jumped down my throat and said there was nothing wrong with it, that he hugged everybody. He used to tell me how lucky I was that I didn't have to worry about boys molesting her, that tennis was her boyfriend."

Through three years of sexual involvement, from the age of thirteen through fifteen, the girl never told anyone. "She thought it would be the end of her tennis career if she told anyone," her mother said. "He always told her she'd never make it without him."

There is tremendous social support for these male coaches. At a high school in South Carolina coach Joe Sutton became extremely possessive of a young Native American athlete, Alana Henderson: incessant telephone calls, gifts, and after-game hugging she couldn't ward off. "I was starting to be afraid of him," she said. Her parents went to the school and eventually to the county's superintendent of schools. When that produced no action, they went to the South Carolina Board of Education. Sutton was eventually suspended, and in a closed-door session with the school board in January 1998 his resignation was accepted with the proviso that he not seek teaching or coaching positions in South Carolina that put him in contact with girls under the age of eighteen. (The conditions became public last fall when Sutton ran unsuccessfully for a seat on the same school board that had suspended him. Talk about denial!)

"We found a pattern of inappropriate behavior that warranted his suspension," the county school superintendent said later. Yet, he averred, "I don't see how we can beef up our harassment policy without putting our schools into some sort of terror state."

This was the man who'd ignored the Hendersons' plea for an investigation until pressured to do so by the Board of Ed. As for his concern about terror states, it was Alana who lived in an emotional hell after making her complaints. Anonymous letters were sent to the colleges that were recruiting her, "warning them I was a troublemaker." Her parents had to transfer her younger brother to a different high school because of the continuing backlash from his sister's case. (Sutton, in the meantime, was free on bail while awaiting trial on the criminal sexual misconduct charge that grew out of the Henderson investigation.)

When sociologists use the term *rape culture,* they are referring to a broader phenomenon than rape per se; they mean the culture that tolerates sexual violence against women in general, one in which the threat of rape is always simmering. It simmers threateningly on college campuses. A degrading and threatening ritual is what fraternity brothers at some universities call "the walk of shame." The men gather on balconies or outside to leer at women returning home late at night, taunting them with comments like "Fuck that bitch" or "Who's that slut?" The "hypererotic male culture" established and maintained by fraternity life is so tainted with violence that insurance companies have designated frat houses the third most costly type of property to insure, after toxic waste dumps and amusement parks. Parties in these dens of iniquity are occasions to disrespect, if not out-and-out attack, female students. At the University of Rhode Island an eighteen-year-old freshman was raped at a fraternity party while five other men watched.

Some fraternities are notably worse than others. In one study comparing "low-risk" houses with "high-risk" houses, behavior at the latter involved heavy drinking and gender segregation, with men drinking on another side of the room from women. Men in the high-risk houses engaged "in jokes, conversations, and behaviors that degraded women . . . [and they] behaved more crudely . . . a brother dropped his pants . . . another brother slid across the dance floor completely naked. . . . Men were openly hostile, which made the high-risk parties seem almost threatening at times," the researchers observed.

Almost threatening?

The general ambience of large universities is often one of extreme viciousness toward women. At Cornell University four male students were charged with sexual harassment for circulating a list of "The Top 75 Reasons Why Women Should Not Have Freedom of Speech" over the campus e-mail. Among the reasons cited were "If my penis is in her mouth, she can't talk anyway" and "If she can't speak, she can't cry rape."

Some colleges today are getting rid of fraternities—or at least attempting to restrict the drinking at parties, known harbors of sexual and physical violence. Why do female students even go to these parties? you might wonder. Perhaps they keep denying the reality, hoping for something better. Or perhaps they've already been abused, and this behavior, in their worldview, is more or less par for the course.

Schools vary in how much help they offer, from high-screeching whistles to "escort" services that ferry girls safely from building to building at night. A coed college in upstate New York with two thousand students gets 1,200 requests a week for its escort service. You could call it a sort of post-tuition-payment caveat emptor when schools write parents of prospective female freshmen that their campuses aren't safe and suggest students take a self-defense course before arriving. Parents cry, "Twenty thousand a year in tuition and my kid has to take judo before she goes?"

Better to play it safe and add a little more to that astronomical fee—protect your investment, as it were, if you're the parent of a girl going to college today. A recent Canadian study found that one female student out of three from six universities across Ontario had been either physically or sexually assaulted *in the year prior to the survey.* At three midwestern universities 42 percent of female students reported having been victims of sexual coercion in college dating situations. Seventy percent had had intercourse when they didn't want to as a result of overwhelming arguments and pressure.

Meanwhile, college women are throwing up. If they were throwing up in high school, now they're *really* throwing up. In 1999 a story so phenomenal as to seem apocryphal was reported in *People* magazine. At a large northeastern university plastic sandwich bags had begun disappearing by the hundreds from the kitchen of a sorority house. When the sorority president began to investigate, she found a disturbing explanation: the bags, filled with vomit, had been hidden in a basement bathroom. Later she learned that the building's pipes, eroded by gallons of stomach acid, would have to be replaced. "Yet in a way it made sense," she told a reporter, because most of her forty-five housemates were worried about weight.

Some have questioned whether eating illnesses in women might be related to sexual abuse. Studies have shown a correlation, if not cause and effect. Both phenomena crescendo in parallel as girls leave high school and enter college, where, if anything, they are even less unprotected. In 1998, according to the FBI, campus rape rose 11.4 percent above the previous year. The University of Massachusetts at Amherst reported more "forcible sex offenses" in 1996 and 1997 than did any other college except Colorado State University and the University of Southern California. The university recently responded to reports of two rapes and two attacks in one two-week period by making available ten thousand alarms that create a "loud screeching noise" when a pin is pulled. *That* must have been reassuring to parents.

A University of South Carolina study warned of "alarming rates" of coercive sexual behavior on college campuses. In Texas researchers studying a large group of college students in the Midwest called the amount of sexual coercion on campus "phenomenal." Intoxication, blackmail, lies, false promises, threats to end the relationship, persistent touching, holding the woman down, "detainment," and threat or use of physical force, including use of a weapon—these were the tactics used in the attempt to force submission. (In this study, female "coercers" were included as well as male. But their coercive behavior tended to be unwanted kissing or touching.)

This is what has not yet been acknowledged: Girls are physically endangered and mentally traumatized to such a degree that their ability to learn is affected. Not only girls who've been raped or molested, but girls who've undergone sexual harassment—an experience that has been abstracted, sanitized if you will, by political controversy—suffer cognitive losses. While different camps continue to argue about whether or not sexual harassment is real, or prevalent, or even harmful, girls' lives are filled with it. Often the very frequency of the experience is taken as reason to dismiss it. Oh, that again. Breasts grabbed, crotches grabbed, what else can you expect? Boys will be boys.

But in the meantime, girls' bodies are registering these infractions. Their bodies—and their brains—are keeping score.

People who've been traumatized can't think straight. Their cognitive processes are distorted by the intrusion upon their mental lives of traumatic memories and images. Their primary goal is not growth, but safety. In *Reviving Ophelia,* Pipher says that girls' thinking is "so chaotic and scrambled," the scoring of psychological tests should be changed to accommodate it, that if you attempt to compare girls to stable adults, "they all look crazy." But what kind of solution is changing the tests? It's an idea based on another of those "it's so common that it must be normal" arguments. It's so common that it might be average, perhaps, but average and normal are not the same.

What makes girls' thinking crazy is their struggle to preserve themselves in a hostile and dangerous environment.

What makes girls' thinking crazy is the altered brain pathways produced by the trauma they endure. The changed neuronal activity German researchers have found in children's brains following high levels of psychosocial stress "threaten the mental and affective stability, integrity, and the future development of the child."

What makes girls' thinking crazy—and difficult to straighten out—is fear.

Only the body, working with the brain, as we'll see in a later chapter (Physical Equality: The Final Stage), can reverse the effects of fear conditioning. Strength and endurance conditioning, and even yoga, can help girls stand up to the hostile environment into which they become indoctrinated at earlier and earlier ages. Yet girls are conditioned to halt the development of their bodies at puberty. During adolescence most turn their bodies into what I call victim bodies. It's a further extension of the shrinking, or self-disempowerment, that begins in early childhood. Victim bodies belong to those who mentally believe they are *incapable* of physical power.

In its report on hostile hallways in the schools, the American Association of University Women didn't advise schools to attempt to provide a risk-free environment ("an impossible task," it insists) but instead recommended a "resilience approach" focusing on building girls' coping skills so they can "withstand stress and weather crises." This is still victim talk. How about coping skills that would allow girls to stand up to the plate, to say, "Back off!"—and mean it?

Becoming physically strong, and the earlier the better, is crucial for girls preparing themselves for participation in a sexist world and buffering themselves against the assault of what is considered, by those like Christina Hoff Sommers, John Leo, and Justice Anthony Kennedy, "normal" female socialization. Today some girls are beginning to get the encouragement they require for developing themselves physically, but they are still the exceptions, and for the rest the toll is great. Girls who grow to feel weaker and less physically competent, less engaged in the functioning of their bodies, as they reach puberty and enter adolescence, are at risk of depression, a lag in mental development, and vulnerability to both premature sex and sexual abuse. They are definitely at risk of becoming victims.

FIVE

Can I Play?:
The Struggle to
Get into the Game

O ne of the great failings of the American educational system is
the continuation of corrosive and unjustified discrimination
against women. It is clear to me that sex discrimination reaches into
all facets of education—admission, scholarship programs, faculty
hiring and promotion, professional staffing, and pay scales. . . . The
only antidote is a comprehensive amendment such as the one now
before the Senate."

With these words, almost thirty years ago, Senator Birch Bayh
introduced Title IX, an amendment to the Civil Rights Act that
would have a major impact on girls' access to physical education.
Title IX requires that "no person in the United States shall, on the
basis of sex . . . be subjected to discrimination under any education
program or activity receiving Federal financial assistance." Various
amendments to the Constitution have focused on the right to due
process (Fourteenth Amendment) and the right to vote (Fifteenth,
Nineteenth, and Twenty-sixth Amendments). In 1964, landmark
legislation led to the passage of the Civil Rights Act. Title VII of this

act addresses equal employment. Title IX addresses equality in education, including physical education; it took a major battle to get this amendment to the Civil Rights Act up and running.

Title IX, or, The Fight for a Physical Education

Many students today fail to comprehend the impact that Title IX has had on their educations. In high schools, prior to this amendment, girls were expelled for being married or pregnant. Even teachers in elementary and secondary schools could be dismissed for these transgressions. To be married or pregnant was a reminder of the existence of female sexuality—and the reminder was thought unseemly.

In physical education classes and athletic programs, boys got the locker rooms, the gym time, the teams, the funding. They enjoyed the uniforms, coaches, and fancy electronic scoreboards. Girls had team practice early in the morning or at night so that boys could get the prime-time after-school use of facilities. Boys had air-conditioned buses transporting them to games, while girls had their parents or whoever else could be dug up to drive them.

Before Title IX women lagged significantly behind men in even getting into college. Once there, it wasn't unusual for them to find certain classes limited to males, different rules of conduct (females had to live on campus, males could live off), and different access to "extracurricular activities." Title IX was the first comprehensive legislation to include the rights of students to be free of what we now call "gender discrimination" in schools. The new law covered the games they were allowed to play, the training they received, and the athletic equipment and scholarship funding that was allotted them.

The struggle to get a physical education equal to men's has been longer and harder for women than gaining equal access to an academic education. Physical power is taboo for females—more taboo even than mental power. The parallels between the battle for educating our bodies and the battle for educating our minds are striking. The very same arguments are used to prevent women's physical education: that giving money to their courses and teams will take money away from men's. That expecting too much of them is futile because their bodies aren't up to it—just as it was once said about their minds. When all else fails, out comes the argument that women aren't really interested in sport, at least not as interested as men, and that any money spent on their physical education is money down the drain.

In the years since Title IX was passed, these arguments have risen and fallen, risen and fallen, as different interpretations of the law have been handed down by the courts, as government administrations, with their different views of women, have changed, and finally, as more and more young women have succeeded in becoming physically educated and in getting their expectations raised for what they want and what they believe they are entitled to. What is remarkable is that men keep challenging the constitutionality of Title IX even as it became painfully clear that institutions that ignore its proscriptions can be hauled to court. And as some *are* hauled to court, and as monetary damages are awarded, and as girls and women successfully sue for the right to play, the organizers of what have been traditionally thought of as "male" sports have become increasingly perturbed. It isn't just fairness that's at issue here, but, once again, gender identity. Sport is male. Muscle is male. Power is male. And as the male power mystique is slowly but surely being punctured, men feel that something is being taken away from them. They feel that something is very definitely at risk, that something very unnatural is happening, and that they are at the mercy of some huge, powerful mechanism that is fraught with injustice—injustice to *them.*

But of course it is injustice to girls and women that Title IX is attempting to redress, and its effectiveness, though it has been painfully gradual, can be deduced from the numbers. In 1971, the year before Title IX was signed into law, fewer than three hundred thousand girls in high school played team sports. Today that number is 2.4 million. In 1972 women made up only 15 percent of college athletes, compared with 37 percent in 1995, and only 2 percent of college athletic budgets went to females! By 1986 the budget apportioned to women's sports had increased to only 16 percent.

Though the law was passed with little controversy, Title IX's implementation was subverted from the start. Right away the National Collegiate Athletic Association (NCAA) and high school administrators began grumbling that boys' sports would suffer if girls' sports were funded equally. Regulations about how to implement the 1972 law were not released for another two years, and schools weren't expected to comply for yet another three. The Department of Health, Education and Welfare didn't issue its final guidelines until September 1979—seven years after the amendment was passed! Even then the Office of Civil Rights (OCR) didn't enforce the law, and few complaints were investigated. By 1982, 150 complaints of gender discrimination in athletics were still pending, some dating back to 1973.

During the Reagan and Bush administrations Title IX suffered a terrific setback. In a 1984 decision, *Grove City v. Bell,* the U.S. Supreme Court ruled that Title IX had never been intended to cover educational institutions, only programs that directly received federal funds. Programs such as athletics that did not receive federal funds would now be left free to discriminate on the basis of gender. The *Grove City v. Bell* decision effectively killed gender parity in physical education. As soon as it came down, *all* athletic discrimination cases pending with the OCR were summarily dropped. This was a major blow for women. The loss of Title IX protection triggered a huge protest by rights groups who wanted the government to stop its weaseling over "interpretations."

In the years after Title IX was struck down, and before it was eventually reinstated, state laws became central in the fight for equality in physical education. *Blair v. Washington State University* was a particularly important Supreme Court case because it set higher standards for determining what was discriminatory in athletic programs than had Title IX. *Blair* raised the amount of athletic scholarship money available to women by legislating that it be based on the female percentage of the total student population, not just the female percentage of the athletic population. Further, *Blair* blasted the stranglehold that football had held on athletic budgets by stating specifically that football could not be conveniently left out when schools were doing the figures for equalizing athletic budgets.

In 1976, California instituted an Education Code that mandated immediate progress in gender equity in CSU intercollegiate athletics. With this state law backing it, the California chapter of the National Organization for Women (NOW) filed suit against all twenty campuses of California State University. In an out-of-court settlement, CSU officials agreed to do what they should have been doing all along—provide equal opportunities and funding for women's and men's athletics on all campuses.

The power of Title IX was finally restored when the Civil Rights Restoration Act was passed by Congress on March 22, 1988, over President Reagan's veto. The OCR made a public commitment to end gender discrimination, calling Title IX a "top priority" and publishing a *Title IX Athletic Investigator's Manual* to strengthen enforcement procedures.

Suing for the Right to Play

In 1992 the Title IX amendment was given much-needed clout when the Supreme Court decided that claimants in sex discrimination cases could be awarded monetary damages. The decisive case, *Franklin v. Gwinnett County Public Schools,* didn't involve athletics but nevertheless supplied an important precedent. A high school girl claiming sexual harassment and abuse by a teacher filed for damages in federal court. The court dismissed the complaint, saying Title IX didn't authorize damage awards. An appeals court agreed with the federal court. But the Supreme Court held that compensatory and punitive damages *were,* in fact, permissible in Title IX cases. This case was crucial in putting teeth into Title IX because it allowed women to find lawyers who would take their cases on a "contingency" basis because of the possibility of damage awards.

Another thing that had made it difficult for students to mount a Title IX complaint had been lack of information on where schools were actually putting their athletic monies. The 1994 amendment to the Elementary and Secondary Education Act required colleges and universities to disclose funding and participation rates. Now, students and prospective students can get a university's athletic department's report on expenditures and participation rates that's broken down by gender.

Hundreds of girls and women have filed lawsuits and civil rights complaints charging gender discrimination in their school athletic programs. Most cases have been resolved in their favor. The first athletics case to win a monetary award under Title IX was filed the year after the *Franklin-Gwinnett* win. In 1993 head basketball coach Sanya Tyler sued Howard University for sex discrimination. She was being paid much less than the head coach of the men's basketball team. Breaking new ground, Tyler was awarded $2.4 million (later reduced to $1.1 million) in damages. It was an important moment for female coaches, though its outcome had an ironic effect: Once salaries for coaching women's teams were forced upward, men decided they wanted those jobs—and they got them. By the end of the century more than half of women's teams were coached by men, while less than 1 percent of men's teams were coached by women.

But the landmark case in stimulating major change in how colleges and universities treat women's athletics was *Amy Cohen et al. v. Brown University.* After Brown demoted its women's gymnastics and volleyball teams from varsity to club varsity status in 1991, a group of women gymnasts took it to court. Brown tried to defend itself against the charge on the grounds that it had also lowered the status of its men's golf and water polo teams. The women were not impressed—nor was the judge. Money was the issue here. Loss of the two women's teams cut a total of $62,000 from the women's sports budget, whereas the demotion of the two men's teams had resulted in only a $16,000 cut from the sports budget for men. The U.S. district court judge immediately reinstated all four teams to varsity status and said Brown could not cut funding from *any* female athletic program until the suit was resolved. It took six years for that to happen and it cost Brown over $1 million in legal fees.

Infuriated by the district court's decision, Brown took its appeal all the way to the Supreme Court and along the way got an outpouring of support from other schools. More than forty individual colleges and university systems along with seventeen educational associations and sport-governing bodies submitted amici briefs. Even the American Council on Education, which represents 1,800 colleges and universities around the country, was against a small group of female student-athletes requesting equity, Ellen Staurowsky reported in a long analysis of Title IX and gender equity published in *Journal of Sport and Social Issues.* As the *Brown Daily Herald,* which was in favor of the plaintiffs, reported: "With the court's finding that Brown—among the nation's leaders in athletic offerings for female students—is violating Title IX, institutions nationwide with less impressive records regarding women's athletics will likely be forced to radically improve their offerings." *Cohen* v. *Brown,* the editors predicted, would probably become a benchmark "with repercussions throughout the world of higher education."

One of the interesting things about this case was that Brown kept claiming in its defense that it had the *best* athletics program for girls of any school in the United States. The Court kept saying, "Yeah, but you're still in violation of Title IX." On June 23, 1998, U.S. district court judge Ernest Torres, in Providence, Rhode Island, approved a plan whereby Brown agreed to ensure that the percentage of women competing in varsity sports would be within 3.5 percent of the school's total female population, to elevate women's water polo from a club sport to varsity level, and to fund women's water polo, gymnastics, skiing, and fencing for at least another three years.

Schools around the country never really expected that Brown would be forced to capitulate. The decision made palpably clear that a university stood to lose a lot of money if it messed with Title IX. Harvard, Stanford, and the University of Iowa were among the first to start making changes, initiating what they called "women's sports enhancement programs." These, in fact, were not additions to already equitable funding but legally required moves to correct longstanding discriminatory practices.

Compliance with Title IX regulations continues to be partial at best. The money spent on men's teams is growing faster than the money spent on women's. Between 1992 and 1997 overall operating expenditures for women's college sports grew by only 89 percent, compared with 139 percent for men. And as of 1998, according to a study by the National Collegiate Athletic Association, *female college athletes still receive only 23 percent of athletic operating budgets, 38 percent of athletic scholarship dollars, and 27 percent of the money spent to recruit new athletes.* Such puny figures, nevertheless, appear to be encouraging to some. *The Washington Post* headlined its report NCAA GENDER EQUITY FIGURES IMPROVING.

In 1997 the National Women's Law Center filed a suit against twenty-five colleges and universities that were violating Title IX requirements for female athletic scholarships. Mary Frances O'Shea, the Office of Civil Rights national coordinator for Title IX athletics, issued a "clarification" suggesting that by 2000–01, the disparity between what is spent on men's athletic scholarships and what is spent on women's should not deviate by more than 1 percent. This "rigorous criteria," as the *Chronicle of Higher Education* called it, provoked instant complaint from many who felt the government was creating too many problems for men's sports. Opponents began yelling "gender quotas" and attempting to confuse Title IX with the preferential treatment that had often been mandated by affirmative action programs. But rather than an affirmative action agenda, and rather than "preferential treatment," the government, in enforcing Title IX, is merely trying to make available to girls and women what has long been made available to boys and men: funding for their physical education. The goal—radical though it may seem to some—is *equal* funding for their physical education.

"I never wondered why baseball remained off-limits to girls," recalls historian Susan Cahn.

Who among us did? Our gender conditioning was far too entrenched. Cahn says she even yearned to play halfback on her high school football team, but *that* dream she kept a secret. It made her feel self-conscious, as if she were nursing a perverse desire. "I assumed these were the private dilemmas of a girl born on the cusp of a new era," she writes.

Private though Cahn's "dilemmas" may have seemed, they were not just personal. Many women who went to school before Title IX are now confessing the desire they had as girls to play just as hard, and as tough, and as frequently as boys—to be actual jocks, if that word had existed then. I had my secret wish to play ice hockey. Others wanted to play basketball with the boys. The thing was this: Most all of us wanted to get into the game. It was a wish that was more or less repressed, depending upon our parents, the schools we went to, and the encouragement we were given or not given. The great breakthrough of Title IX is that it gave girls a structure for fighting for the dream. It made the dream legitimate.

For many years sport and athletic opportunities "have been generously provided for males," writes Sue Durrant, an associate professor in the Department of Physical Education, Sport, and Leisure Studies at Washington State University. "However, movement is a basic human activity in which we all engage, *until we are conditioned not to do so.*" (Italics mine.) That concept, that women and girls have actually been *conditioned* to avoid movement, is essential to understanding what has happened to females physically. Title IX spoke directly to that conditioning. It acknowledged the importance to *everyone* of having a physical education and of being encouraged to participate in sports—not just individual sports, but team sports. "To be able to move ourselves in desired ways increases our confidence, competence, and efficacy," says Durrant. "I can" and "I will" become "integral parts of our approach to future challenges, both in athletics and in other life endeavors." Could anyone have made it clearer that the chance to participate in sports and physical activities is equally important for both males and females?

The frailty myth is not just about women being excluded from "the world of sport," or women "not being allowed to compete," or even about women being discriminated against. It is about women actually being kept from using their bodies—and for a reason. When physically weakened, women become socially and politically weakened. It is not so much that men want women to be frail and incompetent, and certainly individual men have no consciousness of such a wish. What men want, simply, is to keep on being the ones with the power to make the big decisions, and this is easier to pull off when the other—the other race or the other gender—is economically weakened, intellectually weakened, or physically weakened, or ideally all three.

In the past century, through great struggle, women managed to pull themselves out of the first two weakened states. Now they are pulling themselves out of the third. Men are actually quite disturbed to see women leaving their weakened state and gaining physical power, because it is the final power they need—the power that will seal their equality. For this reason society has gone to great lengths to control girls' and women's physical development and to keep them out of the game—a game that is much larger than just the game of sport.

Admission into the Ultimate Game: The Olympics

The most vivid proof that women can develop strength, endurance, and the will to win can be found in their battle to gain admittance to the Olympic Games. It took nearly a century for elite female athletes to fully pry their way in.

From the outset, the history of the Olympics was one of elitism and oppression. Exclusion was the rule, beginning with the ancient

Greek Games fourteen centuries ago. With the institution of the first modern games at the end of the nineteenth century, men were still vigorously opposed to women. Baron Pierre de Coubertin, a French educator who reestablished the Olympic movement, announced that the modern Games were to be sport festivals for white, upper-class male youth. He also envisioned them as training French males for military service and leadership roles in government and business. Women simply weren't up to the demands of Olympic-level competition (or, for that matter, of leadership roles in government and business). "No matter how toughened a sportswoman may be, her organism is not cut out to sustain certain shocks," Coubertin proclaimed. But he gave away his hand when he described the raison d'être of the Olympics as the "solemn and periodic exaltation of male athleticism . . . with female applause as reward."

Promoted as one of the most elevated of human endeavors, the Olympics had a shameful secret at its core: supremacy—men keeping other men out, men keeping other countries out, men keeping women out. "In public competitions [women's] participation must be absolutely prohibited," Coubertin insisted, although his will alone wasn't enough to deter female athletes from finding a way into the game. The first modern Olympic Games, in Athens in 1896, brought together 285 male athletes from twelve nations. According to news accounts from the time, a Greek woman named Meloponeme was barred from competition. She nevertheless ran a marathon, though it wasn't considered official, in four hours and thirty minutes.

In Paris in 1900, seven American women entered the Games, although they did it through serendipity. All were golfers, as it happened, and all came from wealthy families who were in Europe for various reasons when the Games were going on. Margaret Abbott, who belonged to the Chicago Golf Club, was visiting Paris with her mother when she noticed an ad for an international golf tournament. She entered and became winner of the first women's Olympic golf event. Her mother, Mary Abbott, took seventh place.

In 1904, at the St. Louis Olympic Games, American women took part in an archery competition that the American Olympic Committee (AOC) immediately demoted to the level of an "exhibition." The AOC, too, was against women participating in the Olympics. One influential champion of this supremely antifemale position was James E. Sullivan, a founder of the U.S. Amateur Athletic Union who was a friend of Coubertin's. When Sweden announced it would admit women into swimming and diving events of the 1912 Olympics, an American diver, Ida Schnall, wanted to enter, but Sullivan put the kibosh on it. It wasn't until after he died, in 1914, that the gates to the competition began to open a bit for American women. But only a bit, for Sullivan wasn't the only one trying to keep control over what female athletes could and could not do.

Most American women who managed to worm their way into the Olympics in those years did it through the aegis of small, private sports organizations where they were able to get training. Schools weren't offering the training required for high-level competition because they still didn't approve of it for women. American physical educators (as we saw in chapter 1) were fostering a "female model" of sports that had health and "femininity" as its goals. Intense, sweaty, all-out competition was masculine. So in the early decades of the twentieth century any girls who wanted to develop themselves into top athletes had to do it outside the school system.

American women were able to compete in swimming and diving for the first time at the 1920 Antwerp Games. Six of the fifteen of them came from the Women's Swimming Association (WSA) of New York, the first American organization to train women for international competition. One athlete who trained with the WSA was

Ethelda Bleibtrey, who set world records in various distances that year, often competing when strong winds and cold water forced other competitors to withdraw. On August 25 Bleibtrey won the 100-meter freestyle in the record time of 1 minute 13.6 seconds, making Olympic history. Another winner was fourteen-year-old Aileen Riggin, who received the gold medal in springboard diving.

Meanwhile, women from all over the world were petitioning to get into more events, a movement that was not to the Baron de Coubertin's liking. He was particularly dismayed when one of his countrywomen, Mme. Alice Milliat, founded the Fédération Sportive Féminine Internationale (FSFI) and began organizing an international competition for women. Mme. Milliat wanted women to have the opportunity to compete internationally in a broad array of sports. Tired of watching them held back by the controlling reins of the male-run International Olympic Committee, she bypassed Coubertin's objections and in 1922, under the sponsorship of the federation, presented the first Women's Olympic Games. Twenty thousand spectators came to watch female athletes perform in eleven events. A highlight of the occasion was track-and-field competition for women.

Alas, physical education teachers in America found the Fédération Internationale's inclusion of track events unsavory in the extreme. "Where sport in general connoted masculinity, track and field had a particularly masculine image," historian Susan Cahn tells us. It was about power and speed. It was about (heaven forfend!) near nudity. "Thinly clad running, throwing, and jumping athletes appeared to demonstrate 'naked' athletic prowess as they exhibited their strained faces and muscles for an audience entranced by elemental human exertion." Horrified at the prospect of women exerting themselves so plainly, educators tightened their control of the physical development of their students. The New York State director of physical education, Frederick Rand Rogers, published a critique of Olympic track and field for women. These sports, requiring strength and neuromuscular skill, were "profoundly unnatural" for the female, he claimed in a 1928 treatise on the kind of physical education appropriate for girls. The Olympics "are essentially masculine in nature and develop wholly masculine physiques and behavior traits."

As the Women's Olympic Games approached, female sports educators whispered among one another that socially less acceptable (read "working-class") women were planning to compete in track and field. One gym teacher wrote about it to another with dismay: "This Paris meet has appealed to certain classes of women in and about Syracuse. Not college women—and I hear it is true pretty much throughout the state." Her correspondent was more concerned that in fact some college women were about to lower themselves. "It is more surprising the apparently nice girls that are planning to go over [to Paris] in August," she wrote in reply.

In 1924 the International Amateur Athletic Federation (IAAF) denied women the right to compete in the Games. But the handwriting was on the wall: women had started to rebel. Following Mme. Milliat's success in organizing a big competition for women, other, similar events were created, such as the International and British Games. Suddenly, sensing that women were going to up and chart their own course, the IAAF agreed in 1927 to "organize" women athletes and recommended that the next Games include a generous five female events. Mme. Milliat protested that in no way could this be considered a full program. British women athletes, feeling more independent now that they'd put on their own Games, boycotted the restrictive 1928 Olympics. Clearly, mounting political pressure against the monolithically male IOC was causing some of its power to erode. In 1930 the Olympic Congress reversed the committee's decision and voted to let women back in.

The effects of athletic competition on women's health continued to be made into a big issue. Endurance events in particular were considered beyond women. In the 1932 Games in Los Angeles, the Olympic committee finally decided to include a few track-and-field events for women. A breakthrough female athlete was America's Mildred "Babe" Didrikson, who won gold medals in the javelin and 80-meter hurdles and a silver medal in the high jump. But after the women's 800-meter race, a rumor circulated that some of the runners had come across the finish line staggering from fatigue, "pale" and "exhausted." Other racers couldn't even *get* to the finish, it was said. We're talking about a race of less than 900 yards! The rumor about the fated 800 quickly became fact, and world opinion calcified. "The cinder track was strewn with wretched damsels in agonized distress," *The New York Times* proclaimed. The *Daily Mail* of London quoted a doctor who insisted that "women who took part in the 800 meter race and other such feats of endurance would become too old too soon." Even Knute Rockne, the famous Notre Dame football coach, felt he had to chime in, calling the women's race "a pitiful spectacle."

The medical opinion that women were frail still held the day. The 800-meter races were kept off-limits to women for another thirty-two years! When sport historian Lynne Emery reexamined the data on that controversial 800-meter race in 1932, she found that in fact all nine finalists had completed it. Olympic officials had never had a good reason to eliminate the event. By the time Emery's historical revision was published, however, the damage had long been done. The brouhaha after the fateful 800 had overshadowed the victory of sixteen-year-old Betty Robinson, who had come in first, and was the first female to win a track event in the Olympic Games. At sixteen she seemed barely out of childhood. She'd been so nervous before her event that she'd brought two left running shoes with her to the field.

Women's increasing athletic prowess seemed to be producing a certain male hysteria. John Tunis, writing in 1929 in *Harper's Monthly Magazine,* said the Olympics was an "animalistic ordeal for women." And to some, women who put themselves through the ordeal were little more than animals themselves: "Manly women . . . may constitute nature's greatest failures which should perhaps be corrected by as drastic means as those by which the most hideous deformities are treated." That was Frederick Rand Rogers speaking again, the man who had veto power over the athletic opportunities of girls in New York State. Even Pope Pius XI got into the act. In a letter to the vicar of Rome, he spelled out his opposition to girls' athletics—or, it would seem, to any female physical activity not in the service of the spiritual life: "If ever woman must raise a hand, we hope and pray she may do so only in prayer or for acts of charity."

Meanwhile, in the United States, certain influential groups were proselytizing against women competing internationally. *American Physical Education Review,* the phys ed teachers' bible, published article after article criticizing organized sport for females. The women's division of the National Amateur Athletic Federation continued to oppose women in the Olympics. They feared that "lacking the firm guidance of wise educators, enthusiastic young women risked being seduced by the glamour and fun of highly competitive sports," historian Susan Cahn tells us. But try as they might, American physical educators couldn't contain women's rising interest in high-level athletic competition. The compelling prowess of women Olympic athletes was decimating traditional ideas of women's physical capacities.

The first educational institution to prepare women for top competition was Tuskegee Institute in Alabama. Among American colleges and universities in the 1940s, all-black Tuskegee was a notable exception in offering women training for elite-level athletics while most white colleges and universities were still infantilizing their female students with intramural-only "Play Days." In the 1948 London Games three women from Tuskegee—Mabel Walker, Theresa Manuel, and Nell Jackson—were named to the Olympic track-and-field team. That year Francina (Fanny) Blankers-Koen, from the Netherlands, won an astounding four gold medals in track and field. She also won the heartwarming headline THE MARVELOUS MAMA: FASTEST WOMAN IN THE WORLD CAN COOK.

With or without such journalistic tributes to the athletes' femininity, women were making extraordinary gains in running and jumping as the century unfolded. In 1952 Alice Coachman of Albany, Georgia, won the high jump and became the first black woman Olympic champion. She was also the United States' only gold medalist that year.

The intent of the founders of the Olympics had been to promote competition among individual athletes, not countries, but as the world became increasingly divided, the Olympics became a platform for intense chauvinism. International sports competitiveness increased during the cold war. While managing to hold off bombing one another (fear of nuclear holocaust had created a détente), countries substituted the trouncing of one another's athletes. War once again (even the so-called cold war) had the ironic effect of broadening women's horizons. With female athletes adding to a country's prestige, prejudices that had previously barred them from competition abated, at least temporarily.

The Pan American Games in Buenos Aires and the Asian Games in New Delhi in 1951 brought Third World women into the international sports arena. In 1964 women from Ghana, Nigeria, Uganda, Iran, Malaysia, Mongolia, Nicaragua, Peru, and Thailand made their Olympic debuts in Tokyo.

Winning as We'd Never Imagined

The 1960s were a turning point for women in the Olympics. In 1964 women's volleyball (the first Olympic team sport for women), the 400-meter individual medley in swimming, the 400-meter run in track, and the track-and-field pentathlon were introduced for the first time. And the beleaguered 800-meter race was finally deemed "safe enough" for women to reinstate. Four years later, in 1968, an additional six women's swimming events were added to the program.

Television was likely the biggest booster of women in sport, as it was of sport in general. The modern age of sport spectatorship was ushered in when live television entered the living rooms of increasing masses of viewers around the world. The women's movement also ratcheted up interest in female sports, and the two forces—TV and feminism—conjoined to produce a breakthrough sporting "event" in the infamous Billie Jean King and Bobby Riggs "Battle of the Sexes" tennis match in 1973. The idea that a woman would take on a man was considered so preposterous, the match had instant marketability. Organizers went all out, promoting the event in a manner only slightly less sleazy than they would mud wrestling. Billie Jean was carried into Houston's Astrodome on a feathered Egyptian litter borne by bare-chested beauty boys. Riggs entered on a Chinese rickshaw hauled by scantily clothed females cutely named "Bobby's Bosom Buddies." From an advertising point of view, the gender hype paid off. Over thirty thousand watched from the stands, and another fifty million watched on television, making it the biggest TV audience a sports event had ever attracted. King's conquest of the fifty-five-year-old Riggs (she was twenty-nine) focused attention on women's ostracism from serious athletic competition. Despite its folderol, and in spite of the age difference between the two, which clearly put Riggs at a disadvantage, the notorious event slipped into the collective unconscious the heart-fibrillating notion that maybe men *weren't* the stronger sex.

Helping break down the gender division in sport had been King's main motivation in taking on Riggs. "I knew it might provide a springboard for girls and women in athletics," she said. But on the day of the famous match, her very visible role as a model for women upped the stakes. "As I sat in the locker room waiting to vomit, I kept thinking this was not about a tennis match, this was about social change."

And so it was. Suddenly the whole subject of women in sport became hot. *Sports Illustrated* published a series of articles on sexism in sport. *Time* ran a cover story in 1976, "Sex and Tennis: The New Battleground," about life in the world of tennis after the Billie Jean King win. As soon as women begin to really fly in a given sport, two questions get raised: How good *are* they, really? and How do they compare with men? The second question is a self-affirming one, raised only so that its answer can comfortingly remind us that as strong as women might become, they will *never* be as strong as men. *Time,* two years later, was still comfortable enough in its chauvinism to ballyhoo the new female athlete in yet another cover story, this one with the long and heady title "Come the Revolution: Joining the Game at Last, Women Are Transforming American Athletics." This was one of those stories designed to be sufficiently rousing to stimulate newsstand sales but nothing more. "The revolution in women's athletics is at full, running tide," the magazine trumpeted, "bringing with it a sea change—not just in activities, but in attitudes as well."

Well, there's no question that women needed a sea change in attitudes and activities, but this kind of hoopla obscures continuing bias and discrimination. As long as women weren't really perceived as a threat to men, the "full, running tide" made for good copy. No revolutionary toppling of the power structure seemed imminent. In truth, the ordinary woman's physical development was still as systematically restrained as the growth of Chinese women's feet once had been.

In the 1984 Games in Los Angeles, the Olympics finally allowed a women's marathon event. Eighty-eight years after Meloponeme's unofficial accomplishment after sneaking into the first modern Olympic Games, Joan Benoit made it official: women were able to run long distances and stay the course in spite of injury. Three months prior to winning the gold medal in women's marathon running, she'd had knee surgery. That was only seventeen days before the U.S. Olympic trials. She'd been determined to compete, surgery or no. During that brief rehab period she swam, cycled, ran, and had six to ten hours of treatment daily. Three days before the 26.2-mile race she completed a 15-mile test run. "Even as I was jogging to the starting line, I honestly didn't know whether I could manage the race," she wrote in her autobiography, *Running Tide*. But she broke away after 3 miles and held the lead for good after mile 14, cheered by family and friends. "Because I was buoyed by these people I ran what I consider the race of my life that day." By August 5, the day of the first women's Olympic marathon, Benoit was ready.

For American women in track and field, 1984 was a big year. Valerie Brisco-Hooks became the first woman to win both the 200- and 400-meter running events. A women's 49-mile cycling road race and synchronized swimming were also among the firsts for women in 1984. Connie Carpenter-Phinney won the first women's cycling race. And in 1984 as well, Pat Summit's team from the University of

Tennessee claimed the first gold medal in women's Olympic basketball competition.

In 1988 sprinter Florence Griffith Joyner claimed three gold medals and a silver. Louise Ritter won the 1988 high jump championship. Another major breakthrough for women occurred in 1989, when a California microbiology teacher became the first woman to win a mixed-gender national championship, the twenty-four-hour run. Ann Trason completed 143 miles! The best male finisher completed 4 fewer. Male competitors had told Trason they'd "rather die" than let her pass them. But pass them she did.

The history of the Olympics has been a history of contempt—toward nonwhites, toward developing countries, toward women. To break into the Games meant having to armor oneself against demeaning practices and behavior. To break in meant occupying one's place in the pecking order. When the whisper-small runner from Kenya, Tegla Loroupe, first entered the Olympics in the early 1990s, the male athletes from Kenya expected her to wash their clothes, and she did. She had to win the New York City Marathon in 1994 and gain honor for her country before she was able to stand up to the men and say to them, "I am not your wife."

The nineties was the decade of most significant gains for female athletes. Women's basketball, women's ice hockey, and women's soccer all became huge in a very short period of time, which not only pleased women, but entertained both men and women in sufficient number that the networks began covering their games. This gained for them an audience, sponsorship deals, and better pay. Conscious of the economic strides they were making, women players wasted no time in standing up to male-administered leagues that were giving them short shrift. At the end of 1999, six months after their spectacular World Cup win, the American women's soccer team went on strike for a salary increase. They were still getting the same puny

$3,500 a month they'd been getting since 1996, and the U.S. Soccer Federation was waffling. They wanted $5,000 a month, and the Federation, whether out of stupidity, arrogance, or some doomed attempt to take the wind out of their sails, was flatly denying them any increase in pay at all. "The stone-age leadership of the U.S. Soccer Federation has rocks in its head," exploded the *St. Louis Post-Dispatch*. "Even after the fabulous U.S. women's soccer team won the World Cup last year—and the adulation of every red-blooded American within reach of a TV—the USSF continues to lowball, stiff-arm and otherwise mess with the women's team." So a month before they were to begin an outdoor winter tour that would have paid them relatively little, they went on strike. Immediately they set up their own indoor tour, one that guaranteed each of them $100,000. As the Sydney Summer Olympics approached, they would just hang back and let the pressure on the federation mount. They didn't have to wait long.

In February of 2000 they reached an agreement on a five-year contract that will pay veteran players a minimum of $60,000 a year and less-experienced players $42,000. More significantly, they will get the same $2,000-per-game appearance fee that the men's national team players receive. There's no doubt that this will have an effect on what top women in other sports get paid in the future. "There now is a precedent where women are saying we really will not accept being underpaid," said Bruce Levy, a New York–based agent who represents thirty-five WNBA players.

The Abominable Sex Tests

Nowhere is male ambivalence about female strength more blatantly manifest than in the humiliating "sex tests" required of women (but not of men) in international sport competitions. Many sport sociologists are convinced there's no coincidence in the fact that sex testing became institutionalized just as women began storming the upper ranks of athletic competition. As we've seen, the number of women's Olympic events increased dramatically in the 1960s. That was the very decade women in different international competitions began being required to present themselves to a panel of judges for visual examination of their genitalia. Dubbed "nude parades" by the media, these examinations were humiliating for the women as judges searched for evidence of no vaginal opening, an enlarged clitoris that could be a protopenis, a penis, or testicles. Since visual exams proved troublesome and genital anomalies could be corrected surgically, the International Olympic Committee soon switched from visual inspection to the technologically advanced "Barr" sex test, or "buccal smear test," Laura Wackwitz reports in a scholarly article on sex testing. Known popularly as saliva tests, these genetic exams involved scraping tissue from the inside of the cheek and analyzing the cells to be sure each suspect had two complete X chromosomes and no Y chromosomes. Failure to meet this advanced scientific standard bounced the woman right out of the Olympics (and many other international competitions), stripped her of any prizes she might have won in the past, and fated her to ineligibility for athletic competition for life. The stated reason for the tests is that they presumably protect female athletes from any big, beefy Jack in the Beanstalk who might sneak into and unfairly win a women's competition, thereby committing an injustice against the weaker sex. The concept is so paranoid, one can only imagine it as some Gothic blip in the minds of twentieth-century sports organizers, but it is no blip. This is an idea that organizers of international sports find compelling—and is a practice that doesn't stop, even though it's been denounced by the most creditable scientific and medical associations.

The first woman to fail the chromosome test was Ewa Kłobukowska, a Polish sprinter. Kłobukowska had won a gold medal in the 1964 Olympics. She passed her first visual inspection by physicians in 1967. But the more sophisticated chromosome test the following year ruined her chances for the 1968 Olympics. Kłobukowska had "one chromosome too many to be declared a woman for the purposes of athletic competition," doctors reported. A year later the International Amateur Athletic Federation, governing body for the sport of track and field, stripped her of the two medals she had won in the 1964 Olympics and of all other awards and records she had earned during the course of her life. "It is a dirty and stupid thing to do to me," Kłobukowska told the press. "I know what I am and how I feel. I've been very aware of all the unhealthy sensationalism in the press, but I wasn't expecting anything like this."

The Barr test produces false negative results up to 15 percent of the time, owing in part to "errors in interpretation by inexperienced workers." An even greater problem is that the test identifies—and punishes—women who have all the observable female physical characteristics but who have a male sex chromosome. These women have no athletic advantage as a result of their congenital abnormality and reasonably should not be excluded from competition. But they are.

According to Prince Alexandre de Mérode, who established the Olympic Medical Commission in 1968 and had been a prominent member of the IOC since 1964, cross-sex masquerading is the primary concern addressed by sex testing: "We started the sex tests in 1968 at the Grenoble Olympics . . . to end cheating and stop someone competing with women when he was a man," he stated in 1992, when newspapers began circulating the report that the real reason for sex testing, from the get-go, was to identify women who were thought to be profiting from hidden "genetic anomalies." But the prince had already tipped his hand in announcing in Agence France Presse, "We have reached our goal. We stopped an immoral practice that was threatening to grow, an unethical practice that encouraged . . . genetic anomalies in order to win a medal."

So this really was the core of it! The organizers of the Olympics weren't afraid of men getting into women's competitions and cheating the poor things out of prizes. They were worried about female athletes competing with the advantage of hidden "masculine traits." Women who *knew* they weren't really women might unfairly beat those without the precious hidden masculine traits and fool the world in the process. Such thinking is so convoluted, it's testimony to the insularity of the International Olympic Committee that gender tests remained solidly in place—in spite of persistent challenges from the medical community—for over thirty years!

The furor over sex testing continued throughout the 1980s. In 1985 Kirsten Wengler was prevented from competing in an international swim meet. "After the test, the swimmers lined up for their femininity cards, and every woman except Ms. Wengler was handed one. She was told, in front of the group, that she needed to return to the lab," according to a report in *The New York Times*. There, doctors not only told Wengler her chromosomes were iffy, they warned her she might never have children. "I was crying and really freaked out," she recalls. But as it turned out, Kirsten Wengler *had* the typical XX chromosome pattern that should have classified her as "female." The test results had been incorrect. Four months later, after paying for additional testing, Wengler was informed of the error and deemed eligible to return to competition as a full-fledged woman.

In that same year María José Martínez Patino, expecting to compete in women's hurdles at the World University Games, didn't fare so well. She had passed a genetic sex test two years earlier, but the new test revealed a previously undetected XY chromosome pattern, proving to officials that Patino was really—"a man." "I could barely comprehend what was happening," the *International Journal of Sports Medicine* reports her as saying. "I was scared and ashamed, but at the same time angry, because I couldn't see how my body was different from [those of the] other girls."

Externally it *wasn't* different from those of the other girls. Patino had been born with a "male" chromosome pattern; however, she did not have the ability to process testosterone. Her body had developed as a female—that is, she possessed external female genitals and a fe-male build, but she had no uterus. People with this condition are not men medically. "In fact, there is no advantage because they don't have the receptors in their muscle to even benefit from male hor-mone," according to Dr. Robert Voie, former U.S. Olympic medical examiner. "So they don't have the muscles of a male. So they're very much female. But they just have this genetic birth defect."

Four months after failing her first test, Patino was instructed by the IOC to fake an injury to end her career. She refused to do this. "I knew I was a woman—in the eyes of medicine, God, and most of all, in my own eyes. If I hadn't been an athlete, my femininity would never have been questioned."

Patino defied officials and ran anyway. After finishing the race, she was publicly humiliated in the press and banned from competi-tive sports forever. She lost her job, her boyfriend, and many of her friends. But incredibly, in 1988, her status as a female competitor was reinstated by the International Amateur Athletic Federation, making her the first woman to successfully challenge the results, and pursuant ruling, of a genetic sex test. "Women must fight, and not just for a day or a year," she warns. "What happened to me was like being raped. I'm sure it's the same sense of incredible shame and violation. The only difference is that, in my case, the whole world was watching."

Ironically, there has been one—and only one—male impostor who managed to make his way into the 1936 women's Games as "Dora Ratgent" and was never even tested. A German Olympic high jumper, Hermann Ratgent came forth with the admission, years later in 1955, that he had been forced by the Hitler Youth Movement to compete in the 1936 Berlin Games as a woman, at which time he succeeded in setting a world's record as a woman. In the following Olympics, however, he lost out to three women who jumped higher than he did. End of Dora. When he "came out" in 1955, he said bitterly, "For three years I lived the life of a girl. It was most dull."

Though sex testing has revealed no attempts to defraud women, their humiliating "protection" continues. Each year about twelve women fail the Barr test and are banned from competition for life. After the tests most withdraw in shock and humiliation, feigning an injury, as advised to do by tournament officials, to disguise the real reason for their dropping out. The IOC has done its best to keep a veil of secrecy over its historical persecution of female athletes. Nor has it yet to give up, not even in the face of protests from organized medicine. The American College of Physicians and the American College of Obstetricians and Gynecologists both have opposed sex tests on the grounds that they lack scientific basis and are discriminatory. Still, the Barr sex test continued to be used.

All during the first half of the 1990s, sex testing was a hotly debated issue. The IAAF eliminated all genetic sex-testing requirements, replacing them with a requirement that all athletes—male and female—undergo a complete medical examination that would "include simple inspection of the external genitalia." Some critics thought this left too much room for cheating. "This is horrific," a

British sports medical officer said about the new IAAF approach. "With cosmetic surgery a woman with physiological advantages . . . could easily pass the [visual] test."

The IOC wasn't ready to quit. Yet another genetic sex test—the "PCR test"—had been designed by biochemist Dr. Bernard Dingeon. "The old test sought to establish that a woman was female," said Dingeon. "We set out to prove she is not a man." When the PCR test was introduced at the 1992 Albertville Winter Olympics, a group of French scientists requested that the French government stop the testing, saying, "The use of this genetic test is an aggression and manifests sexual discrimination towards women. . . . This practice sets the definition of femininity, which, in any case, should not be established by a simple genetic determinant." The Ethics Commission of the French Medical Association threatened to take disciplinary action against any doctors who performed the tests. Still, the IOC held to its position and prevailed. "We won't be lectured to," said Prince Alexandre de Mérode, head of the IOC Medical Commission.

The sport of boxing entered the sex-testing controversy as the presence of women in both amateur and professional boxing in the United States grew. In 1995 women were introduced into the prestigious Golden Gloves amateur boxing tournament and into the realm of professional boxing. In New York State the first professional boxing match for women received live television coverage. Controversy erupted when the New York State Athletic Commission ordered gynecological tests as a prerequisite for the fight. The commission mandated these tests be performed in spite of certification of testing from the women's own physicians. Clearly genetics plays a role in the relative success of individual athletes. "But sex testing is not an issue of how tall a woman is or what percentage of her mass is composed of muscle," writes Laura Wackwitz, "it is an attempt to maintain control over women who challenge the expectations of femininity by entering a stereotypically defined 'male' arena."

In 1996 the very physicians whose department had been responsible for granting "sex passports" to Olympic female participants for more than twenty years announced the fallibility of these tests in the *International Journal of Sports Medicine.* Having by then examined a total of 364 Olympic female athletes from sixteen to twenty-nine years of age and having found only 3 "chromatic negative" individuals, the doctors proposed a "return to the original criteria"—that is, to the face-value assessments made during the humiliating nude parades.

Back to square one. Revealingly, the IOC has never, in all these years, published a reason for its requirement of sex tests for females. Could this be because once such a practice is put down on paper, the risk is much greater of being nailed—for discrimination?

Media, Marketing, and the New Female Contender

It was one thing for women to get into the Olympics, quite another to break into the male world of organized professional sport. Earth-shaking, to men, or at the very least amusing, was the National Basketball Association's announcement that it would back a women's basketball team. What *could* they have been thinking?

Well, any number of things, none of which had much to do with the concept of gender equality. First, there were the amazing women's teams in the Olympics of 1996, which had come to be known as "the Year of the Women." Then there was that long empty

summer lag when basketball just disappeared from public imagination, a time when advertising sponsors and the NBA could have
been making money. There was also the problem of the increasingly
disruptive male players. The men of the NBA were getting too well
known for beating people up and getting in trouble with the police.
They were giving the NBA a smarmy image. Wouldn't it be constructive, from a marketing point of view, if the NBA could put a
team of "mature" female athletes on the court in the summertime,
when nothing else was happening anyway? Provide some good,
wholesome family entertainment?

"Mature" meant not those teenybopper athletes of fourteen or
fifteen, but a tough, competitive group of women with muscle—
women who were over twenty-one, some married, some actually
with children. They would be wearing baggy shorts, not tinselly little outfits, and showing sweat in the televised close-ups. Was America ready for this? If the marketing was sophisticated and things
went right, it could be dynamite. Think of the publicity! Think of the
potential revenue.

Newsweek jumped onto the bandwagon, pushing all the right
buttons: "Jammed into the nexus of prime-time sports and gender
politics, the WNBA offers an untested combination of old and
new, a game of naked female aggression played below the rim." Get
the "naked." Get the "female aggression." Fun. Shocking, but fun.
A big issue for the Women's National Basketball Association
(WNBA) was representing itself "in a way that would counteract
the American public's fears about the players (and thus, by association, the sport) being homosexual," Sarah Banet-Weiser wrote in
a penetrating analysis in the *Journal of Sport and Social Issues*. It
was important to the NBA to keep the women's team appropriate
for the slot for which they were developing it: good wholesome

family entertainment. Sports that are trying to attract a paying audience are those for which it is most important to wipe out the possible taint of lesbianism. Strategies are needed to redefine and recast "male" sports as feminine or womanly. Female tennis players are described as playing for their love interest in the stands, notes Banet-Weiser. Professional female basketball players are promoted as models and mothers. When WNBA star Sheryl Swoopes of the Houston Comets became pregnant in the first season, the image of the whole league seemed to become more acceptable. Asked how league officials felt about Swoopes's pregnancy, the chief marketing officer for both the NBA and WNBA said, "We embrace maternity."

You bet. Sheryl became an MVP not because she was top scorer, but because she had a baby and six weeks later was back on the court. When she returned to the game, every mom in the crowd stood up and cheered. "Hey, Sheryl! Go, girl! Can you believe how good she looks! She had a baby! Go, Sheryl! You still nursing? Sheryl, you look great."

Other maternal players get similar adoration. On the official WNBA Web site there's a section called "Ask Olympia" that allows visitors to the site to post questions to Utah's Olympia Scott-Richardson. Banet-Weiser says a full three-fourths of these posts had to do with the player's recent pregnancy, what sex the baby would be, what her name would be, whether or not Scott-Richardson would take the baby on tour with her. In the promotion of the WNBA there's also a lot of "girls just wanna have fun" stuff. Lisa Leslie is portrayed as swinging comfortably back and forth between her role as a fashion model and her job playing basketball. "That's what I call my Wonder Woman theory," she says. "When I'm playing, I'll sweat and talk trash. However, off the court, I'm lipstick, heels, and short skirts. I'm very feminine, mild-mannered, and sensitive."

There is still no quicker way to put women in their place than by portraying them as sex objects. Consider a *GQ* cover with Martina Hingis displayed in a short white dress with huge cutouts on the sides. First the magazine editors dressed her like a slut, then they called her one. "The Champ Is a Vamp" was the cover copy splashed across Hingis's body. Of course no one chains these women to the camera. Many female athletes have a vested interest in proclaiming their femininity. The theory of "sex-role conflict" argues that contradictions between athleticism and femininity can feel so extreme that many women choose not to participate in sport, and those who do often experience debilitating conflict between their roles as athletes and women. Some athletic women try to resolve the conflict by overemphasizing their feminine side with lots of jewelry, short skirts, and references to their boyfriends.

What the writer gets to focus on when doing stories about the women's league is influenced by the WNBA's marketing plan. Keep those players looking heterosexual—even, if possible, maternal. There's a "rhetoric of purity" the marketers are going for here. There's also a secondary agenda for the women players of the NBA (the NBA *owns* the WNBA, horrible thought). Pure and wholesome, the women will hopefully offer a corrective to the wild, unruly, bad-boy image of the male players. The marketing division has cleverly positioned them as the "moral guardians" of the game, on guard to save it from the "thugs" of the NBA.

Since the beginning, the WNBA has been compared with the NBA and its players found lacking in particular skills. The women were great athletes, yes, but could they play as well as the boys? Where were their slam dunks? Where were their rebounding skills? The press could be vitriolic in its comparisons. "The WNBA is to the NBA as the Special Olympics is to the Olympics," one columnist wrote. "The game they play bears only superficial resemblance to basketball as it is played by men, even at the larger high school level."

Here we have the old "women can't play as well as schoolboys" argument. But in fact they were good, and everyone knew it. How could the NBA escape the lash of cynical male columnists and also forestall the possibility of the women's team actually becoming "too good"? League officials hoped to kill two birds with one stone by changing the rules for the women players. The WNBA plays with a smaller ball, narrower lanes, and a shorter three-point distance. It also plays twenty-minute halves rather than twelve-minute quarters.

You might imagine that the changed rules could produce a somewhat different game, having the effect of "delegitimizing" the women's game and potentially infantilizing its players. As it turned out, though, the "different game" played by the women helped regain some respect for the league. The WNBA played a good clean game of fundamentals and camaraderie, without the increasingly obnoxious showboating and scene stealing of the rich, inflated, hypermasculine NBA.

Last but not least, the role-modeling function of the women players has been used to great profit by the advertising sponsors. It is, of course, to the good that girls now have someone other than Barbie and Miss America to look up to, but it is interesting to see how Nike and Reebok, the major sponsors of the WNBA, have adopted a sly feminist rhetoric in their advertising. A Nike ad shown on Lifetime had Cynthia Cooper of the Houston Comets looking into the camera and saying, "We get out in the malls and we're laughing and joking, and I actually took a picture with the first person—she hasn't sent it to me yet—with the first little girl that I saw with my jersey. It was awesome. I wanted to cry. She came up to me and she said, 'Would you please sign my autograph?' I said, 'Can I take a picture with you, pleeeease?' It was great. It was amazing."

The ad ends with a black-and-white image of Cooper and the words *I can inspire* merging with *I can aspire*. Like most women, I can get a tear in my eye when I see commercials like these that are so positive and seemingly mold-shattering. What isn't so apparent is how narrowly the role of the new female athlete is actually being cast. *Newsweek* describes the WNBA as "the good apple in the increasingly rotten barrel of professional sports." Beware the tempting apple. Someone out there is creating that old Madonna/whore dichotomy again and pushing these fantastic female athletes onto one narrow side of it. Forget your muscles. Forget your rebounds, or luge slides, or wicked slap shots. You've got a job to do here, and a place to be. Project those good old family values. And when you play, be a "good apple" so that you can maintain your role in television's profitable (if hidebound) family entertainment slot. Finally, play a game with a shrunken court and a smaller ball. That way no one will *ever* be able to compare you—favorably—to the men.

The press has created a sense of hierarchical difference in the way it "names" gender in its sports coverage. In tennis and in basketball, one researcher found, female players are named "girls," "young ladies," and "women." Gender naming can be ludicrous in its confusion, as when Steffi Graf was called "the wonder girl of women's tennis." Male athletes, in a study of TV sportscasts, were virtually never referred to as "boys." "Young fellas" was about as infantilizing as it got. Even attributions of strength in women were expressed ambivalently: "big girl," "she's tiny, she's small, but so effective under the boards," "her little jump hook," and so on. But there was little ambivalence in the descriptions of men, noted the authors of the TV study: "These were 'big' guys with 'big' forehands, who played 'big' games.'" Even men's weaknesses were framed positively, as in "He created his own error." When male athletes showed nervousness, it was made to seem like strength and heroism. The authors of the study heard this exchange between two commentators covering a men's tennis match:

"They're both pretty nervous, and that's pretty normal."

"Something would be wrong if they weren't."

"It means you care."

"Like marines going into Iwo Jima saying they weren't nervous, something's a little fishy."

Speaking of Iwo Jima, sports commentators often use martial metaphors (such as ambush, explode, whip, misfire, attack, stalk, squeezing trigger, fully armed, duel, shoot-out, blasting away, drawing first blood, and so on), and they are much more likely to use them as power descriptors of male athletes. In tennis, commentators used twice as many martial metaphors when discussing men's play. In basketball, it was closer to three times as many. The descriptors used for women are often less evocative of power. A man will "attack" a hoop, whereas a woman is more likely to "go to" it. A man's play will be "aggressive," a woman's "active." He "crashes through" the defense; she merely "moves against" it. Even when the outcome is negative, a man can be counted upon to do it more robustly: he "misfires"; she simply "misses."

One *Sports Illustrated* writer, discussing the comparative successes of Boris Becker and Steffi Graf after they'd both won the 1989 Wimbledon, found a way to favor the achievements of Becker. Although he mentioned the strength and athleticism of both players, he ended his report by quoting Becker as saying, "I used to be the worst of the boys and she was the best in the girls . . . [so] I had to hit with her." Readers are thus guided to compare the talents of Graf and Becker in light of the "worst" boy having once competed against the "best" girl. This type of treatment clearly creates a male-female hierarchy: even the worst man can beat the best woman. And so once again we are reminded who the "real" athlete is.

In chapter 1 I talked about the nineteenth-century exclusion of women from sport and showed how Victorian attitudes about women's frailty dominated the first half of the twentieth as well. In this chapter we've seen how, during the past fifty years, old biases began breaking down as women pressed for equality, including the right to develop their bodies and physical skills. As in their fight to be allowed to develop their minds, women would not gain the right to develop their bodies without a long and difficult struggle. The ages-old "battle of the sexes" was, as much as anything, a physical battle—a battle about body strength, body power. The reason we have not been able to see and grasp the implications of the war against gender equity in physical education is that as a group we never before posed a threat to men's dominance, so they had nothing to fight. Isolated instances of women's athletic prowess were viewed as just that: isolated instances. It was even easy to dismiss the female Olympic athletes as somehow freakish.

But as ordinary women began gaining ground, and as elite female athletes began competing with men for audiences, sponsors, and advertising dollars, the balance of power in the world of sport shifted. In the final decade of the twentieth century, what seemed an almost evolutionary leap occurred as women began closing the strength gap. Things that had been unimaginable only a few short years earlier were now stunningly demonstrated: that females didn't fatigue as quickly as men; that they could run, and swim, and cycle farther than men; that their muscles responded equally well to training. Even that they were not, by nature, afraid of body contact or of the possibility of injury. This physical courage, it would turn out, belonged not only to Olympic-level athletes but to ordinary girls, high school kids who'd begun putting on face masks and jumping into the fray of tackle football—actually playing with the boys, and against other boys, on their school teams.

In the United States the blossoming of women's long denied physical potential required the intervention of law and then a full sixteen-year battle before that law actually went into effect. It required standing up to an intense battle to exclude women from the Olympics. It required three decades of humiliating "sex verification" tests in which women had to prove that, though strong, they were actually female and not male. In the past century women athletes have been pushed down each time they gained a toehold in the rock face of male resistance. Why have women had to struggle so hard to be included in competitive sports? It isn't so much that men don't *want* women playing, they kept insisting, they just don't want funds taken away and their own opportunities compromised. This was the very argument used when women first began entering the workplace—men didn't want women taking their jobs.

Getting into the world of sport has been no easier for women, the threat to men being if anything even more disturbing than females entering their offices and sitting in their boardrooms. It is as though the ground men stand on turns to sand when women show the possibility of physical equality, so steps are taken to make sure they don't get there. This, at root, is what has kept women from having equal access to physical education: Men haven't wanted them to. By century's end the myth of the weaker sex lay in tatters, but that didn't bring an end to inequity. Over a quarter of a century after Title IX was passed, less than 40 percent of college athletic scholarships are awarded to women. Male college athletes receive over $179 million *more* in scholarship dollars every year. Men's sport programs command 77 percent of athletic operating budgets. Clearly there's much to be done if women are to have equal training, equal funding, equal acceptance. And gaining these is not in itself the ultimate goal but rather the underpinning required for a much larger paradigm shift: the change that has to take place if girls are going to throw off the shackles of restrictive gender conditioning and fly out the door and run and kick and throw as early in life as boys—and not stop when they enter puberty.

SIX

Closing the Strength Gap

I grew up in a house where my mother had the Metropolitan Opera on the radio every Saturday afternoon and my father had on at least two ball games, one on television, one on the radio. For the longest time I hated baseball. Only much later, when suddenly (it seemed) women had become pitchers, and tight ends, and goalies, when they were risking life and limb and rib cage to play in even the most rugged of contact sports, did I begin wondering why women had been excluded from certain sports (baseball among them) to begin with. Who, and what, had interfered with women's sense of their own physical possibility, so that as they came of age, sport had seemed the all-too-unpeaceable kingdom of men? What was the message being given to females of all ages about risk, courage, and the potential—hideous thought—for getting hurt? What was making us so bloody *scared*?

Day after day, when I was a child, I saw the same images on television and in the sports section: male muscle, male aggression, male explosive power. Men in face-slashing fights with gloves and sticks. Men jumping vertically. Men in huge pileups, tackling one another. Men, men, men. How bored I was by men's sports, as a girl growing up in Baltimore. And how I repressed the underlying message: Men are on top. My father wore a tie and a white shirt, always, whether to work, or to dinner, or on weekends. I never saw him do more than throw the occasional ball with my brother in the backyard, even then in his white shirt. But the shirt was a ruse, a kind of genteel drag, for what I really associated with my father was not the primness of his dress. What I associated him with were the loud voices of sportscasters calling the plays. I associated him, and my brother, and the boys I grew up with, with men in boxing rings knocking hell out of one another, men in giant pileups on the football field. I associated them with the lacrosse sticks so popular in Baltimore, invented by Native American men in the early days of our country and slung in such a way that the ball could knock your eye out with the force of its velocity. I associated them with the raucous cheers and stomping that made the stands quake around me on the rare occasions when I was taken to a game. I associated them with screams of "Blood on the ice!" I associated them with raw physical power that seemed only barely contained by the rules of a game. For wasn't there a connection between "Blood on the ice!" and blood on the war fields, blood in the streets? Violence was symbolized, ever present, in the reined-in but eminently unleashable explosive power of the male. There was rage in it. And there were people who got caught in the rage and hurt by it. There was always the possibility of injury, always the possibility of things getting out of control. And so we girls were warned: Don't stay out after dark; avoid narrow streets; keep your eyes down; don't look at them; don't take the chance; if you get hurt, you've only yourself to blame. All of this, from the belief in our own weakness to the excessive fear of male strength and power, is pumped up by the cultural institution of sport.

Sport is more than just the swinging of a bat, the jumping of a hurdle, the sliding, all mud-covered, to a base. It is a male-defined agenda no less powerful than education or even, for that matter, religion (to which it is often compared). Sport has always been an agenda, from the time of the Greek city-states, when, by excluding slaves and women, it contributed to their subjugation, to the nineteenth-century preparation of middle- and upper-class boys for the military. Sport has been used to perpetuate racism and classism, and it is used, still, to dominate women. The body, after all, is an instrument of power. Through sport, the male body signifies "better than," "stronger than," "more than." And this superiority appears to be inevitable—a "natural" result of differences in size, strength, and physical power.

The more I examined this obvious-seeming but misguided idea, the more disturbed I became. *On average,* males are 10 to 15 percent larger in physical stature than women. There are many women who are larger than men, of course, just as there are many smaller men in relation to large men. How big a power difference could really be legitimated by the fact that *some* men are larger than *some* women? Hasn't a mystique been generated here? And what would happen to that mystique if women—more women, *most* women—actually had the knowledge, the training, and the encouragement to make the most of themselves physically? How would things change if women knew how to use their bodies for power, and leverage, and social position, just as men do? If they used their bodies not for surrogate power, through passively pleasing men, but directly, getting what they want in their lives through a sense of their own physical agency and competence?

Women today compete at levels comparable to men. The threat this creates, conscious or not, produces a steady effort on the part of sports officials to slow their advance. It's too late now to keep women out of sports, so the tactics for undermining their accomplishments have had to grow subtler. Today the goal is more one of deflecting attention from just *how* physically similar males and females actually are.

One method has been to divide and conquer: keeping men's games separate from women's. When the chips are down, men don't want to contend with the other sex. The reasons put up against doing so, when they're put up at all, are laughable. In a variation on the "no women in the locker room" theme, bass fishermen excluded females from competition on the grounds that women shouldn't watch men urinate over the side of the boat. It took an organization no less auspicious than the Army Corps of Engineers to confront male modesty by refusing to allow use of a lake for a bass tournament unless women were admitted. (This was in the early 1990s, still the Dark Ages in the male world of fishing.)

Another tactic has been the creation of minor differences in the rules, which makes it harder to compare men's and women's increasingly similar abilities. In archery, for example, men shoot at 30, 50, 70, and 90 meters, women at 30, 50, 60, and 70 meters. What's the point of such a minimal distinction—a false distinction, some would say. Female athletes began to get the sense that the rules were being changed as soon as it appeared they were catching up. They found it suspicious, for example, when, after Chinese skeet shooter Zhang Shan became the first woman to win a gold medal in a mixed shooting event, in 1992, the IOC immediately decided to separate men and women skeet shooters in the next Games. (This was not an unprecedented move. The International Shooting Federation quickly segregated most of its mixed events when a woman took first place in rifle shooting, in 1976.)

Earlier in the century, women who defeated men simply had their titles taken away. When Helene Mayer beat the men's U.S. fencing champion in 1938, the Fencing Commission not only imposed a ban on male-female competition, it revoked the winner's title. The grounds? Mayer had won in an unfair fight, since men can't go all out when playing against a woman. To continue mixed-sex fencing, the officials decided, would be "almost as bad as punching a girl in the eye."

Since body contact in fencing involves the tip of a foil pressing up against a thickly padded player, there isn't much danger involved. We can only assume the commission didn't want women beating men.

The fear of female physical power is cross-cultural. When Barbara Mayer Winters became a finalist at the Acapulco cliff-diving championships, she was promptly disqualified from further jumping—for "her own protection," she was told. The men had complained about having to compete against her. "This is a death-defying activity," one male diver protested. "What would be the point if everyone saw that a woman could do the same?"

What would be the point indeed? In some cultures the very rites of passage into adulthood require men's being able to scare the hell out of women with their physical daring. Young boys from Bunlap, on the island of Pentecost in the South Pacific, are taught to hurl themselves from absurdly high platforms, making twenty-five-foot dives when they're as young as five, then going on to higher and higher jumping platforms as they grow older. A *National Geographic* reporter watched a sixteen-year-old dive from seventy feet. When his lianas, vines tied to the ankles to break the fall, snapped, the boy remained facedown on the ground, pretending to be dead, until his mother and sisters broke out sobbing, whereupon he leaped up shouting and laughing.

I wonder what this youth would have made of the eighty-three-year-old woman who recently bungee-jumped from a bridge over a gorge in Queenstown, New Zealand, dropping 150 feet and bobbing on her line like a yo-yo. Was she scared? Not really. She said it was exhilarating.

Men's Fear of Women's Strength

Historically men have been able to disempower and subordinate women, use their labor, influence their thoughts, and secure their co-operation mainly because of the power they have held over women's bodies. At a conscious level this has manifested itself in actual physical servitude, wherein women have been coerced into performing duties deemed appropriate to their sex. That Tegla Loroupe's fellow male athletes from Kenya expected her to launder their dirty clothes during the Olympics is an example. But there are subtler forms of domination. Most effective of all has been getting women to experience their bodies in ways that make *men* more comfortable. This conspiring of women in their own physical oppression can be seen in female bodybuilding. The sport became serious with the creation of the American Federation of Women Bodybuilders in 1980. But from the beginning women took care to establish their femininity by posing differently from male bodybuilders. They affect dancelike, less static postures that prevent onlookers from being able to see the full extent of their muscular development. This has been encouraged, if not required, by male officials, who have focused entirely on the feminine image as a judging criterion. "First and foremost, the judge must bear in mind that he or she is judging a woman's bodybuilding competition and is looking for an ideal feminine physique," the International Federation of Bodybuilding states unambiguously in its guidelines. "Therefore, the most important aspect is shape, a feminine shape, and controlling the development of muscle—it must not be carried to excess, where it resembles the massive muscularity of the male physique."

Here at last we see, written out and unvarnished, the message females have been getting since they were girls: *Don't get too muscular. Keep yourself smaller, so as to seem weaker than the boys.* Bodybuilding is a contest that is about being strong. It is about developing oneself physically to the max. But lo and behold, as women got more muscular, the event was redesigned for female competitors so that it has less to do with looking strong and more to do with looking female. The old bottom line was right there in the black and white of the International Federation of Women Bodybuilders' criterion: For females, it's not what you do, it's how you look while doing it. The beauty of the surface is what's relevant for women. In addition to rewarding smaller muscles and more feminine dance poses, judges of female bodybuilding are instructed to *take off points* for typical female wear and tear: stretch marks, surgical scars, cellulite. So get rid of them, girls, if you want to have a chance on the bodybuilding stage.

When it comes to muscle, the question "How much is too much?" is, for women, continually being reassessed and redefined. In female bodybuilding truly muscular women have always been at a disadvantage. The irony was not lost on two filmmakers, who used it to hype the drama in *Pumping Iron II: The Women.* To create a documentary effect, two actual bodybuilders, Bev Francis, a muscular power lifter, and Rachel McLish, who describes herself as a "powder puff," were used as the film's main characters. Bev can deadlift 520 pounds. Here was a woman, as sociologist Ellis Cashmore puts it, "who had not only challenged traditional concepts of femininity, but crushed them like an aluminum beer can in her mighty fist."

Rachel, by comparison, is a lifter of another dimension—someone who poses for magazine photo sessions in superfemme costumes: for example, a zebra-print bikini and feather headdress with gold chains around her belly. In the story, the contest between Bev and Rachel, who are preparing for a staged competition, structures the film's plot. "On one level, the film is about the competition between these two female bodies. But at another level it is a film about ideologies of femininity," says feminist scholar Anne Balsamo.

Pumping Iron II shows by whom—and for what—women body-builders get rewarded, and its message is clear: They *don't* get re-warded for out-and-out strength. Of eight women lifters, Bev finished last—not because she didn't lift great, but because she didn't *look* right. Her last-place finish was used to symbolize her body's "trans-gressions against the cultural norm," says Balsamo. A judge was shown explaining that "women with 'big grotesque muscles' violate the natural differences between men and women"—just in case the film audience didn't get it.

In the end, Rachel didn't win, either. That would have been too obviously retrograde. To finish off the story, the scriptwriter brought in a third woman, neither too massive nor too feminine. That Carla Dunlap is a black athlete, however, threw a new variable into the mix, so that the initial tension between macho woman and powder-puff girl was never resolved, it was simply dropped. Carla became the way out of a plot dilemma that seemed, to the filmmakers, im-possible. Though apparently they were entranced by the drama of women exhibiting great strength, they couldn't find a way to extri-cate themselves from the very issue they found so dramatic. They couldn't bring themselves to say that a woman capable of deadlifting 520 pounds is a woman like any other.

In the real world of female bodybuilding, 1993 was a big year be-cause the federation finally lifted its ban on big muscles. The achieve-ments of Bev Francis were instrumental in the rule change. By the end of the 1990s the bigger and harder shape had become the norm, with women competitors being judged on virtually the same criteria as men. Today women bodybuilding champions can actually make as much money from appearances and endorsements as male body-builders—perhaps the final indignity for many men.

While extreme muscular development in women is still a turnoff to many, there has been, in fact, a growing acceptance of bigger and harder muscles. In the women's sports magazines, showing bodies that are highly developed and even big has become the norm. The fashion magazines trail behind, although today even models show off bodies that are subtly shaped with muscle. Before the 1990s, muscle in models was total anathema.

The Myth of the "Mannish" Woman

No less an authority than Lewis Terman, the creator of the first IQ test, got involved in the pressing issue of masculinity and femininity in sports. He concocted what would become the extremely influential Attitude Interest Analysis Survey. One's attitudes and interests, he believed, were the key to determining where a given individual fell on the masculinity-femininity spectrum. An interest in sport, in Terman's schema, was a major indicator; indeed, he declared that an interest in sport was "the most masculine interest" a woman could have. His tests, he believed, showed that college athletes, male *or* female, were high scorers in "masculinity."

One of Terman's students, E. Lowell Kelly, took all this masculine/feminine insanity to its inevitable conclusion when he came up with a system to tease out "potential homosexuality." Based on a ridiculously small sample, the research results, highly publicized, caught everyone's eye. After analyzing a test group of eighteen lesbians, he had found—oh boy!—that they were "slightly less masculine" than a group of thirty-seven female college athletes. Terman and Kelly's "scales" lent supposedly scientific validity to the idea that women athletes not only lacked femininity but were even more masculine than the much-feared lesbians. This was exciting stuff. Popular magazines published articles on the new studies, articles with titles like "How Masculine or Feminine Are You?," accompanied by clever little male/female surveys that encouraged anxious readers to rate themselves. Football, skating, and tennis were the possibilities from which one was to choose a favorite sport. If one chose football, that was two points. Skating and tennis were gender neutral enough to confer zero points. The higher the total points (there were other scoring categories besides sports), the greater the masculinity. Terman and Kelly's vaunted M/F scales fed into and supported midcentury gender proscriptions. If a girl wanted to play on her school football team, there was clearly something wrong with her. End of story.

The threat of seeming masculine has kept a lot of girls and women from entering sports in a serious way—and understandably. Formidable female athletes have been shamelessly ridiculed, reduced to little more than sideshow freaks. The stronger and more athletically brilliant, the freakier their portrayal in the media. The story of Martina Navratilova is *the* classic example. A young defector from Communist Czechoslovakia, Navratilova was sworn in as a U.S. citizen in 1981 and went on to take the world of women's tennis by storm. Over the course of her career she netted eighteen grand slam singles titles and a record 1,438 single match victories. By 1985 she had accumulated $8.5 million in winnings, more than any other player in the history of the sport. This athlete's stunning achievements might have been construed as an example of using natural talent, hard work, and first-rate training to reach a new level of performance. Yet the media took the position that anyone who performed as well as Martina couldn't possibly be a real woman, she could only be some sort of overly aggressive misfit. Navratilova was characterized as a "bionic sci-fi creation," an "Amazon," even "some kind of hulking predator who kept 'beating up on all those innocent girls.'" A writer for *Sports Illustrated* referred to her as "the bleached blonde Czech bisexual defector" who "bludgeoned" and "teased" her hopelessly inferior opponents and suggested she was something other than a "natural" female. *Time* magazine wrote that in order to play so well, Navratilova "must have a chromosomic screw loose somewhere."

Within a few years other women had developed their skills to the point of being able to beat Navratilova, but the smear of virilism didn't stop there. Instead of returning talented female athletes to the category of normal as their ranks swelled in all sports, male writers became yet more hostile and suspicious. Even in the 1990s top women athletes were ridiculed as unfeminine. A story in *The Washington Post*, "The (Lesser) Games Women Play," said of female basketball players in the 1992 Barcelona Games, "They walked like men, slapped hands like men."

They may have behaved like men, but of course they didn't *play* like men. Rather, this sportswriter gibed, "They played like junior high school boys."

Women who are successful as athletes invariably have the experience, at some point in their careers, of being described as masculine. The British golfer Enid Wilson could "punch out an iron with masculine vigor." Tennis players were robotlike, exhibiting "cold, tense, machine-like qualities." Aggressive male players were praised. Aggressive female players were not talented, they were cruelly merciless. When Helen Wills played tennis, it "was almost as though a man with a rapier were sending home his vital thrusts against a foeman unarmed."

In women's sport the underlying tension has always come from the presumed contradiction between physical intelligence and womanhood. From the 1930s to the 1950s, Mildred "Babe" Didrikson's fabulous athletic accomplishments were shredded in the journalistic mill. Tabloids were littered with comments about her "mannish" appearance, her "hawkish and hairy" face, and her "unusual amount of male dominance." Reporters were always asking Didrikson if she ever intended to marry. "It gets my goat," she said. "They seem to think I'm a strange, unnatural being summed up in the words Muscle Moll." Poor Babe. It's no wonder she finally took a husband (who knew about her lesbianism). As a career saver, it worked. "Babe Is a Lady Now: The World's Most Amazing Athlete Has Learned to Wear Nylons and Cook for Her Huge Husband," *Life* magazine raved. But with all the brouhaha about Didrikson's femininity, her remarkable athletic ability got less attention than it deserved. First starring in basketball, track and field, and baseball, she then, between bouts of cancer, became the top woman golfer in the United States. When she died of the illness in her forties, the press spent less time celebrating Didrikson's athletic accomplishments than her achievement of "femininity."

Men didn't stop at slapping the label of gender abnormality on female *children* who were good athletes. At a girls' soccer match in Lewisville, Texas, fathers whose daughter's team was defeated charged out onto the field and demanded that the three best players on the winning team be sent to the bathroom to have their sex verified. (This was in 1990!) After the game one of the fathers further humiliated the team's nine-year-old star goalie, calling out to her, "Nice game, boy!" and "Good game, son." Young Natasha Dennis, to her credit, didn't fold but instead remarked that someone should take the men "and check to see if they have anything between their ears."

The soccer fathers, of course, were revealing their own insecurities. Historically men have dominated the playing fields, with athletic qualities such as aggression, competitiveness, strength, speed, and power being viewed entirely as masculine. And now not only women but girls, *kids*, were demonstrating those very traits. "Nice game, boy!" meanly and deliberately addressed to a girl of nine is the sound of the world tilting.

Not all girls are as clearheaded as Natasha. The implication of lesbianism is still a fearsome challenge—for young females especially. It

was partly a result of homophobic attitudes toward strong, athletic females that girls' participation in high school sports barely increased
during the sixties and seventies. Post–Title IX, far fewer girls entered
sports than progressive educators would have hoped. It was because if
you were a girl, you had to have guts if you wanted to play your heart
out. Even in the 1990s you could be chewed up and spat out for that
transgression.

The taint of homosexuality is the modern-day equivalent of the
mark of the tar brush. For the woman so marked, it changes everything. It certainly dissuades women from pursuing careers in coaching or athletic administration. A former high school athlete and later
a coach, Laura Noah knew when she was young that much of her
identity was wrapped up in sports: "My mother says I was an athlete
in the womb. I could pick up a basketball before I could walk." Yet
she was constantly feeling that she could be successful in sports
"only as long as I still looked and acted like a 'girl.' " Laura was a soccer and basketball star in high school and a four-year soccer starter at
Division III Kenyon College in Ohio, and she won all-conference and
all-regional honors and the North Coast Athletic Conference's
scholar-athlete award. But she was also a lesbian. By the time she
was a senior in college Laura was "out" to the team captains and
dearly wanted to come out to the rest of her team. The team captains
didn't think so. They said if she came out, it would be too upsetting
and disruptive to the team. To Laura it seemed as if she couldn't be
both an open lesbian and an athlete. "I was holding back. I didn't feel
whole." When she left coaching at the age of twenty-six, it was because she feared she'd have to remain in the closet if she wanted to
succeed in her field.

Some say homophobia has gotten worse as women get stronger. It
has always been a big issue for female athletic coaches, whether or not
they're lesbian. If they are, they're advised not to "come out." If they're

not, they're categorized as lesbian anyway. For some, like Laura, the whole atmosphere is so destructive, they're forced to leave the profession to protect their integrity.

People's confusion about gender and athleticism is nowhere more dramatically revealed than in the story of Richard Raskind, a six-foot-two high-ranking player in the thirty-five and older men's division of the United States Tennis Association (USTA). Richard became a surgically constructed female in 1975, changed his name to Renee Clarke, and in 1976 thrashed the defending champion in the women's division of a local tournament in La Jolla, California. A suspicious reporter looked into the situation—the winner *was* six-two—and discovered that Renee Clarke was actually Renee Richards, the name Richard Raskin had taken after becoming a transsexual. Talk about a media circus. The clamor might eventually have died down had Richards not accepted an invitation to play in a national tournament that was a warm-up for the U.S. Open. That did it. The USTA, the Women's Tennis Association (WTA), and the U.S. Open Committee leaped to the challenge by requiring *all* women competitors to take a sex chromosome test. Richards refused and one year later took the case to the New York Supreme Court, which ruled that "this person is now female" and that requiring Richards to pass a chromosome test was "grossly unfair, discriminatory and inequitable, and violative of her rights." How ironic that the court finally deemed sex tests unlawful in the case of a biological male surgically turned female. The decision opened the way for Richards to play in the women's singles in the 1977 U.S. Open, where she promptly lost in the first round to Virginia Wade. That's right. Husky, six-two Renee lost to a woman. What *had* everyone been so afraid of? "[T]hat the floodgates would be opened," in Richards's words. That through them "would come tumbling an endless stream of made-over Neanderthals who would brutalize Chris Evert and Evonne Goolagong. . . . Some player who was not quite good enough in men's tennis might decide to change only in order to overpower the women players."

Here, perhaps, is the most peculiar possibility of all. Did Richards lose his game as part of his makeover? Did he subconsciously weaken himself in order to play—in Bob Dylan's famous refrain—"just like a woman"?

New Ways of Assessing Performance

The idea that women are unable to achieve the same levels of physical development as men is today under question. The only reason some women don't perform at similar levels, suggest some sport sociologists and even physicians, is that women have been cast as biologically incapable for so long. In the new edition of the *Oxford Textbook of Sports Medicine,* Per-Olof Åstrand, professor emeritus of Sweden's Karolinska Institute, is one who suggests how close women's records may end up coming to men's, despite physiological differences.

Ellis Cashmore, a professor of sociology at Staffordshire University in England, has done a historical analysis of marathon results, comparing changes in men's and women's running times. Over a thirty-year period, between 1964 and 1995, the world record for women improved by 1 hour, 5 minutes, 21 seconds. During that same period the male world record improved by only 5 minutes, 2 seconds. By the last year of the period studied, the glaring ability gap between men and women was no longer so glaring. The difference in the world's bests was down to 12 minutes, 13 seconds—or about 9 percent.

"*Is* the performance of women inferior to that of men?" asks movement analyst Jackie Hudson. "It depends on the terms of comparison: Who, and what, is being compared?" A method developed for comparing male weight lifters is finally being considered a fairer and more accurate way of assessing performance comparisons between males and females. Based on biomechanics, the calculation converts fixed race distances into units of competitor height. An example: Suppose you stand 1.67 meters (5 feet 5¾ inches) tall and run the 10K in 50 minutes, or 3,000 seconds. Convert the length of the race to heights by dividing race length by height. That's 10,000 meters divided by 1.67 meters equals 6,000 heights. Velocity is then computed by dividing heights by time. Using this method, says Hudson, it's possible to get an accurate comparison of male and female world record holders. She used it to make a comparative analysis of Carl Lewis and Florence Griffith Joyner. A runner of the 100-meter dash, Lewis, who stood 6 feet 2 inches tall and held the men's world record of 9.92 seconds, had a relative velocity of 5.36 heights per second. But was he faster than Flo-Jo at the 100 meters? You probably have guessed the biomechanical answer. Joyner, who was 5 feet 6½ inches tall, ran the 100-meter dash in 10.49 seconds and thus had a relative velocity of 5.64 heights per second. "In other words," says Hudson exultantly, "the fastest woman is 5.3 percent faster than the fastest man!"

What about men's vaunted upper body strength and relatively wider shoulders? Would they be better equipped for an upper body sport such as swimming? Not necessarily. Hudson compares Janet Evans, a 5-foot-5-inch women's world record holder with 15:52.1 minutes in the 1,500-meter freestyle, with Vladimir Salnikov, the 5-foot-11-inch men's record holder with 14:54.76 minutes. When a biomechanical assessment is made, Hudson shows us, Evans's velocity is .949 heights per second and Salnikov's is .926 heights per second, a difference of 2.5 percent in favor of Evans. (Let's hear it for fancy math.) When measurements are made in absolute terms, the males are faster. However, when these fairer biomechanical measurements, which take into account an individual's size, are made, the physical abilities of elite-level females appear to be equal, and sometimes superior, to those of elite-level males.

What happens, skeptics may wonder, when the base of comparison is broadened? When fifty-seven women and seventy men who swam the 100-meter freestyle in the 1988 Olympics were compared inch for inch, the men were 2.1 percent faster. This difference appears to support the hypothesis that swimming, because it's an upper body sport, favors men. However, other characteristics of the contestants are relevant: age is significantly related to velocity, and the men were 2.8 years older. Might the women reduce the velocity differential with 2.8 more years of training? That is an unanswered but tantalizing question.

But surely males have *some* physical advantages. Well, yes, but females have their advantages, too. On average, men can carry and use more oxygen. They tend to be heavier—an advantage in football—and taller: handy in basketball and volleyball. Men have more lean muscle mass, convenient in sports requiring explosive power. Less muscle-bound, women generally have greater flexibility, useful in gymnastics, diving, and skating. Their lower center of gravity helps in hockey, golf, tennis, baseball, and even basketball. Women sweat better (less dripping, therefore better evaporation), which is critical, since bodies need to remain cool to function efficiently. A physiologist at the University of Virginia tested athletes under various conditions of heat, humidity, exercise, and nutritional intake and concluded that women are better able to adjust to environmental changes. "In every case, females were better able to handle the stress," she says.

You might be wondering whether closing the strength gap is something only elite female athletes are capable of. Significantly, the difference between elite and ordinary female athletes is greater than it is between elite and ordinary male athletes. As an example, the *average* female eighteen-year-old needs 10 minutes, 51 seconds, to run a mile, whereas the women's world record holder needs just 39 percent of that time (4:15). By contrast, the male champion completes the mile in about half (49 percent) the time taken by the average male eighteen-year-old (7:35). Young women, then, are farther from their athletic potential than young men.

Much of the gap has to do with predictable differences in level of skill. Jackie Hudson's research found that when novice, intermediate/advanced, and elite college women basketball players were compared on free-throw-shooting technique, for example, the novice players were more likely to use restricted—or partially "frozen"—range of motion and to veer off balance. She deduced that the limited range of motion may have been a function of the instability, and that improving balance might be a goal for players in the *novice phase*. At the *intermediate/advanced phase* of skill development, reduced range of motion correlated with missed shots. This led Hudson to speculate that tasks for improving range of motion might be a general goal for players in the intermediate learning phase.

Analyzing jumping in men and women, researchers tested military trainees on the task of maximal vertical jumping while carrying a rifle and wearing an eighty-pound backpack. The women and men differed significantly in three ways: the men jumped higher, took longer to jump, and created greater forces against the ground in preparing to jump. From this the researchers concluded that the men were "better performers" than the women. Yet biomechanics experts like Jackie Hudson will tell you that the differences in jump scores probably would have been insignificant if the trainees' heights had been taken into consideration. And taking longer to jump is a characteristic of poor performance, she points out. Also interesting, the trainees' performance declined when subjects were wearing the eighty-pound pack as opposed to no pack, and the decline was similar for both 135-pound women and 160-pound men.

Most comparisons of male and female strength are crudely determined and misleading, and these are what we're most likely to hear about. We hear, for example, how a woman's hand span is too small for single-hand gripping of a fire hose (the reason given by the New York Fire Department for the small number of female firefighters it hires), but we don't hear that grip strengthening can compensate for the size difference. The New York Fire Department has recently offered a training program for women to strengthen their physical skills before taking the firefighter's test. In the most recent test the women who didn't make the grade were also the women who hadn't taken the training program. Apparently word isn't out yet on the degree of difference two months of three training sessions a week can make.

What does all this mean for women? It's the importance of the training effect again. What biomechanical models do is break down skill problems into precise units with clear-cut techniques for correcting them. As the performance mystique is penetrated by more sophisticated assessment tools, it becomes clearer not only what is required for better performance, but that the potential for improvement has nothing to do with gender and everything to do with know-how.

The Backlash

With women around the world developing physical intelligence, using strength to justify a power difference between genders is on its way to becoming history. Just as we're uncovering historical evidence of women whose physical feats had been lost to us, so, now, are we gaining scientific evidence that women are no more physiologically frail than men. The breaking through of this information, with all its unsettling implications, has brought crashing down the boom of male backlash. As Susan Faludi so solidly nailed it in her Pulitzer Prize–winning book, *Backlash,* the negative reaction to women's progress is a recurring phenomenon. Its chilling effect can be counted on whenever women appear to be making another leap toward equality.

Virtually everyone involved in the forward movement of women's sport has been subjected to male hostility. Sometimes the backlash is personal, sometimes institutional. Sometimes it is ridiculous in its effect, sometimes devastating. But this much can be said without risk of rebuttal: Men don't like women's bold new intrusion into the insular, comforting, historically antifemale world of sport. As Faludi wrote, backlash is triggered not by women's achieving full equality but by their demonstrations of an increased possibility of doing so. "It is a preemptive strike," she writes, and it "stops women long before they reach the finish line."

Even women once removed in the fight for the right to play—not the players themselves but those who write about the players—have been punished for their temerity, especially if they were writing about men. Jeannie Roberts, a Florida sportswriter, recalls entering male locker rooms in the early 1970s: "I had things like jockstraps 'accidentally' thrown at me . . . and my fellow reporters would pretend that they didn't see a thing." A male fraternity of sportswriters felt too "embarrassed," Roberts says, "to show any kind of support for female reporters." Empathy was "a sign of weakness." To show any allegiance at all was to become "a traitor to the fraternity."

Only a dozen or so women sportswriters had broken into the coverage of men's sports when Time Inc. sued to allow *Sports Illustrated* reporter Melissa Ludtke to enter the New York Yankees clubhouse—the first time a woman had breached this hermetically sealed bubble of masculine sweat and self-aggrandizement. It was 1978. Certainly getting into the clubhouse, or locker room, or any other fortress of male exclusivity had never been pleasant for the women pioneering the break-ins, but in the arena of sport, the very physicality of the atmosphere heightened the men's hostility. And the hostility didn't abate with time. In September 1990 Lisa Olson, a sports reporter for the *Boston Herald* whose regular beat was football, was sexually harassed in the New England Patriots locker room. Zeke Mowatt shook his genitals at her while making lewd remarks. Team members watched and cheered. Management took no action.

Supported by her peers, Olson launched a protest. The owner of the team, Victor Kiam, ignored it all until media attention convinced him the public was taking the incident seriously. Eventually, Kiam sent Olson an apology, but the smarm continued. Four months later Kiam found himself in the indefensible position of having to apologize once again—this time for having made a sexist joke about the reporter at a Patriots banquet.

Olson, in the meantime, was receiving threats and harassing phone calls. The incident in the Patriots locker room had apparently touched a chord, and the reaction was widespread and venomous. Inflatable "Lisa" dolls were sold outside Foxboro Stadium, and male fans amused themselves by engaging the dolls in "lewd and suggestive acts." This jolly romp spread to other venues. In Fenway Park the following year, male spectators at a baseball game tossed plastic, life-size female blowup dolls from spectator to spectator. It was a gang-bang atmosphere. "Yeah, yeah, do her!" men yelled, fists punching the air. Reporter Bella English wrote, "They were touching her breasts. . . . They threw her around to each other. These are grown men we're talking about. It was disgusting. It was like an advertisement for rape."

Reports of harassment of female sportswriters mounted: a football player running a razor up a woman's leg; another player sending a female sportswriter a rat in a pink box; the hurling of jockstraps and obscenities at women writers as they tried to get the after-game story—as any male sportswriter would do—in the locker room. There were those in the world of sport, like Frank Deford (six times named Sportswriter of the Year), who tried to explain away the hostility toward women. "It's not a matter of . . . breaking into a profession," he said. "It's a matter of breaking down a culture, and that is eminently harder to do. We [men] think we need you for procreation and recreation, but we don't need you for sports."

Nowhere is misogyny more blatantly on display than in male rugby culture, where, postgame, men sing songs depicting women as "loathsome creatures with insatiable sexual appetites and dangerous sexual organs." They talk about raping other men's girlfriends and mothers, sociologist-anthropologist Steven P. Schacht informed a meeting of the North American Society for the Sociology of Sport. In a presentation on the misogyny that flourishes in rugby culture, Schacht described witnessing a coach telling a player, "Fuck you, you pussy. Just shut the fuck up, or I'll bend you over [and] fuck ya like a bitch." Code terms for plays included "Fucked your mother"; "Your mother's a cunt"; "Gang-banged your girlfriend"; and "Suck my dick."

"There is a seamy side to sport that involves inequality, oppression, discrimination, scandal, deviant behavior, and violence," write the authors of a book on the sociology of sport. "For many years this seamy side of sport remained hidden." The seaminess came out in the open as women's inroads into male sport cut deeper. The misogyny of the sort Schacht describes in rugby culture isn't an encapsulated instance of violence and hatred; it is a reflection of society's attitude in general. Athletic skill *is* masculinity, as far as men are concerned. Nor is it only the strongest, most aggressive female athletes who create a threat. For what they can do, others can obviously do if they put in the training effort. "All of us, collectively, are a threat," wrote basketball coach Mariah Burton Nelson. "A threat to male privilege and to masculinity as defined through manly sports."

The Estrogen Effect

In the nineteenth century anatomists believed that one's sex was not limited to one's reproductive organs, but affected every part of the body. The skeleton itself was thought to prove woman's inferiority, particularly her smaller (and thus, presumably, less intellectually capable) cranium. By the end of the nineteenth century female and male bodies were virtually understood as opposites, each having different organs, different functions, and even different feelings.

In the 1920s and 1930s, the discovery of the hormones estrogen and testosterone added a new dimension to medicine's beliefs about sexual differences. The findings of endocrinology seemed profoundly to validate male-female polarity. Estrogen and testosterone (which today are no longer viewed as "sex" hormones, both being necessary to the health and functioning of males *and* females) became the new scientific bedrock of the view of women as soft and weak and men as tough and strong. In the popular imagination hormones almost replaced genitals as the signifiers of sex. This endocrinologic view of male and female persisted all the way to the year 2000.

Women are "the disadvantaged gender." You think no one would have the nerve to say that anymore? Not so. It was the entire point of an article on the glories of testosterone, "The He Hormone," published in *The New York Times Magazine*. Its author, Andrew Sullivan, spelled out with damning certainty the biological deficiencies limiting women from ever making it—in the electorate, in the military, and even in venture capitalism. They just don't have the *cojones*.

Since the hormone was discovered in the male testicle in the 1930s (it was subsequently discovered in the female ovary and adrenals), testosterone has been falsely equated with greater male aggression in humans (the literature doesn't support this theory), greater assertiveness, and even clearer thinking. Historically, such luminously "male" qualities have been used as the rationale for job discrimination in every imaginable field, from construction work to firefighting to tenure-track college teaching.

What a stunning throwback to centuries-old, presumably medical, misogyny Sullivan's highly controversial article was! The bandying of testosterone to perpetuate discrimination against women, as we enter the twenty-first century, is no more scientifically justified than was late-nineteenth-century medicine's advice to women to refrain from physical and mental work so that they could preserve their limited energies for childbirth. Female physical frailty is not a reality but a myth with an agenda.

The long-standing perception that women are "the weaker sex" continues to affect women's attitudes toward sport and physical activity. But this is changing as the extraordinary breakthroughs of elite-level women athletes shatter the remnants of the frailty myth. Consider, as one dramatic example, Sweden's Ludmila Engquist, the thirty-two-year-old runner who won the gold medal in the 100-meter hurdles in the 1996 Summer Olympic Games in Atlanta and then, in the spring of 1999, went on to face the greatest trial of her life so far. In March of that year she discovered a lump in her breast. In April she had a mastectomy. In May she began chemotherapy. But then, stunningly, after the fourth of her six scheduled chemo sessions, she was back in action, competing at a track meet! When her name was announced as she stood behind the starting blocks, the other racers clapped. Finishing that race would have been triumph enough, but lo! she won it—won it in 12.68 seconds, shaving $^{18}/_{100}$ of a second off her Olympic gold medal time.

Ludmila's physician, Dr. Arne Ljungqvist, vice president of the International Amateur Athletic Federation and head of the cancer foundation in Sweden, explained that the athlete's strength had been a bonus in the healing process. Engquist didn't let enough time pass to lose muscle. Five days after surgery she was using small weights; a month after, she was doing clean-and-jerk exercises with over 120 pounds of weight. She continued training throughout the balance of her chemotherapy.

Farewell to the cult of female invalidism. Yes, many men have more lean muscle mass than women—owing, in part, to their having more testosterone—but women have physical advantages that come from having more estrogen. Recent studies suggest that the hormone long associated with women's reproductive functioning buffers them against muscle soreness after exercise. Soreness results from microtears in muscle tissue. "The animal data are very clear," says Dr. Priscilla Clarkson, an exercise physiologist at the University of Massachusetts at Amherst. Male rats show much more muscle damage, postexercise, than female rats. "Estrogen seems to explain the difference." When male rats were given estrogen, they sustained less muscle damage. It's not clear yet how estrogen does its protecting, but Clarkson speculates that the hormone "may be able to insert itself into cells, like muscle membranes, and stabilize them, which would protect them from tearing."

The sex difference in muscle soreness may help explain why women can endure longer exercise sessions than men. "Women may accumulate less damage over the course of the long event, which would enable them to perform better," one physiologist suggests.

New hormone research challenges the traditional view of osteoporosis as a "women's" disease linked to menopause. Of the 10 million Americans who have osteoporosis, more than 1.5 million are men, and 1 in 8 men over fifty will suffer an osteoporosis-related fracture. In an ironic reverse of the frailty myth, osteoporosis is actually far more prevalent in men than had previously been thought. Medical textbooks used to describe osteoporosis in men as the result of low testosterone levels caused by hypogonadism, a quite rare phenomenon. But new studies show that estrogen is the more central player in men's osteoporosis. In Framingham, Massachusetts, researchers studied 385 elderly men for eight years, tracking both their bone density and their estrogen levels. The correlation was startling: Men with the best bones had the highest estrogen levels. The connection between hypogonadism and low bone density in men was in fact negligible. "This is surprising," said Dr. B. Lawrence Riggs, a professor of medical research at the Mayo Clinic in Rochester, Minnesota, who found that estrogen naturally falls in men after about age sixty-five. "Three years ago none of us would have thought estrogen loss was a factor in male osteoporosis."

Historically, men's reproductive capacity has never been suspected of being compromised by physical exertion, but that idea is being shattered by modern science. (Medicine giveth, and medicine taketh away.) A recent study, for example, found that sperm count was lowered in men following long-distance racing. And as endocrinology advances, we are beginning to find that the precious "sex hormones" sometimes provide advantages for the *opposite* sex. For example, androgen (testosterone) *enhances spatial ability in women but inhibits it in men,* according to a fascinating study published in *Perceptual Motor Skills* in 1998. Researchers tested spatial abilities (visualization and orientation) in 150 men and 150 women collegiate athletes in different varsity sports. Across the board, women scored significantly higher than men in their ability to visualize and orient, but in basketball their superior spatial capacities were off the charts.

It is no coincidence that the great jaws of sex discrimination clamp down at particular moments in history. At the turn of the nineteenth century, changes in work and family, urbanization, and the increasing female domination of public schools created a crisis of masculinity that led to the cults of the "he-man" and the invalided woman. At the turn of the twenty-first century, women's growing physical competence in every conceivable sport from soccer to rock climbing has apparently produced another crisis in masculinity. Now, suddenly, we are hearing about testosterone again, as if it were the magic potion conferring kingship on men.

The "cult of invalidism" dogged women throughout the entire twentieth century as they tried to get into the Olympics, to be allowed to run races longer than 400 meters, to get into contact sports (finally girls by the thousands in this country are playing ice hockey and contact football), and even to get into Little League. Talk about a masculinity crisis. But now women's advances in elite-level athletics are challenging the entire concept of significant strength differences between the genders, wrecking any justification for male dominion. Men are not better equipped to deal with life's slings and arrows because they are stronger. Nor are they required to protect women because women are weaker. The argument for the whole social structure—men stronger, women weaker; men in charge, women their subservient helpmates—collapses as the strength gap between males and females closes. Testosterone, however mistakenly, appears to men to be the final saving grace. This is precisely why "We have more than you do" has once again become men's plaintive schoolyard cry.

The New Physical Woman

In New York City there's an outdoor basketball court on the corner of West Fourth Street and Sixth Avenue that's been there for years. It's called "the Cage." Men slam into one another in the Cage every day of the year. In the summer of 1999 a girl walked into the Cage one day. Natasha Green, a high school basketball star, had taken the subway down from the Bronx to try out her skills against the men and boys. Sixteen years old and five feet nine, Natasha jumped right in. "She stayed with her man as he tried to switch directions and drive to the basket," said a newspaper reporter, Chris Ballard, who happened to catch her act. "Reaching out her hand, she poked the ball loose as he headed by"—"stripping him clean," as the expression goes. She turned, took five hard dribbles, and charged back to the basket for a layup. Hoots and whistles of appreciation came from a couple of fence-hanging spectators who weren't used to seeing a woman hold her own on the blacktop, much less at this particular spot, the most revered of all for pickup basketball in Manhattan.

Guys "playing her like a guy" is the supreme compliment a female player can receive, Natasha told Ballard. It's not because she wants to be like a guy, but because she wants to improve her game. "Coming out here is how I get better," she says. "So if a guy's not going to play me hard, I'd rather he not even play."

Women's attitudes change when they push themselves athletically. Nicola Thost of Germany represents a new breed of female snowboarders, "going bigger" than ever before. At nineteen she brought a gold medal home from the 1998 Olympics in Nagano. She's so extreme in her moves, spectators often mistake her for a boy. "It's a pleasure to see other girls improving so much: like Shannon Dunn with a 720 and so many girls with a good, clean McTwist," she says. "We have to push the limits all the time."

It's a matter of understanding the particular challenges of any given sport. With snowboarding, it's important to get height. You have to be strong, but strong isn't the whole game. As Nicola says, some of the guys who snowboard are "so tiny, so muscular. It's clear it's technique."

Technique and attitude. "You must get in your mind that you can do it." Nicola says she has no "scary feelings." Fear plays no part in it for her. "I just take speed, and don't speed-check, and then just see how high I can go. It's such a good feeling to go big. If you think, Oh, my gosh, I can't fall hard, I'm afraid I'll injure myself, then it's already too late."

Overcoming the fear of falling is a challenge for today's woman, just as overcoming the "fear of flying"—the fear of risk and adventure—was something for Erica Jong's generation of overly protected females to overcome. A best-selling book in the 1970s, *Fear of Flying* celebrated *emotional* risk taking and sexual adventure for women. Today it's fear of *physical* risk taking that women have come to see is holding them back. They want the courage to go the distance, to raise their sights past what they'd thought they were capable of. Modeling this so dramatically are the exploits of elite women athletes, women who started out with ordinary skills but kept pushing. In doing so—although this was rarely if ever the intent—they began seriously challenging the concept of male physical superiority.

Going the Distance

"In 1967 people thought women couldn't do long runs. It wasn't supposed to be 'feminine,'" says Katherine Switzer, the woman who opened the gateway to women's phenomenal success in long-distance sports. That year an irate official had tried to pull Switzer out of the then all-male Boston Marathon. She dodged him and kept running, becoming the first woman to officially complete the race. Her run made headlines, the twenty-year-old college student made history, and women's competitive running took off. Switzer would be the one to push women's distance running all the way to the Olympics. In 1974 she won the women's division of the New York Marathon, then went on to launch a series of international races that led to the establishment of the first women's Olympic marathon, in the 1984 Summer Games. Now in her fifties, Switzer brings the message of running to women of all ages via her work promoting the Avon races. She's inspired by her own mother, Ruth Rothfarb, who began walking to recover from heart surgery at age seventy-two and completed her first marathon at eighty-one.

Some of the elite women athletes' most compelling advances have been in swimming. In marathon and long-distance cold-water swims, women usually outswim the men. In 1995 Australian champion Shelley Taylor-Smith set the record for both men and women when she swam around Manhattan in 5 hours, 45 minutes, 26 seconds. In 1998 she did it again, this time pulling ahead to win after she'd dropped half a mile behind two male swimmers. "I call it 'catching up with the boys,'" she said.

Seana Hogan recently cycled the four hundred miles from San Francisco to Los Angeles in 19 hours, 49 minutes, breaking the previous men's record by almost an hour. Helen Klein's world-record distance in a twenty-four-hour race—109.5 miles—exceeds the best distance for an American man in her age group, which was sixty-five to sixty-nine.

The phenomenon of the older woman athlete is one of the more amazing aspects of the shattering of the frailty myth. If women keep training, they can retain endurance capabilities into late life. I am thinking in particular of a woman who looks forward each year to participating in the Avon Running Global Women's Circuit. In the summer of 1998 Mary Hanes was eighty-three and preparing to run in Connecticut, in the Hartford 10K, when I heard her story. She'd started running fifteen years earlier, at the age of sixty-five. "I lost twenty-two pounds when I started and have kept it off," says Hanes, who also plays tennis and basketball and throws javelin. "Once you get going, you'd be amazed at what you can do."

Today, results of medical studies are encouraging to the woman who wants to keep moving no matter what her age. A study in *The New England Journal of Medicine* found that walking/strolling just two miles a day cuts the risk of death almost in half for people in their sixties, seventies, and eighties. A 1995 Harvard Medical School study noted a 40 percent reduction in the risk of heart disease for women who exercise.

As amazing as the marathoning octogenarians, on the other end of the age spectrum are the football-playing girls. Girls began playing football in the late 1980s and by the 1990s had graduated to *tackle* football, all padded up and helmeted, playing on their high school football teams with and against boys their own age. As the century turned, a sixth-grader in New Orleans who'd been playing tackle football for five years became the first girl to play on the all-star team in her parish. Her coach says she's one of the best offensive players he's ever worked with.

It's not just tokenism, either. At Lincoln High School in Los Angeles, four girls play on the football team. One of them, in the fall of 1999, was a finalist for homecoming queen. "The world as we knew it has changed forever," said *Time* magazine, reporting the girl's double accomplishment. In 1998 there were 708 girls playing high school football, according to the National Federation of State High School Associations.

Efforts are under way to launch a professional tackle football league for women. In December 1999 the New York Sharks played an exhibition game with the Minnesota Vixens. "This is a dream come true for all of us," said lawyer Lyn Lewis, who plays offensive tackle for the Sharks. "I grew up playing football with the guys. Then when you got to a certain age you couldn't play anything organized. . . . Out of all the major sports, this is the last one that brought women to its playground."

Women, there is no doubt about it, are going the distance. America's women's ice hockey team made its Olympic debut in 1998—and won the gold its first time out! "These were warriors, hard-charging competitors who came to win, not just play," said *The New York Times*, describing the 1998 Olympic women's ice hockey team. The social implications of the win were not lost on the sports world. Said Tara Mounsey's hockey coach, "This is the final public knell of the artificial construct of what is masculine and feminine in sports."

It's apparent that no one foresaw the radical changes Title IX would lead to—that girls were not only going to catch up with boys, but in some sports they would even surpass them. That in the process they would flood the gyms and athletic fields. Not only would they enter the competition, they would take on the most challenging and aggressive sports. By the end of the century they would be playing football, ice hockey, and rugby—and would be starting these sports at younger and younger ages. Even preschool girls were learning contact sports—ice hockey, for example—spurred on by fathers and brothers.

By century's end the excitement over competition, team sports, and personal best had become thoroughly contagious. Two million girls were playing soccer. Sixteen million women were playing softball. The breakthroughs of young females were carrying over into the lives of older women—mothers, aunts, grandmothers. As female athletics became huge in the television ratings, the effect on the rest of us was like the blowing of the whistle at the beginning of the game. Suddenly, it seemed, sixty- and seventy-year-olds were in-line skating. The young were rock climbing and challenging themselves with wilderness expeditions. Teenagers—even *preteenagers*—were excelling at "extreme" sports: aggressive skating, half-pipe snowboarding, skateboarding. Females of all ages had discovered that they no longer had to hold themselves back.

———

It is now, as we've entered a new millennium, that we are finally seeing the truth: Women don't have to restrict themselves physically because of being mothers. Not only can they handle the rigors of elite-level sport, they can manage their children while they're doing it. Thirteen members of the WNBA are mothers, many taking their children along with them, and nannies and grandmothers to help, as they travel around the world. They were upset, in the spring of 1999, when Pamela McGee, who'd played the previous season for the Los Angeles Sparks, lost custody of her three-year-old daughter after her former husband said she had missed several scheduled visits with her child. In court the husband's lawyer argued that McGee's basketball career interfered with her parenting. Forced to choose between child and career, McGee retired. "Being a professional woman, in the spotlight, making good money, would put a strain on any relationship," she said. "Then with the travel. A lot of people can't handle that."

Fortunately not all husbands squelch their wives' athletic ambitions. Suzie McConnell Serio had four children ranging in age from one to seven when she decided to reenter the competitive world of sport she'd left six years earlier. An Olympic gold medalist in 1988, she had dropped out in 1991 to raise a family. It was her husband, Peter, who looked at her one day in the summer of 1997, while the two were watching women basketball players on TV in their Pittsburgh home, and said, "You're as good as they are." She was nursing her newborn fourth at the time. "You should think about playing next year."

Ten months later she was back in the WNBA, playing for the Cleveland Rockers. It was fun; she was excited; she hadn't realized how much she missed it. In August of 1998 she was the WNBA's player of the week, having played thirty-six minutes in one game, taken five shots, and become her team's most indispensable player.

Her husband, a coach of high school girls, was proud. He saw his wife as a leader.

Players for the WNBA are rarely away from home more than several days at a time, so those who are moms can generally manage their time spent as mothers and as athletes. It doesn't work that way for soccer players. Joy Fawcett and Carla Overbeck are basically gone on a six-month road trip, except for a week's break each month, while they prepare for the World Cup. So the kids go with them. "Breast-feeding at halftime, or on the sideline, that can get interesting," Fawcett told a reporter. "It's like, 'I'll be back in a minute.'"

Fawcett has two daughters, three and six, Katey and Carli. When Carli was born in 1997, Fawcett was coaching the USLA women's soccer team, commuting two hours each way from her home in Orange County, California, and also coaching a youth team—all while playing on a national team herself. Overbeck, who is thirty-two, was running stadium steps through her ninth month of pregnancy to stay fit. She lifted weights the day she delivered her son, Jackson, now three.

The women's team travels with a load of equipment, from car seats to strollers and diaper bags. They have a nanny who gets paid $750 a week—by the U.S. Soccer Federation! But soccer-playing women traveling with their kids are still a rarity. Japanese women who came to the U.S. tune-up for the World Cup seemed "wistful" to find that Overbeck and Fawcett could continue their careers after becoming mothers. An American who played professionally in Japan for a year says that Japanese women quit the sport once they marry. "Seeing our players doing it as mothers gives them hope that they may be able to do it, too."

Greg Overbeck, who stays home in Chapel Hill, North Carolina, tries to see his son every two weeks. "It's tough, it's hard, but I understand why we go through it, and I totally support what Carla is doing," he said. "To see how far they've come is amazing. Before the 1991 World Cup, they didn't get paid, there was no insurance, no exposure, no endorsements. Not enough to make a living at it. Carla worked at an elementary school."

Overbeck sees it as a triumph—physical, emotional, professional—for his wife, for her teammates, and for all women. To him the women are heroes: "They had sacrificed relationships and career, put everything on hold, then they reached the pinnacle. . . . It's great for women."

"In the beginning, I questioned whether this [life] was good for the kids," says Fawcett. She'd talked to other moms whose kids eat and sleep on a regular schedule. "My kids eat when they can, sleep in the stroller. But they're adaptable. Things don't bother them too much. I think it's good. They get to see the world, and it allows me to play soccer."

Learning these stories about the personal lives of the World Cup mothers and their husbands and kids, and the even more challenging situation facing the players who are single moms, made me think once again: I never thought I would live to see this. It was exciting to see these women playing, unencumbered and free and beautiful, in the final game against China. But knowing their personal histories, their fight to do what they have done, to get the support they need from husbands and relatives and officials holding the purse strings, and to do it while traveling thousands of miles a year and sleeping in motels with their kids, was even more overwhelming. It brought me to tears.

The independence women are achieving today is not independence *from* anything, it is the independence to *be*. To lift huge loads. To run for miles. To defend themselves, ourselves, whether against sexual discrimination or sexual aggression. This, it turns out, has been the missing link in women's emancipation. Physically they are now able to occupy their full stature, to stand tall, chest open, and face the world.

SEVEN

Physical Equality: The Final Stage

Fear of "mature" sexuality used to be considered a female illness, a childish defense against the demands of adulthood. Freud and his followers decided that the unpleasantries of which so many of their patients spoke were largely imagined: mental products haunting the minds of frightened women whom they labeled "hysteric." That label has long since been abandoned by all but the most die-hard Freudians. What really affects women—and this was as true in Freud's day as it is in our own—is fearsome reality. But the social denial of fear in women's lives—and of the reasons for their fear—continues to this day, its most vitriolic expression coming from a small but influential group who refer to themselves as "power feminists."

In one of the more notorious questions posed in the controversial book *The Morning After*, Katie Roiphe asked, "If 25 percent of my friends are being raped, wouldn't I know it?" The young writer made an impassioned argument against the unhealthy positioning of women as victims and in doing so felt compelled to denounce what has come to be called a "rape culture," by which other feminists (the so-called victim feminists) mean a culture in which sexual violence and fear of sexual violence are an accepted norm. Roiphe was concerned about the effects on women of infantilizing them, of making them seem weaker than they are, but she developed her argument at the expense of both women and reality: she threw out the baby with the bathwater. Spoken from her protected turf as a graduate student at Princeton University, where, she says, walking "over the golf course to the graduate college, I was more afraid of wild geese than rapists," Roiphe's position was astoundingly naive.

But it wasn't original. Betty Friedan was singing the same tune in the early 1980s, when she wrote, "Obsession with rape, even offering Band-Aids to its victims, is a kind of wallowing in that victim state, that impotent rage, that sterile polarization." Friedan's outburst came on the heels of Susan Brownmiller's treatise on the destructiveness and prevalence of rape, *Against Our Will*. That book, shocking as it was in 1975, brought rape out of the closet. It reassured women, psychologically, with its persuasive thesis that rape wasn't just personal, it was political. It wasn't about sex per se or even them per se, as much as it was about men controlling women by keeping them physically intimidated. It was a theory that detonated any shred of personal responsibility women felt for having been singled out for the crime. Women, by then, were ready to hear it, for Brownmiller's well-documented book became a best-seller.

Some twenty years later Roiphe joined Friedan's bandwagon, angered by the wimpishness of women students in her college town: "Considering how many things there are to be afraid of, being frightened to walk around Princeton, New Jersey, late at night does not seem like one of God's greatest injustices."

The Morning After was a reactionary harkening to the previous century's cult of invalidism, when doctors were making women out to be weaker than they are and at the same time refusing to sympathize with their complaints of sexual assault. Writers like Friedan and Roiphe disassociate themselves from the suffering of trauma-tized women, suggesting things would be otherwise if only they were to pick themselves up, dust themselves off, and stop talking about what happened to them. It's a kind of double assault, not unlike the subtle blaming of cancer patients for their illness that Susan Sontag first identified in *Illness as Metaphor*. But with feminists the odd twist has been in saying that women who cry about rape are giving *other* women a bad name. They're not good for feminism, that is.

Power feminists gain a hollow strength by criticizing their less for-tunate sisters. Roiphe ridiculed women's efforts to come to terms with having been violated, their solidarity marches and the Take Back the Night protests that were drawing crowds on college campuses all over the United States in the eighties and nineties. "There is power to be drawn from declaring one's victimhood and oppression," Roiphe wrote. "There is strength in numbers, and unfortunately right now there is strength in being the most oppressed. Students scramble for that microphone, for a chance for a moment of authority."

Why "unfortunately"? Why shouldn't women who've been raped gather strength from their collectivity? And why shouldn't they want to regenerate some sense of authority in their lives by making the fact—and prevalence—of rape public? At that time, it was the only way women had of reconstituting themselves after they'd been sex-ually abused. Not even therapists were very adept at treating the raped. Now, a burgeoning new self-defense movement is teaching women that learning how to defend themselves physically is not only the best way to protect themselves against attack, it's also cen-tral to healing themselves once it's happened.

Learning to defend ourselves is not an extreme measure; it's cru-cial in a world where power differences are tied to strength differ-ences. The power feminists' concern about the victimization of women is in at least one respect constructive. Women need to come out of the cloister of femininity and develop their physical strength—those, at least, who want to be free to walk around Princeton or any other college town late at night. Either they must learn how to fight offensively (and many are doing just that) or they must learn how to fend off attackers by throwing their energy around, as the martial arts teach. Basically, they need to develop strength in the same ways that men develop it, and, as do smaller men who want to be able to defend themselves against bigger men, they can get training in compensatory defense skills. Some women were highly skilled in martial arts centuries ago, but—as with sports skills—there has been a systematic attempt to keep modern women *un*defended and physically insecure. Fortunately, this is changing. Even girls today are beginning to get the picture that learning how to protect themselves can alter their relationship to the rape culture. It can give them power. It can put them in charge. It can lessen their fear in the world.

Physical Assault: Keeping Women Down

A third of the women interviewed in several urban centers across the United States said the possibility of being physically harmed, especially raped, was their greatest fear. Those under thirty-five feared rape more than murder, assault, or robbery. More than half the women reacted to their fear of crime with self-isolation; many said they stayed inside at night and avoided visiting friends or going out for entertainment. Ninety percent of the men in this study lived in the same neighborhoods but took no steps to reduce their vulnerability to crime. These findings suggest that women live under a feeling of threat particular to their gender, a "special burden," one researcher put it, "not shared by men." Approximately one in four women will be the victim of a sexual assault in her lifetime, according to a report conducted by the

American Psychological Association. C. Everett Koop, the former surgeon general, identified domestic violence as the number one health problem for women in the United States, causing more injuries to them than automobile accidents, muggings, and rapes combined.

Talk to any woman today and you'll hear stories—their own or of women they know—of running: running down alleys, running across dunes, running up dormitory stairs. You'll hear of weapons, of threats. The worst cases sometimes show up in the news. Some of us, sitting at home in our robes and pajamas as we watch such reports on television, find it impossible to identify with the women because their state of deterioration is so extreme. *Our* stories are likely quieter, the bruises less livid, the outcomes less public. *Our* stories are likely to be blanketed by years of repression.

I didn't start remembering things that had happened to me until many years later: the creepy piano teacher, when I was eleven, hovering over me, breathing over me, sitting too close on the piano bench. The divinity student who tried to rape me in a dorm room at Union Theological Seminary in New York, when I was twenty. Or the other man, a college student at a beach party who kept pushing my head underwater in the ocean and then, on the way home, kept acting as if he were trying to shove me out of a fast-moving convertible. I didn't know if he was really intent on doing it or just trying to scare me. It made little difference, since I was terrified and powerless to do anything about it, either way. Why had it taken so long for these memories to come back to me? It wasn't that I had really forgotten the things that had happened, but rather that I'd stashed them away as irrelevant, so that their details, their "pictures," the extreme terror I'd felt, had melted into something tolerable.

Women live with fear in their bones, and then, when something *does* happen, they are often held responsible, even by women. "This woman *knew* better," said a teacher I interviewed, speaking of an acquaintance who'd been attacked a few years earlier. "She was a journalist and traveled all over the place. But this time she wasn't careful. She'd ordered something from room service, and when the knock on the door came she didn't check, she just opened the door."

The journalist was raped, and her face was slashed with a knife by a man who was never caught. The woman telling the story sounded almost angry, and not at the attacker.

"Does she still stay alone in hotels?" I asked.

"Oh sure," the woman said. "I'm sure she does. She's tough."

Tough, but she should have known better. Tough, but one can't slip for a moment, making such careless assumptions as that the person who knocks on the door ten minutes after room service was ordered is actually from room service. No, it's necessary to live on guard. And as we grow older we stop even questioning it. We learn to accommodate violence, thinking, What else is there to do? We try to forget because what does remembering do besides make us anxious? We try to be mature, to accept, to rise above, to get on with.

But eventually the memories return. Over the years there have been sporadic and always surprising references friends have made to "the time I was raped." Or "the time my husband hit me." I would ask for the story, and they would tell me, their faces clouding. Some had never told anyone but a sister or a best friend. Some had never told anyone, not even their therapists. Some had thought no one would care, or that the incident was no more or less relevant than any of life's other unpleasantries, or that they were somehow implicated in the crime, which made them feel guilty. Some would cry.

True, these conversations bear no statistical relevance, only personal, but statistics abound. In a recent national study, 18 percent of female respondents said they'd been raped or had suffered an attempted rape. As many as 60 percent of those who are raped never report it. Rape is most likely to happen to the young. A random study of 930 women found that 12 percent had experienced sexual abuse by a family member and 25 percent had been abused by someone not in the family—*before they'd turned seventeen!*

One out of four high school girls has been sexually or physically abused. Fifty percent receive unwanted touching in school. One out of three has suicidal thoughts. Many girls end up with post-traumatic stress. And this may not be a new phenomenon. Freud first noted the emotional shutdown of girls entering adolescence when he wrote, in 1905, of the "fresh wave of repression" girls seemed to undergo after reaching puberty. Similar observations were made by the renowned psychoanalysts Karen Horney in the 1920s and Helene Deutsch and Clara Thompson in the 1940s. All of these women wrote about the startling "regression," in adolescence, of girls who previously had seemed healthy and strong. But it was not until the 1990s that researchers began connecting the sexual abuse of girls and women with an illness—post-traumatic stress disorder (PTSD)—that produces emotional shutdown. Studies began to appear showing that adolescents who'd been abused manifested classic symptoms of PTSD: rage, self-destructive behaviors such as self-cutting, nightmares, physical tremors, and recollections of the traumatic events therapists describe as "intrusive" because they are so vivid and uncontrollable.

Deborah Miranda, who was seven when her mother's boyfriend first began raping her, remembers the old orchard down by the barn and what went on there. "At seven years old I have no words to describe the pain thrusting into my vagina—a hand wrapped around my throat—sound of a man's ragged breath next to my ear," she wrote. "I hate that he is still in me, that cells in my brain hold his image." Some people forget being molested, she says, but "my problem is that I can't forget."

Much of the research being done by developmental theorists has ignored the massively violent—and traumatic—environment in which girls live. The ramifications of what is happening to girls' bodies—and what subsequently gets imprinted on their brains—have not been fully grasped. When a group of male high school athletes calls itself "the Spur Posse" and goes around raping girls as young as ten and telling everyone their conquests are sluts, ruining the girls' reputations and making it impossible for them to stay in the same school—no one denies that's traumatic.

But so, too, are more hidden forms of abuse in girls' lives. Concerned about the increasing numbers of girls in abusive relationships with their boyfriends, experts believe that those who've grown up with traditional beliefs about men dominating and women being submissive are particularly at risk. Even if they haven't grown up seeing physical abuse in their families, girls can have a hard time identifying abusiveness in their relationships. The culture of fear becomes increasingly suffocating as they get older. By the time they reach college, some are seeing friends get killed by boyfriends or acquaintances. Or they are being abused themselves, with slaps or more serious violence, as is one out of five female college students.

The culture of date rape causes young college women to be fearful not only on campus, but on their bikes, jogging, in public places, even in their own homes.

The "necessity" of women constricting their lives is thought to be a rational response to the condition of being female. It becomes a way of life. "I know young girls who, without being at all timid, find no enjoyment in taking walks alone in Paris," Simone de Beauvoir wrote, "because, importuned incessantly, they must be always on the alert." Girls and women are advised, Stay in at night. Don't walk across campus without a security guard by your side. Don't forget to carry your pepper spray. Use your whistle. This is a life? We are conditioned to restrict ourselves for the sake of safety the way dogs are conditioned to stay back from an electrified fence.

"Constriction" has actually been identified as a medical symptom of a psychological state, a state of trauma-produced fear. It is Pavlovian—a conditioned response to environmental threat. But there's so much cultural support for the wisdom of women living their lives in this way, it's considered normal—even womanly, reflective of a certain demure sensibility in which one doesn't live too public a life or certainly doesn't make public spectacles. We learn that constriction not only is the road to safety, it is mature, rational, adult behavior—for females. But what has only recently been learned is that trauma, and such psychological effects as constriction, actually get wired into our brains. To some degree, as we'll see, this wiring happens to all of us, not just to women whose abuse has been extreme.

Trauma: Freud's Little Detour

In the late 1800s the pervasiveness of the abuse of women remained a huge social secret long after medicine had begun trying to treat what it thought of as mysterious female complaints. Women would go to doctors for certain bodily problems: a deadness to sensation, a tendency to space out or go into fleeting trance states, sleep difficulties, in rarer cases even muteness. The well-to-do sought help from distinguished physicians like Sigmund Freud. The poor banged on the clinic doors at the Hôpital Salpêtrière, a huge hospital complex for the down-and-out of Paris. There, Jean-Martin Charcot, a famous neurologist, was finding among the prostitutes and beggars and other abandoned women who were his patients a syndrome of symptoms he named "hysteria," from the Latin word for uterus. Charcot's lecture-demonstrations, where assistants poked and prodded the women, who went into self-protective trance states and called out for their mothers, were famous. People from all disciplines attended them, for the mysterious illness had caught the public imagination. Charcot himself was interested in the symptoms mainly as evidence of neurological damage: motor paralyses, sensory losses, convulsions, amnesias. He didn't connect these with actual experiences in his patients' lives. Still, his work was valuable. Freud credited Charcot with "throwing the whole weight of his authority on the side of the genuineness and objectivity of hysterical phenomena." Up until then, women reporting mysterious bodily symptoms had been considered malingerers. Charcot's work gave credibility to the so-called hysterical experience. "Little by little, people gave up the scornful smile with which the patient could at that time feel certain of being met," Freud wrote.

In Vienna in the late 1800s and early 1900s, Freud was hearing stories from his women patients that appalled him—stories of sexual assault, abuse, and childhood incest. These women were manifesting the same kinds of symptoms as Charcot's patients. After a decade, psychologist Pierre Janet in France and Freud and his collaborator Josef Breuer in Vienna arrived independently at very similar conclusions: Hysteria was a condition caused by psychological trauma resulting from having been physically abused. And it was found not only among the poor and disenfranchised, patients like Charcot's. Freud wanted it known that traumatic experience sometimes underlay the psychological difficulties in "people of the clearest intellect, strongest will, greatest character, and highest critical power." Molestation and its effects, in other words, were not related to station in life. Whether a woman was rich or poor, from the city or the country, with or without an education, she could still end up traumatized and knocking on a doctor's door.

By the late 1800s, Freud and Breuer had clearly demonstrated that when traumatic memories, and the intense feelings that accompany them, were retrieved and put into words, bodily symptoms could be alleviated. The treatment Freud devised for traumatized women, which he named "psychoanalysis," would become the basis of modern psychotherapy. At that point in his career he was convinced that "at the bottom of every case of hysteria there are one or more occurrences of premature sexual experience, occurrences which belong to the earliest years of childhood, but which can be reproduced through the work of psychoanalysis in spite of the intervening decades." Lest there be any doubt, he wrote in a renowned paper, "The Aetiology of Hysteria," "I believe that this is an important finding . . . in neuropathology." This paper has relevance today, notes Judith Herman, a professor at Harvard Medical School and an expert on trauma, in its similarity to "contemporary clinical descriptions of the effects of childhood sexual abuse. It is a brilliant, compassionate, eloquently argued, closely reasoned document."

But the notion that women were suffering as a result of being sexually abused as children was repellent, if not virtually inconceivable, to many of Freud's Victorian contemporaries. Within a year of the famous paper's publication Freud was privately repudiating his "important finding." Correspondence shows he was worried about the effects on his reputation of talking about the *extent* of sexual abuse of females and children. "Hysteria was so common among women that if his patients' stories were true," says Judith Herman, "and if his theory were correct, he would be forced to conclude that what he called 'perverted acts toward children' were endemic, not only among the proletariat of Paris, where he had first studied hysteria [under Charcot], but also among the respectable bourgeois families of Vienna, where he had established his practice."

Buckling under social pressure, Freud took a sharp detour from his initial instinct to believe women when they told him they'd been physically and sexually harmed. Freud started diagnosing women's reports of being violated as "intrapsychic"—that is, mere manifestations of their own deluded minds. He formulated an elaborate theory to explain why their minds would make up these vivid scenarios and called it "conversion." The poor neurotic things were so sexually repressed, they could only fantasize sexual gratification—and even *that* they could permit only by imagining themselves passive recipients of violence. Turning their sexual longings into fantasies of rape and incest supposedly relieved them of intolerable guilt. Convoluted as it may now seem, Freud's notion of "conversion" would influence the treatment of women's psychological symptoms for almost a hundred years. It would be a long and difficult journey before women reporting traumatic assault would again be believed. "By the first decade of the twentieth century," Judith Herman writes in her classic book, *Trauma and Recovery,* "without ever offering any clinical documentation of false complaints, Freud had concluded that his hysterical patients' accounts of childhood sexual abuse were untrue: 'I was at last obliged to recognize that these scenes of seduction had never taken place, and that they were only fantasies which my patients had made up.'"

Sexuality remained the central focus of inquiry with Freud's female patients, but the abusive social context in which so often they had to struggle with sex "became utterly invisible" again once Freud decided to make his turnaround. How ironic, Herman continues, that "the dominant psychological theory of the next century was founded in the denial of women's reality."

Women's mental response to physical abuse would not be fully understood until the same syndrome of symptoms was first acknowledged—and then identified as a legitimate illness—in men in the 1970s. The twentieth-century story of physical trauma began when veterans of World War I and World War II, neurologically damaged by their brutal experiences on the battlefield, were labeled "shell-shocked." People believed that proximity to the blast of shells had made the men crazy—and in some sense, perhaps, it had. I can remember, as a child, a man wandering around our village dressed always in his olive green World War II uniform and the red poppy insignia of veteran status in his buttonhole. People gave him a wide berth. The understanding of the phenomenon—including how to treat it—was very limited. Doctors and psychiatrists considered themselves successful if they could calm these guys down enough to return them to battle. And there was stigma attached to the soldiers' illness, as if they had somehow lacked the strength to withstand the horrors of what had happened to them. Only a major cultural shift, in part inspired by the Vietnam Veterans Against the War movement, got people thinking, at last, that combat might be highly psychologically destructive, as well as morally reprehensible. "Many soldiers began to act like hysterical women," Judith Herman reports. "They screamed and wept uncontrollably. They froze and could not move. They became mute and unresponsive. They lost their memory and their capacity to feel." Flashbacks, nightmares, intrusive imagery, attentional difficulties—these were not trifles. Maybe men who had been exposed to the worst horrors of war could not *but* be traumatized.

In 1980 the syndrome earlier called "shell shock," having at last been adequately assessed, was given the name post-traumatic stress disorder and listed in psychiatry's *Diagnostic and Statistical Manual of Mental Disorders*. With a more accurately described illness to attribute their troubles to, and massively supported by the society that had sent them to war, Vietnam veterans were in a political situation to push for research funding. An explosion of scientific work on the neurobiology and treatment of acute stress disorders resulted.

Women with a strikingly similar syndrome of uncontrollable crying, nightmares, flashbacks, and dissociation or trance states—symptoms often arising after rape, incest, or other forms of molestation—made feminist therapists wonder: Were their women patients with these symptoms also suffering from post-traumatic stress disorder? Doctors and therapists eventually began viewing women's traumatic episodes in a new way. Women were *not*, as in the Freudian view, expressing a "conversion" phenomenon in which they projected their erotic longings onto some malevolent figure so they wouldn't have to own up to their desires. Women were reporting assaults that had actually taken place, and the assaults had been so terrifying that they had developed the same illness that affects many war veterans. This was a remarkable discovery, and Judith Herman was in the forefront of this new understanding of women. "Hysteria is the combat neurosis of the sex war," she wrote.

Clinicians working with rape victims were encouraged to learn more about the psychological experience of trauma. In 1972 a psychiatric nurse, Ann Burgess, and a sociologist, Lynda Holmstrom, began a study of what rape actually does to victims psychologically. They arranged to be notified at any time of day or night so that they might interview, and counsel, every rape victim who came to the emergency ward of Boston City Hospital. Studying ninety-two women and thirty-seven children in the course of a year, Burgess and Holmstrom discerned a pattern of psychological reactions they called "rape trauma syndrome." They found that women tend to experience rape as life threatening and often fear mutilation and death while they are being assaulted. In the aftermath, victims complain of insomnia, nausea, startle responses, and nightmares, as well as dissociation and "numbing"—all symptoms resembling those reported by combat victims, the two researchers noted.

Three years after their study, the National Institute of Mental Health created the first research center for the study of rape. A sophisticated epidemiological survey had unearthed shocking statistics: One woman in four had been raped. One in three had been sexually abused in childhood. For females, the likelihood of being exposed to a traumatic event in the course of a lifetime is close to 70 percent. "The implications in the present day are as horrifying as they were a century ago," says Judith Herman.

Because the use of force against women and children has been so deeply embedded in our culture, it has only recently been recognized as a basic violation of human rights. Widespread patterns of coercive control such as battering, stalking, sexual harassment, and acquaintance rape were not even named, let alone understood to be crimes, until they were defined by the feminist movement. Today these crimes are being widely studied. The prevalence of aggression against women in the workplace is the latest shocker, work being a place where some modicum of professionalism might be expected to provide a buffer for women. Here, if nowhere else, they might be able to feel safe. But on the contrary, one in approximately two women will be subjected to some form of sexual harassment over the course of her working life.

A century has passed since Freud and Breuer and Janet first identified the connection between the violence done women and the symptoms they displayed. Now modern brain science has come along to nail the neurological connection: Violence actually causes changes in the neural pathways of the brain. Even verbal violence, when it's repeated often enough, can affect an individual's ability to think, to grow, and to live a full life. In the 1990s PET and MRI scans proved the no longer deniable: Fear solders the neural circuitry of the brain into a state of hyperarousal—a readiness to respond at a moment's notice to the slightest sensory suggestion of the traumatizing event. A prominent neuroscientist at New York University, Joseph LeDoux, says that one horrible experience can be all it takes to produce a memory that will last a lifetime.

Brain scans show that trauma damages the connection between right and left sides of the brain. Fearful memories remain in the right, or "emotional," part of the brain. The left, or "language," side of the brain receives no information on the traumatic experience. As a result, those deep feelings and the bodily sensations that go with them don't get processed by the part of the brain that would normally mediate them, explain them, give language to them. Those who've been traumatized often can't connect such symptoms as sleep disturbance, inability to concentrate, and tendency to startle to a specific thing, or things, that happened to them. The shocking experiences that triggered the symptoms are split off from the region of the brain that makes sense of them, names them, and allows them to be integrated into one's autobiographical "story." Thus does trauma become locked into its own memory network, Debra Niehoff explains in *The Biology of Violence.*

Here is how it plays out in the life of the individual. Pam Spencer, a corporate executive at Neutrogena, told a 1999 rape speak-out in Los Angeles of having been raped twenty-two years earlier by an intruder who came into her home and wondered aloud, during the entire rape, whether or not he was going to kill her. She says there are days now when she is free of the memory, but the smallest thing can bring it shudderingly back. "Sometimes, it's when a man looks at my body before he looks into my eyes."

The images, physical sensations, and beliefs about the event remain, as if frozen in time, exactly as they were experienced, says Niehoff. A man who survives a train crash continues to be afraid of trains. The sight—even the sound—of them stays locked in his nervous system because he has been unable to process it. Certain sensory experiences can trigger the memory of the crash in its entirety. This is a "flashback." Women who've been assaulted have them all the time. The whiff of someone's Camel cigarette may be all it takes. People may not understand this when they blame women for "obsessing over rape," as Betty Friedan put it. Those who've been assaulted cannot help obsessing. It's *physical*.

But there are ways of undoing the conditioning. For women who've been threatened or harmed by being physically overpowered, healing comes from developing their own physical power. This isn't just a "spiritual" type of healing. Working with the body can change the neural pathways in the brain. Women's self-defense training, as we'll see later, can be a reprogramming regimen for the body. The reprogramming is necessary because the socialization into femininity has made women believe that defending themselves physically is not only something they are incapable of, it's something that is wrong. It's better to die than to defend ourselves: women have died because they believed that.

Dangerous Lessons in Passive Resistance

The frailty myth is deeply supportive of women's fear of rape. Women are taught that they need to be wary in the extreme in determining whom they'll attempt to defend themselves against and what measures they'll take to do it. They are crimped in their beliefs about what they are actually capable of. You can see society's ambivalence about female self-defense in the rape prevention advice given to women, which shifts dramatically—now telling women to hold back, now telling them to strike out—in accordance with whatever general attitudes toward women prevail, and especially in accordance with what the nation wants from women at any given moment in time. A look at changes in defense manuals for women over the past fifty or sixty years is revealing. Proponents of women's self-defense at the time of World War II encouraged much more forceful behavior than those who were writing in the sixties and seventies. Why would they be going backward at this point, in the direction of the frailty myth? Precisely because women were going forward.

Cases in point: Two self-defense manuals that came out during World War II, both written by military men, generously encouraged women to assume a positive attitude about defending themselves. One stated, "It goes without saying that a woman should know how to protect herself. In wartime—in America at war—this is doubly so." There was a reason Corporal William Underwood was suggesting that women feel free to put up their dukes. The confidence they could gain from knowing how to protect themselves would "immeasurably" increase their "value to the war effort." Female adults were needed, alive and healthy, to run the country when so many of the men were off doing battle.

A whole body of advice developed instructing women on just what sort of aggression against attackers was necessary, appropriate, and possible for the female. Without ever mentioning rape or sexual assault, Underwood's self-defense book for women broke out three different categories: "simple nuisances" (this included "theater touches" and the overly persistent handshaker); "serious but not deadly" threats; and, finally, "deadly serious" threats. Even simple nuisances were not for a moment to be tolerated. Women readers were instructed to "grab the hand of the hapless handshaker, twist his arm around, throw him to the ground, and, finally, give a punch to his Adam's apple or a kick behind his ear." Should a stranger ask for a light, another manual, *Hands Off!* by Major William Fairbairn, shows, in an illustration, how a woman might throw a punch in his face. Should a man stop a woman on a dark road and *demand* a light, *Hands Off!* instructs women to light the entire matchbook and throw it in his face. "Clearly these books teach women serious and violent defense moves even against dates," commented Martha McCaughey, a professor of women's studies at Virginia Tech who has written about self-defense culture and what she calls a "new" feminism.

But by the 1970s the type of demeanor suggested to women being harassed or threatened was considerably more passive. By now, it's important to note, women had become much stronger, socially and politically. And note that rape was at this time being reconfigured by the feminist movement into a crime of violence. How odd that suddenly women were being advised to back off. To refrain from becoming angry. To run if they can. Now the advice had changed to, Don't carry a gun because you may not be able to get to it in time. Or, You're likely to fumble when you try to use it. Women's incompetence was the big message, even though women who *did* use weapons, a study in the journal *Criminology* shows, were more likely to injure people than men were. (When weapons were not used, men were four times as likely to injure, in a violent attack, than were women.)

Violence in defending themselves was strongly discouraged in women in the 1970s. Instead they were instructed to try any of a number of passive, undignified, but hopefully distracting tactics. Defecate. Urinate. Faint. Fake a seizure. *Vomit,* if you can bring yourself to! "Yes, it pays to be deceptive!" one cheerleading male self-defense expert advised. "Be an actress if you must. Someday, God forbid, you may *need* all of your theatrical skills." But above all, don't enrage them by suggesting they're not capable of completing what they originally planned. In short, don't mock the weenie.

Advice manuals of this era were distinctly disabling in tone, as if women might be foolhardy enough to strike out in anger when any fool knows they don't have the strength, or will, to defend themselves with violence. "If he's skinny, you may smash his chest," one male writer cautioned. "But how are you to know he's skinny [if he grabs you from behind]—reach back and feel? And what do you think he'll be doing while you're hitting him? He'll be tearing you apart." Better to just start heaving on the guy's shoes.

The notion that it was actually okay to fight back didn't start gaining favor until after the Vietnam War. Enter the Green Berets or, more particularly, one female Green Beret. Lisa Sliwa made headlines when she took on the cause of women's self-defense, challenging the old "Stay meek" rule. Sliwa was no mouse. She wanted women to stop going around feeling passive and affraid. She wanted them to stand up for their dignity and do it with attitude. "Boldness is better than guilt," she wrote in a self-defense guidebook in 1986. "Don't romanticize the hero. Rapists are parasites with a distorted view of reality. It is your responsibility to set them straight by saying, 'Hey, Jack, your number's up.' "

According to the old school, a woman should do anything *passive* she could to avoid penetration, which was tantamount to death. The new school teaches women to fight, and yell, and go all out. The goal today is to surprise the attacker immediately by taking charge of the fight. Studies show this approach to be more effective.

The sassiest advice for women encountering sexual harassment can be found on the Internet. Women get on-line and advise one another. No more experts telling them what to do, just girlfriends. "Keep your head or lose it, babe," warned one, whose Web name is "Tyranny." Tyranny says an effective favorite technique is "the eyes of death," whereby one advertises to any potential harassers, "There is no soul here, only unspeakable violence and insanity." This is "Grrl Power" in action. It includes using the worst language you can think of, and all the better if it's gender-bending. "You're walkin' down the road, keepin' it on the QT, minding your own business," Tyranny says, "and this dick-smack in a car asks you if he can eat your pussy." Would such a scenario fluster the likes of Tyranny? No way. In this very situation, she informs her Web audience, "I turned to the freak and brandished my power-finger and said, "*No*, you can suck my dick, butt-fuck." There's a physical swagger in her language, to say the least. This girl is not about to be intimidated.

Of course, there are situations in which it's smarter to rein in one's gleeful anarchism, and even Tyranny reminds Web surfers to be aware of when provocative behavior might be unwise. But in most situations tough talk actually *is* effective in turning harassers away, according to recent studies.

Another technique Tyranny suggests as effective in harassment situations is giving mixed messages about what gender you are. Say a bunch of construction workers are hanging off a scaffolding and ogling a big muscular blonde walking down the street. When they start in with their verbal abuse, the blonde (in Tyranny's heated parable) says something like "Suck my dick." This creates humiliating uncertainty about whether the big blonde is really a woman after all! The construction guys end up "trying desperately to process the situation."

Media images offer girls and women new fantasies of power that "rest on women's abilities to set boundaries, defend themselves, and enter into combat, especially with aggressive men," says Martha McCaughey. She cites the gun-toting women in such films as *Eve of Destruction, Point of No Return,* and *La Femme Nikita,* and the women who go one-on-one with men. In *Terminator 2,* Linda Hamilton enjoys combat with men, warning one who moans that she's just broken his arm, "There are 215 bones in the human body. That's one."

Women's rock bands celebrate retaliation against violence to women. Seven Year Bitch shouts out the lyrics "Dead men don't rape." At the 1994 Michigan Womyn's Music Festival, Tribe 8, a female punk band, staged a fantasy castration against a gang rape, cutting off a penis with a knife while singing "Frat Pig." Some feminists objected to the violence of the act, but in McCaughey's analysis, "Tribe 8 does not advocate castration of rapists, but they do believe that fantasized violence can be a cathartic ritual for displaying women's anger at past and potential sexual aggression."

Feminists express concern about women entering into a world of "patriarchal violence" by engaging in violent forms of self-defense. In a 1994 *Ms.* magazine issue on women and guns, Ann Jones warned that confronting violent men is "not a job to be done piecemeal by lone women, armed with pearl-handled pistols, picking off batterers and rapists one by one." Who said anything about pearl-handled? Women need more than dainty philosophies of nonviolence when men come breaking into their houses.

Judging by the applause for media images of females being violent, women are not so interested in feminist interpretations of what's appropriate, or isn't, in matters of self-defense. When Thelma, apprehending a rapist in the act, shouts out, in *Thelma and Louise,* "You let her go, you fuckin' asshole, or I'm gonna splatter your ugly face all over this nice car," the audience in the small town where I saw the movie roared its approval. It was fun in a film that was challenging old ideas about femininity. But it was Susan Sarandon's feisty "I'm not taking any truck from anyone" attitude that had women in the audience flipping. Clearly that's the attitude we'd all like to have; the question is, *Can* we have it without necessarily relying on a gun to shield us?

More thrilling by far was the fantastic white-water run masterminded by Meryl Streep in *The River Wild.* She had in her raft two criminals and her son of about seven. It was a death-defying trip through the rapids, and only *she* could get them through it. Standing up in the back of the raft and giving orders to the men, being less frightened by far than they were, Streep, in her role as an athlete and mother, was stunning. In the end, once they were all safely to shore, she couldn't bring herself to shoot the bad guy. He played to her morality, reminding her that she'd wonder for the rest of her life whether she'd done the "right" thing. (What better way to get to a woman?) But then he got the gun in his own hands and immediately threatened her son's life. She got the gun back and without wasting another second shot him through the heart. It was so rousing, I could hardly sleep that night. But the difference—and it is huge—between Susan Sarandon's kill and Meryl Streep's is that Streep had fully empowered herself, physically, to survive. Not only could she take the rapids, she could keep the men's violence in check by her own expertise. She shot and killed to defend her child. The Thelma character shot out of a kind of vindictive glee. Sarandon's role in breaking down gender barriers against violence in women was an intermediary one. Streep's, only a few years later, was far more powerful.

Self-defense experts talk about "will to fight" as something that's hard to instill in women. *Everything* in our conditioning has gone against fighting. Fighting is obscenely "male." It's something we don't believe in. We are pacifists; men are war makers. And besides (bottom line), suppose we should lose? Women who are going to be able to defend themselves physically have to have "will to fight." All the eye-gouging and groin-kicking techniques in the world won't help if they're unwilling to use them.

But will to fight alone won't do it, either. You have to have gained the physical skills to defend yourself. In self-defense courses for women, the fighting techniques and the will to employ them are developed at the same time. Of the two, women may find developing "will to fight" even more antithetical than learning the skills. Men have been developing the will to fight, and the wherewithal to do it, since they were boys. Not to say that all men could defend themselves adequately in a fight; they have to have actually learned how to do it. The difference is that learning to fight enhances a man's sense of gender identity. It diminishes a woman's. The gender conditioning about violent self-defense is powerful. Just to read, in a book by a self-defense expert, "It's not that hard to break a kneecap," makes me cringe. *Break* someone's kneecap? The very idea of deliberately setting forth to accomplish that task seems, well, monstrous. Even now it's hard to imagine surviving a knee crushing; not the victim surviving it, but *me* as the perpetrator. It's as if to defend myself violently against violence would bring something terrible down on me—the wrath of God, or at least the wrath of the guy's friends. Violence is bad karma, at least for a woman.

But what are the possibilities here—only violence or constriction? Only the willingness to be on guard for any potential danger or the willingness to "beat the crap out of anyone" who messes with you (as young Jeff from the Weston Middle School put it in an earlier chapter)? Aren't there options in between? Would the *knowledge* of physical self-defense make us more comfortable with it—make it more likely that we could walk the beach at dusk—or even, heaven forfend, walk it at night? Would the *knowledge* of how to use our bodies in effective self-defense change the inner attitude of victimhood? And would changing the inner attitude alter the way we self-present? And might that, in itself, go toward making us safer?

Weakened bodies and weakened body language make women unnecessarily vulnerable to assault. Attackers are not gallant. They go for the weak and defenseless. Researchers had prison inmates incarcerated for felony crimes watch videos of women walking down the street and point out what sorts of body language are used by those most vulnerable to being attacked.

Women who actually fight the rapist are less likely to be raped, studies show. Four out of five rape attempts fail—and they are more likely to fail if the woman puts up a fight. And the more aggressive the better. In a University of Nebraska study of 150 women who had been targets of rape, those who had screamed, bit, kicked, scratched, or ran were half as likely to be raped as were women who had done nothing.

Fighting Back

It was about two in the morning on a warm summer night in Manhattan when my partner, Lowell, and I decided to walk the block from our apartment on West End Avenue to get something from the car, which was parked on Riverside Drive. Riverside is split, in the nineties, between the main avenue of traffic at the foot of a steep slope and a service drive for the apartment buildings at the top of the slope. As we approached the service drive I had a gut feeling about how isolated we were. It was so late, no doormen were out in front of the buildings. That very moment a car drove up and slowed as it went by. "Those guys are stopping," I said to Lowell, and the next thing we knew they were out of the car and running toward us. One man was flashing a knife. There were four or five of them. Lowell, who had studied aikido for some years, began jumping about like a dervish, arms and legs aswirl. It took them by surprise. Even the guy with the knife seemed taken aback. I saw my opportunity and began to run. Lowell was inches shorter than I but stronger—of course. I knew I couldn't fight. My taking off down the hill might distract them. There was also the chance of flagging down a passing car on the main road. I remember feeling very free flying down that hill—free, and confident in my legs, in their strength, and in my speed. By the time I reached the bottom and looked up to see what was happening, the men were packing into their car and driving off. Lowell and I congratulated ourselves on avoiding injury. I was glad I'd had the instinct to just get the hell out when there was trouble. But I also wished I'd been able to do what *he* had done, to know how to defend myself should anyone ever flash a knife at *me*. Whoever had such competence was a freer person than I.

Still, knowing how to run like the wind—or, more to the point, knowing that I *knew* how to run like the wind—helped me protect myself in the situation with the knife-bearing muggers on Riverside Drive. I had never had to run away before, but in the crisis I was able to pump my legs as hard as the young, hockey-player wannabe I had been in girlhood. Those pumped quads were doubtless part of my inner picture of myself. I actually believed—in that split second of decision making—that I could outrun those guys, and the truth is, I probably could have. And the way they hunkered around the guy who was doing the knife flashing didn't say much for their own body confidence. I think I was able to intuit this on some level. The adrenaline rush of the moment gave me the focus to figure all this out very rapidly. But it was a certain level of body competence that let me take off like a bat out of hell.

I knew I'd passed to a different stage of body consciousness the day ten years later when I encountered a threatening dog. By then I'd been working out for several years and walking almost daily up the steep mountain road behind my house. Toward the top I always passed a house where two German shepherds were penned up. They began barking even before they could see me. I invariably felt jolted by the barking, even though I knew it was coming. One day, after I'd been doing this for months, I heard a different sound as I walked past the site, the sound of a chain being dragged. I turned and saw a dog charging up the hill toward me, its chain having broken. In a split second I decided not to pick up a stick, lest I further incite it. But I was very angry, angry enough to face up to the dog. It was only yards away from me when I raised my arm shoulder height, pointed toward the house, and shouted, "Go home!" The dog turned and ran back down the hill. I proceeded on my walk, feeling both surprised by my effectiveness and quite powerful.

A few years later it was a bear that I came upon on a remote road. In the mountains surrounding Woodstock there are a lot of black bears. Usually they stay high up in the hills, but during a drought they come down seeking food and water. Once or twice I'd seen bears before, lumbering across my drive at midnight, cubs in tow. I'd seen huge claw holes in my garbage cans, and cans that had been picked up and flung away in disgust because the bungee cords couldn't be sprung. I'd even seen a cub fifty or sixty feet ahead as I was out walking. But one day on another, more desolate road—it was during a drought—I looked up and saw a full-grown male about ten feet from me. Male black bears weigh up to 600 pounds. It was hard to know which of us was more surprised to see the other. I turned, walking slowly in the opposite direction, and heard the crashing away into the woods of an animal that wanted this encounter no more than I but whose tremendous power, expressed in the sound of foliage being crushed beneath it, caused me to resonate like a tuning fork. I continued at a slow, deliberate pace for about a minute, then broke into a run. The next day I put myself back onto that same road. I figured the chances of encountering another bear were about the same as being struck by lightning a second time, and I didn't want to become phobic about walking in my beautiful, isolated countryside. It was body confidence, a connection with my own physical reality, that allowed me to do this. But afterward this thought struck me: I felt safer coming face-to-face with a 600-pound male bear on a desolate stretch of road than I would a 150-pound man. I'd been conditioned to fear men more than bears! It was at that point that I thought: Something is wrong with this picture. Could I really be as helpless and vulnerable in relation to the male of the species as I have been led to believe?

I began to understand that I was a victim, yes—a victim of what I call "the rape mystique." In using that term I'm not questioning the pervasiveness of rape or the suffering it causes. What I'm suggesting is that *rape's power to hold women captive, to keep them constricted and fearful in their lives, grows in proportion to the depth of the belief that women are incapable of standing up to rapists.*

Men need not be particularly aggressive, strong, or physically violent to accomplish rape, feminist self-defense experts note. What they need more is a *belief* in their power. It's the story of the emperor's new clothes again. What we believe is more powerful than reality. It is the broad cultural belief in the physical superiority of men that gives men so much power—that becomes, in the words of legal scholar Catherine MacKinnon, "the myth that makes itself true." We could as conceivably live in a culture in which women fondle and penetrate drunk men in bars and at parties, Martha McCaughey points out, or in which women bearing weapons assault men on the streets and in their homes. But we don't, and *that* we don't is a matter of culture, not nature.

Rape is a learned behavior. It's been mythologized as a drive rooted in natural sex differences. The idea is that rape, if not *caused* by men's greater strength, is certainly enabled by it. But rape doesn't require superior size or strength so much as the fantasy that men are capable of physically dominating women. This fantasy allows *both* men and women to see women as viable targets for abuse. The rape mystique encourages women to believe that any effort they might make to defend themselves would be futile.

The very word *rapist* has a monstrous connotation, as if every man who rapes is no less ghoulish and unstoppable than the demented Hannibal Lecter. In fact, the crazed psychopath is actually the exception to the rule. The rapist is more likely to be the guy next door who wants to get some and is too arrogant, oblivious, or drunk to care what you want. This, as compared to the ghoul version, is just down-and-dirty acquaintance rape. Acquaintance rape is actually more psychologically damaging than stranger rape, some experts believe, in part because it is harder for women to acknowledge and stand up to. Our sugar-and-spice conditioning leaves us confused. How could good old Harry *do* this? And while we're pondering, good old Harry's doing it.

Let's say Harry is your friend's husband. He's drunk at a party and has been leering at you all night, and now he's followed you into the bedroom where you've gone to get your coat and—click!—locked the door in the hope of convincing you to go along. It may not be his conscious intention, but damn if he won't try to overpower you if you don't want to play. Can you take this guy on, and if not, why not? It's the rape mystique that makes you think you can't—and even, in the case of the neighbor guy, say, or your "overzealous date" (as midcentury sex manuals put it), that you *shouldn't*. It's the rape mystique that conflates the notion of "stranger" with the notion of criminal sexual violence, both perpetrating the "ghoul" concept and undermining women's ability to assess—and deal with—danger. Eighty percent of rapes are committed by someone the victim knows. We need to prepare ourselves for rape attempts by acquaintances.

In a culture of violence against females, women nevertheless have an overdetermined fear of rape based upon distorted notions of men's greater strength. But women are piercing the rape mystique by learning to defend themselves against physical violence.

Most violence against women has a point: to reaffirm that women are incapable of responding. A batterer or rapist is basically enforcing his authority by causing pain. Self-defense courses treat violent assault as "scripted interactions" that women are capable of interrupting.

Unlearning Passivity

Gender is a system of ideas about men and women that we live our lives by. The more we live the system, the more internalized it becomes, and the more it actually gets translated into our bodies. The system we have grown up with is embarrassingly simplistic. Man strong; woman weak. Man violent; woman not violent. Man bad;

woman good. As long as women keep buying into this way of looking at gender, it will be impossible for them to see that they are capable of disrupting the rape culture, says Martha McCaughey, "by embracing the very violence that men have used to keep women in line."

"Embracing" violence? It sounds crazy at first. Shouldn't we all be moving in the direction of nonviolence? Can women really free themselves by joining in this "patriarchal" notion of survival? Are we merely animals? And finally, if women resort to violence in the course of defending themselves, what will happen to their souls—not just *their* souls, but the "soul" of the culture, as it were? For that, no less, has become women's charge: keeping gentility and spiritual-ity alive, even if at the expense of their own lives.

In the last decade a small but increasing cadre of feminist experts in self-defense has been challenging such suicidally destructive ef-fects of the frailty myth as remaining passive in the face of an attack. They have been teaching women what it takes to be able to defend themselves—and they have been teaching them how to overcome their learned weakness and reap the benefits of feeling physically con-fident in the world. I think this movement will be revolutionary. First, it challenges women's belief that they can't do it. Second, the self-defense movement attacks ideas that have been central to our con-cepts of manhood and womanhood: that aggression in men is natural and that in women it is unnatural—or, if not unnatural, prohibited. Teachers teach this. So do politicians, lawyers, and the church. Ag-gression is part and parcel of what distinguishes male from female. Feminists have been actively fighting this idea of women's "natural" submissiveness for years without ever eradicating the belief. That's because the belief has been in our bodies as well as in our brains, and only now is the body part being addressed. "I learned to jab, punch, poke, pull, kick, yell, stomp, shoot, and even kill with my bare hands," McCaughey says of her experience in what is called a "padded attacker course." Looking back, she wonders how she could ever have been a feminist activist and not practice, or advocate, self-defense.

As I wrote about in chapter 2, we *learn* to "throw like a girl"—withholding our strength, refusing to develop it, approaching physical tasks as if we were to the Victorian fainting couch born. "Women do not perceive themselves as capable of lifting and carrying heavy things, pushing and shoving with significant force, pulling, squeezing, grasping, or twisting with force," says McCaughey. "When we attempt to do such tasks, we frequently fail to summon the full possibilities of our muscular coordination, position, pose, and bearing." Honey, could you open the pickle jar? When McCaughey asked self-defense instructors what was the biggest hurdle their female students had to overcome, the answer was "femininity." They had to get over "being nice," their fear of hurting people, and their disbelief in their own physical power. Self-defense training gives women the opportunity to "rehearse a new script," McCaughey says. "They develop a new self-image, a new understanding of what a female body can do, and thus break out of the expectations under which they have acted—expectations that have cemented themselves at the level of the body."

At first students have to be assured, "I know you don't think you can do this, but trust me, you can." This is the first stage of deprogramming in virtually any self-defense course, whether the weapon being used is a gun or the body. "From birth, most women are brainwashed into thinking the only proper response to physical aggression is submission," a female rifle expert wrote in *American Rifleman.* "On the playground we're told, 'Girls don't hit'—even if we're striking back in self-defense to flee a much larger and stronger school bully. Later, we're told women should 'submit to criminal attack for fear of injury'—as if the crime itself were not an injury." That's why, she adds, the experience of learning to defend oneself is life altering.

And apparently it is.

The triumphs women experience as they begin to change are shared in the classroom and become, themselves, a part of the transforming agenda. In her padded attacker course, McCaughey told her fellow students how she'd verbally confronted a man who'd harassed her in the street by turning around and yelling at him—something she'd never done before. Another woman produced applause when she told the class how her defensive clamor had affected a man who'd faced her with his pants down, in a parking lot where she worked, and begun to masturbate. She'd made so much noise, he'd had to release his penis before the critical moment so he could put his hands over his ears.

What women learn in self-defense courses is an armament of "don't mess with me" techniques. They learn to "mark" a man with their eyes—a brief but direct glance, as opposed to looking away or looking down—which sends the message, "You're not looking at a victim here, bud." Self-defense courses teach scrappy, practical things like gouging eyes, kicking and punching, and learning to shoot a gun while your hands are shaking. "I can't kick, but I can gouge their eyes," said a seventy-one-year-old widow who decided to learn self-defense because she didn't want fear blighting her solo travel plans.

Some courses include antiharassment exercises like teaching students to yell obscenities or having them practice responding to another's hand being placed on their knee by stating firmly, without smiling, "Take your hand off my knee." Repeating such techniques over and over, women begin to unlearn their self-destructive feminine demeanor. Instructors in padded attacker courses are continually shouting out reminders like "He's in your space!" and "Set your boundaries!"

Workshops offered by Impact Personal Safety Inc. teach both physical and verbal responses to life-threatening situations. The program shows women how to gather strength from their most powerful muscles, in the hips and thighs. And it shows them how to deploy that strength. They practice their most aggressive moves against a male instructor they call "Bif" who's dressed in a twenty-five-pound protective suit. They practice yelling, "No!" from deep in their guts. "For many women, long taught to be quiet and demure," says one Impact student, "this was like asking them to give a speech on a public street corner."

Women need to learn they can take a hit without collapsing. Knowing you can do this is almost as important as knowing how to deliver one. Rene Denfeld had decided to get over her fear of men by studying boxing. Before her first match she realized the fear of getting hit "frightened me more than I had imagined. . . . I was afraid I would freeze. I was afraid it would hurt. I had visions of women being hit in the movies: cringing, helpless, and pleading."

Once the bell rang and Denfeld began sparring with her partner, all the long months of training returned to reassure her. She threw out a few jabs. He popped her in the nose, "a stinging jab," but it didn't hurt as much as she'd thought it would. "Somehow, that realization was more exciting and fulfilling than I could ever have imagined. I was being hit by a man. But I wasn't falling to pieces. I was going to be okay."

Learning to "stay in your body" is central in martial arts courses, where students are taught to find their "chi," a mental force that increases strength and control. Students learn to focus and think quickly. They learn to "coil up" their energy when they need to break out of someone's hold. Body memory is what makes these skills stick around until they're needed. Even verbal assertiveness alone (often taught at rape crisis centers) can enhance a woman's confidence. Of course, the more potentially lethal the techniques learned, the greater the sense of freedom. "It felt great to kick the shit out of a six-foot-two-inch guy," a student said, referring to a padded attacker in her Model Mugging class. A karate student knew her training had really taken hold when she started defending herself against attack in her dreams.

Most women come into these courses relatively paralyzed. They leave empowered, having learned to make decisions about how to move their bodies in specific types of encounters: when grabbed from behind, for example; when attacked by a "walk by" assailant; or when forced fellatio is attempted after one has been pinned to the ground.

Not surprisingly, women who learn to physically defend themselves don't stop there. "They move on," said one instructor, and the transformation is exciting. "They end unhealthy relationships, they quit their jobs, they go back to school. They jump out of planes! They climb mountains. They start new businesses. I mean, they just reach a place within themselves where they can do more than they have, and they unleash that chain, or wall . . . or however you want to label it."

Maybe they *don't* change their careers but are changed in how they are within them. A nurse who took three Model Mugging courses (they're offered at different levels of advancement) didn't realize until afterward that around the doctors she'd always felt "like I didn't exist. I felt like I was this little mouse running around between all these big, important men and . . . that I didn't even have a right to expect them to recognize who I was, and that they were obviously superior to me."

Anyone who's been a patient in a hospital knows whose care is more important, nurses' or doctors'. And the nurses themselves know it. But the system has enforced in them an attitude of submission. Model Mugging gave this nurse a sense of "I have a right to be here, I do exist, you have to recognize me, I have a right to challenge you, and I have a right to tell you what I want." In the end, she said, she felt equal to the doctors.

Such a transformation is, indeed, "life altering." The helpless female is no more. The unstoppable male is stoppable. And the woman's new physical effectiveness is not due to the release of some dormant instinct—any more than rape is. It's due to adopting a model of behavior—just as rape itself is. When necessary, a woman must be able to tap into her fighting spirit and do what she needs to do in order to survive. But the philosophy of self-defense goes beyond the individual's ability to protect herself against attack. It goes straight to the heart of made-up femininity and of the inequality between the sexes that the concept of gender has so insidiously supported. Physical equality—even when it needs to be accomplished compensatorily, through self-defense courses that level the fighting field between people of unequal size and strength—puts an end to domination. This, it has become increasingly clear, is the final stage of women's liberation. By *making* themselves physically equal, women can at last make themselves free.

Epilogue

Women have been excluded from so much in life because of the frailty myth. First we believed we were weak. Then we began to suspect that we weren't but kept getting told that we were. Then we began proving that we weren't and were mocked as men because we were strong. Women have thrown themselves over hurdle after hurdle during the course of the past century, demonstrating extraordinary physical powers and skills, and still we're being kept back for no reason other than that we're female. In the physical trades, for example, there is still a backlash, especially against women doing work associated with masculinity. Jobs that use muscle power to protect others—jobs like soldiering, policing, and fire fighting—are particularly important to male identity. Even mental professions like medicine and law and engineering have traditionally been thought of as requiring some kind of masculine grittiness, or bigness, or male sweat. Because they haven't experienced their own physical strength, women, too, buy into the "men's work" myth. Looking at a bridge that soars high over a river, we would just assume a man had labored over the drawing board to design it. A woman neurosurgeon mucking around inside someone's brain? Impossible. That requires male expertise. So, too, flying. And men weren't the only ones to ridicule the very idea of a female pilot. Even women were prone to say, "I would *never* take a plane that was flown by a woman." The requirements for these kinds of work were not particularly physical but had to do with some ineffable combination of courage and visual acuity that we thought eluded women.

In the thirty years between 1970 and 2000, much of the mythology of "men's work" has been toppled. Today we don't think twice about a woman ferrying a monster 767 through the friendly skies. We may be inclined to trust a female neurosurgeon more than a male because she isn't afraid to relate to us as well as fix our gray matter. It's a given, now, that female cops shoot just as well as male cops. Female spies spy just as well. So much is different, it's almost hard to imagine it was ever any other way.

Yet not everything has been righted. When Rachel moved to Nantucket two years ago, wanting to get away from city life and write, she took a construction job to support herself. Nantucket is a wealthy island with a lot of house building going on, so getting a job was easy. Even being at the bottom of the heap was fine, at least in the beginning. The male contractors told her she needed to develop her "skills." But she was required to sand baseboards and remove paint from shutters far beyond the point at which she'd learned how. She'd spend eight hours a day sanding. Her hands grew callused. "It's not bad. I like it," she told me, "and the views out here are fabulous when you're able to work outside." It fascinated me that she found a positive side to such grueling labor. She got a job driving a cab to supplement her income. But not many months passed before she had to acknowledge that she was being deliberately held back. She quit a job with one contractor who wouldn't promote her to house painting, got a job with another who promised rapid advancement, and quit that one when it became clear to her that it would be a cold day in hell before she got past the sanding detail. These guys didn't *want* her learning to make a perfect bead with a caulk gun.

So she got out. Now she teaches in the local high school and sells her own painted furniture for hundreds of dollars on eBay. So much for her not being "ready" (as one guy told her) to paint a Sheetrock wall with latex. It had been an interesting lesson in gender discrimination. On an island thirty miles out to sea, men who wanted to keep the primo work for themselves could still get away with it.

Not to say that women on the mainland aren't also stifled when they try to get the real boyo jobs. When a woman in California asked a local fire department what she had to do to get a job, she was told she needed to attend the firefighter academy and get her license as an emergency medical technician before she'd be eligible. So she went off and did as she was told, but it turned out she didn't need either of those things. "The captain I talked to in the beginning was blowing me off. He just didn't feel like taking me."

In the early 1990s, after four and a half years of training and attending school, a journeyman sheet metal worker, Vidette Galvin, went out on her first job. The construction site outhouse—unisex, she was the only woman on the job—was high up on the roof. After entering the outhouse that first morning, she noticed it rocking back and forth. "Afterward I got out and I turned around and I looked and the crane cable was hooked to the top of the outhouse and they had raised me while I was in it."

Attitudes about women in nontraditional jobs fluctuate, but such women all have to prove themselves. "For such a long time [men] have worked in the trades, and some fellas think that we're not capable of doing it," says Nancy Kiniery, a bridge painter. "But there's a few of us that are showing the world that we can do it. And do a good job at it."

Kiniery remembers the first time she was sent out to paint a section of the San Francisco Bay Bridge. As an apprentice, she was given the equipment to carry: goggles, a respirator, a chipping hammer, and other tools—all the stuff needed for painting a bridge. It was two days before an earthquake hit and a section of the bridge dropped out. Kiniery climbed the stairs to the top of the bridge, the tools in a bag on her back. "I remember thinking, Oh man, am I going to be able to do this every day? When I got up there . . . they put me in a basket on the outside of the bridge, so it was over water." She would be lowered down the bridge tower in a basket. "They said, 'Just go down painting it inside and out,' and I was thinking, Yeah, right, are you going to get in this basket and show me how to do it? I will never forget that day."

Physical competence is also making a big difference to women in professions. Eighty percent of women in top jobs in Fortune 500 companies have a background in sports. Candace Carpenter, a founder and chief executive officer of the huge women's Web site iVillage, credits her professional success to her involvement with rock climbing: "In climbing there are real consequences of blowing it. You don't have much time to recover. You are climbing a route that you usually have not seen before, and you have to make decisions without knowing what is ahead." It's not unlike the Internet business, she says. "You have to make a lot of the right moves under time pressure and without much information."

The same challenges could be said to accompany the job of being a mother—even more so when you're young, and poor, and trying to raise a child on your own. Meeting rigorous physical demands can give a tremendous boost to the self-esteem of the underprivileged, as Mount Holyoke College in Massachusetts discovered when it decided to offer a rowing program to young single mothers on public aid. The idea was to build their self-confidence in the hope that it would spill over into other aspects of their lives. The college offered not only its boats and coaches for training, but day care for the rowers' children. The young mothers learned faster than some of the other novices who had more time to practice, the coach reported. Before long they were participating in the Mount Holyoke Invitational, the oldest women's regatta in the country, competing against teams from Amherst, Middlebury, Smith, and other colleges known not only for their academic programs but for their rowing prowess.

I think it is part of the passing of the frailty myth that I began to covet the greater physical freedom of my daughters. I saw how positively it affected their lives. To celebrate her thirtieth birthday, Rachel took a five-week trip to Vietnam, traveling alone, with no advance reservations and only a rough outline of a plan. Seeing her exuberance when she returned—hearing of her train ride into the mountains near the Chinese border, her monkey bridge crossings in the Mekong Delta, her crawling on her belly through the hideout tunnels of the Viet Cong—I knew I wanted to be able to have more adventure in my life.

A few months after Rachel returned I had to go to Tokyo on business. Since my way to that part of the world would be paid for, I decided to take my own trip to Vietnam. I began my adventure in Saigon, with no reservations, carrying few clothes, and relying on my Lonely Planet guidebook for company. I would have physical struggles while I was there, bouts of dysentery. I feared mosquitoes because I'd been prescribed an ineffectual medication for malaria before leaving home. I avoided the high noonday sun and couldn't get myself to go out into the South China Sea on a snorkeling boat. I didn't cross the monkey bridges in the Mekong Delta or crawl through the hideout tunnels. But I did more, saw more, *felt* more than I had ever imagined doing, and seeing, and feeling. I walked the streets of Saigon and Hanoi in the day and the night. I flew around on the back of a motor scooter driven by a young Vietnamese man who graciously became my guide, touring me through the open markets, having dinner with me at sidewalk restaurants, taking me to visit his family. I felt the freedom of charting my own path, thinking my own thoughts, facing the challenges of entering, alone, into a very different culture. And when I returned home, it was with a different view of my life and what I would do with the rest of it. Looking back on it now, I can see that that experience wouldn't have been possible without the modeling of my daughters, the reengagement with my own body, and the feelings of entitlement given me by the women's movement.

And I don't consider it over, by any means. There are more risks to be taken in the future. Next time I hope to go back with my daughter. I'll be ready to engage more physically with the land in Southeast Asia and its particular mysteries. The thing is this: At sixty-two I don't feel deprived of physical possibility. I have gotten back something I had when I was younger, the sheer joy of being able to trust my body. I don't believe in shutting myself down physically because I have reached "a certain age." When things get tough I go kickboxing. I've been fortunate enough to outlive the frailty myth, and for that I will be forever grateful.

Notes

Introduction

xxii *mesomorphic* physique: E. B. Lenart et al. "Current and Ideal Physique Choices in Exercising and Nonexercising College Women from a Pilot Athletic Image Scale," *Perceptual Motor Skills* 81, no. 3, pt. 1 (December 1995): 831–48. Note: Women who reported their current shape as moderately mesomorphic had the lowest body dissatisfaction scale scores.

xxii "I have a big intellect": Gabrielle Reece, quote reported in *Glamour,* June 1997, p. 109.

xxiii "Ila is": Neal Karlen, "Diamonds Are a Girl's Best Friend," *The New York Times,* September 6, 1998, Sec. 9, p. 6.

xxiii "like Jackie Robinson": Jim Yardley, owner of the Duluth Dukes, as reported in *The New York Times.*

xxiv "One thing is clear": Sandra Lee Bartky, "Foucault, Femininity and the Modernization of Patriarchal Power," in *Feminism and Foucault: Reflections on Resistance,* ed. I. Diamond and L. Quinby (Boston: Northeastern University Press, 1988), p. 73.

Bartky describes women tending to sit and stand with legs, feet, and knees close or touching as "a coded declaration of sexual circumspection in a society that still maintains a double standard, or an effort, albeit unconscious, to guard the genital area." Woman's tight, constricted posture is an expression of her need to ward off real or symbolic sexual attack.

Chapter 1

5 the forces keeping women: The importance of physical development to success in living has been grasped relatively recently in academe, where a field known as "sport studies" has emerged over the last decade. "Sport," singular, is now regarded by social scientists as a lens on human behavior, by economists as a growth industry, and by feminists as a vehicle for both examining—*and changing*—sex roles.

7 Ice Age females': Heather Pringle, "New Women of the Ice Age," *Discover*, April 1998, p. 62.

7 "set snares": Ibid., p. 64.

7 "They even hunted": Ibid., p. 66.

7 The new research opens to question: Stick-and-line drawings discovered in European Paleolithic caves, for example, were originally thought to be weapons—harpoons, arrows, and spears—though later interpretations saw many of these drawings as stylized depictions of plant life. June Kennard and John Marshall Carter, "In the Beginning: The Ancient and Medieval Worlds," in *Women and Sport,* ed. D. Margaret Costa and Sharon R. Guthrie (Champaign, Ill.: Human Kinetics Books, 1994), p. 16.

7 "If one of these Upper Paleolithic guys": Pringle, p. 66.

The fact that these discoveries haven't been made until now, Olga Soffer and others believe, is related to sexist male assumptions about women's main use—for example, that they couldn't possibly have participated in important survival activities because they had to stay in the cave with the kids. That assumption altered the way men looked at archaeological finds—not noticing the marks of netting in fossils, for example, or signs of edible plant material. Soffer and her colleagues have cast the Ice Age in an entirely new light.

7 worked as bull-vaulting teams: Reynold Higgins, *An Archaeology of Minoan Crete* (London: Bodley Head, 1973), p. 21. Cited by Riane Eisler in *The Chalice and the Blade*, p. 35.

8 "The equal partnership": Riane Eisler, *The Chalice and the Blade* (New York: HarperCollins, 1995), p. 35 (originally published in 1987).

8 Forced to live: They controlled produce, medicine, and textile wealth and were landowners. With so much economic power they became strong political influences in the community.

8 "cheerleaders for chivalry": Kennard and Carter, in Costa and Guthrie, p. 24.

9 Margaret Evans: Roberta J. Park, "From 'Genteel Diversions' to 'Bruising Peg': Active Pastimes, Exercise, and Sports for Females in Late 17th- and 18th-Century Europe," in Costa and Guthrie, p. 31.

9 In 1765: Ibid., p. 33.

9 *Sporting*: Ibid.

9 "significantly *more* frequent": Peter F. Radford, "Women's Foot-Races in the 18th and 19th Centuries: A Popular and Widespread Practice." Paper presented at the 1993 International Congress on the History of Sport, June 30–July 4, Berlin, Germany.

9 "In music halls": Dahn Shaulis, "Women of Endurance," *Women in Sport and Physical Activity Journal* 5, no. 2 (1996): 5.

10 "became part": Nancy L. Struna, "The Recreational Experiences of Early American Women," in Costa and Guthrie, p. 35.

10 "nothing of ruggedness": Martha H. Verbrugge, *Able-Bodied Womanhood: Personal Health and Social Change in Nineteenth-Century Boston* (Oxford, England: Oxford University Press, 1988), p. 196. Cited in Costa and Guthrie, p. 51.

11 "They lusted": Stanley B. Alpern, *Amazons of Black Sparta* (New York: New York University Press, 1999), p. 32.

11 "superior muscular strength": Edmond Chaudoin, *Trois mois de captivité au Dahomey* (Paris, 1891), p. 186.

11 "honorary males": Antonia Fraser, *The Warrior Queens* (New York: Vintage, 1990), pp. 239, 331–32.

12 "We liberated": Ian Fisher, "Like Mother, Like Daughter, Eritrean Women Wage War," *The New York Times,* August 26, 1999, p. A1.

13 "with relaxed": Mary Wollstonecraft, *A Vindication of the Rights of Woman,* ed. Carol H. Poston (New York: W. W. Norton & Company, 1988), p. 25.

13 "but were made": Ibid., p. 280.

13 "The boys were": Hedwig Dohm, *Schicksale einer Seele* (Munich: Verlag Frauenoffensive 1988 [original 1899]), p. 24. Quoted in Chris Weedon, *Feminism, Theory and the Politics of Difference* (Oxford, England: Blackwell Publishers, 1999), p. 24.

13 " the strength of body": Wollstonecraft, p. 81.

14 "how far": Ibid., p. 85.

14 In the 1800s: Ellis Cashmore, *Making Sense of Sport* (London and New York: Routledge, 1990), p. 89.

14 "spend the year": Thomas E. Addis Emmet, M.D., *The Principles and Practice of Gynecology* (Philadelphia, 1879), p. 21. Cited in Patricia A.

Vertinsky, *The Eternally Wounded Woman* (Urbana: University of Illinois Press, 1994), p. 50.

15 "of a masculine": S. K. Westman, *Sport, Physical Training and Womanhood* (Baltimore: Williams and Wilkins, 1939), p. 140.

15 "enfeeblement": J. Madison Taylor, *Pediatrics,* July 15, 1896.

16 They withheld: Bruce Kidd, "The Men's Cultural Centre: Sports and the Dynamic of Women's Oppression/Men's Repression," in *Sport, Men and the Gender Order,* ed. Michael A. Messner and Donald F. Sabo (Champaign, Ill.: Human Kinetics Books, 1990), p. 35.

16 "the future of the white race": Ibid.

16 20 percent of her energy: Vertinsky, p. 70.

17 "anabolic": Ibid., p. 180.

17 "Most women": Elizabeth Robinson Scovil, *Preparation for Motherhood Manual* (Philadelphia: Henry Altemus, 1889), p. 39.

17 "the pelvis alters": C. Roberts, M.D., "Bodily Deformities in Girlhood," *Popular Science Monthly* 22 (January 1983), p. 324.

17 the "Misses Languid": This was a phrase used by Diocletian Lewis, a reformer who believed girls weren't getting enough exercise.

    One of the earliest and most influential reformers was Catharine Beecher (sister of Harriet Beecher Stowe, author of *Uncle Tom's Cabin*). Beecher invented a form of calisthenics, wrote a textbook on it, and founded a girls' school in Hartford, Connecticut, in 1824, but she was no feminist mover and shaker. Beecher believed in women's subordination to men and the importance of domesticity. The exercise system she developed was intended to correct female form and better fit women for work in the home.

18 lifting weights: Vertinsky, p. 207.

    Charlotte Perkins Gilman also became involved, historian Patricia Vertinsky tells us, in "rigid forms of self-discipline." (Ibid.) She became "preoccupied" with exercise and dietary restrictions.

19 "Have your child": Charlotte Perkins Gilman, *The Living of Charlotte Perkins Gilman: An Autobiography* (Univ. of Wisconsin Press, 1991), p. 96.

20 Increasingly: Vertinsky, p. 227, fn. 37. Vertinsky also notes that Mitchell was known to make $70,000 in a good year—an astronomical amount at that time. Most of the money came from consultations.

    Vertinsky notes that businessmen who became fatigued were also prescribed rest, but they were allowed to continue working, and the moral element was missing from the prescription. They were responsible only for taking care of themselves—that is, not the entire human race. Also, men's fatigue had to do with work, women's with biology. Since all women had the biology, many learned to suspect their own bodies when they became mentally clouded.

20 "As a body": "The Obstetrical Society Meeting to Consider the Proposition of the Council for the Removal of Mr. I. B. Brown," *British Medical Journal* 1 (1867): 396.

20 *The Yellow Wallpaper*: Gilman's episodic depression eventually lifted on its own, and she became reenergized. A year after she first went to Mitchell for help, Gilman left her husband and child and moved to California, where she became involved in socialism and the women's movement. Her husband, once an admirer of her athletic skills, now complained to newspapers that his wife had become too involved in the development of her muscles.

20 attracted attention: Vertinsky, p. 219.

21 "the fittest possible": G. Stanley Hall, *Educational Problems*, vol. 1 (New York: I. D. Appleton, 1911), p. 200. Cited in Vertinsky.

21 "the constraint and joy of pure obligation"; "the conduit through which the 'mansoul' might some day become a 'superman' in a 'superstate'": G. Stanley Hall, "Education of the Will," *Princeton Review* 10 (November 1882): 321. Cited in Vertinsky.

21 "first to know": G. Stanley Hall, "Child Study and Its Relation to Education," *The Forum* 29 (August 1900): 702.

Male leaders wanted to control the amount of energy women spent on thinking as well. Again the rationale was biological. When women used their brains, they spent all their energy, resulting in fewer children, doctors believed. "It is probably not an exaggeration to say that to the average cost of each girl's education must be added one unborn child," a protégé of Hall's wrote in *Popular Science Monthly*.

21 "to that country": Ibid.

23 "a crisis of masculinity": Michael S. Kimmel, "Baseball and the Reconstitution of American Masculinity, 1880–1920," in Messner and Sabo, p. 57.

"Men were jolted by changes in the economic and social order which made them perceive that their superior position in the gender order and their supposedly 'natural' male roles and prerogatives were not somehow rooted in the human condition, that they were instead the result of a complex set of relationships subject to change and decay," according to M. Hartman, "Sexual Crack-Up: The Role of Gender in Western History" (unpublished paper, Rutgers University), cited by Kimmel in Messner and Sabo.

23 "reverse the feared decline": Mary Roth Walsh, "Men's Behavior: Is the Mythopoetic Men's Movement Creating New Obstacles for Women?" in *Women, Men, and Gender,* ed. Mary Roth Walsh (New Haven: Yale University Press, 1997), p. 399.

Walsh cites a report from the 1905 *Records of the Commissioner of Education* describing the pathetic state of American boys, who were not being taught to punch one another's heads and be punched "in a healthy and proper manner."

24 "muscular Christianity": Michael Kimmel tells us of the muscular Christianity movement, which was preached through books like *The Manliness of Christ* (1880) and *The Masculine Religion* (1906), in Messner and Sabo.

24 "We are soldiers": G. Stanley Hall, "Christianity and Physical Culture," *Pedagogical Seminary* 9 (1902): 377. Cited in Vertinsky.

24 the "he-man" mystique: Advertisements from the last decade of the 1800s show the ideal male body as having put on about two dozen pounds.

A century after the first liberation movement was squelched by he-man culture and the concurrent cult of female invalidism, the alarm of "the feminization of American manhood" was once again sounded in the 1990s. Men were encouraged to beat their drums and their chests and get in touch with the "wild man" within. In its attempt to connect religion, physical strength, and masculinity, the men's movement of the late twentieth century was not unlike muscular Christianity. The Promise Keepers, for example, claim that men should be head of the family because of their "natural" (that is to say, biblically supported) greater strength. It is this strength that is supposed to endow them with the obligation of protecting the weaker members of the family—including, of course, their wives.

25 An 1877 article: Mary Putnam Jacobi, *The Question of Rest for Women During Menstruation* (New York: G. P. Putnam's Sons, 1877).

25 "using professional authority": Vertinsky, p. 112.

25 "dissipating": Mary Putnam Jacobi, "Social Aspects of the Re-admission of Women into the Medical Profession." Paper and letters presented to the First Women's Congress of the American Association for the Advancement of Women, New York, 1874, p. 173.

26 "but why exaggerate": Florence Pomeroy, Viscountess Harberton, "Rational Dress for Women," *Macmillan,* 1882, quoted in Janet H. Murray, *Strong-Minded Women* (New York: Pantheon Books, 1982), p. 70. Cited in Vertinsky, p. 76.

26 "There is a new dawn": Louise Jeye, *Lady Cyclist,* August 1895, p. 224.

26 "rescue thousands": W. H. Fenton, "A Medical View of Cycling for Ladies," *Nineteenth Century* 39 (1896): 797. Cited in Vertinsky, p. 77.

27 "incalculable harm": Gordon Stables, M.D., "Health," *Girls' Own Paper,* August 1901, p. 4.

27 masturbate: E. B. Turner, M.D., "A Report on Cycling in Health and Disease," *British Medical Journal* 1 (May 9, 1896): 1399.

27 "bicycle face": Patricia Vertinsky, "Women, Sport and Exercise in the 19th Century" in Costa and Guthrie, p. 70.

27 mobility to get about: "A woman known as Mrs. A.M.C. Allen, while setting a record in 1897 for the most miles (21,026) pedaled in one year, was bitten by a dog but drew out her revolver and shot it," Mariah Burton Nelson writes in the introduction to *Nike Is a Goddess*. "She then pedaled another sixteen miles before seeking medical treatment." Ed. Lissa Smith (Boston: Atlantic Monthly Press, 1998), p. xii.

28 peaks toppled: Descriptions of women's ascents of Mount Rainier are in P. W. Kaufman, "Early Women Claim Park Lands for Adventure and Aspiration," *Courier* 3, no. 10 (1986): 16–18.

Another example can be found in the Alpine Club of Canada in 1906. One year after its inception, a third of its 250 members were women, and within a decade that percentage had risen to nearly half. Cyndi Smith, *Off the Beaten Track: Women Adventurers and Mountaineers in Western Canada* (Jasper, Alta.: Coyote Books).

28 Even cheerleading: In a clear example of how behaviors and activities that are presumably "gendered" can change over time, by the 1970s cheerleading was considered a "natural" female activity. Its original masculine roots had been completely forgotten. Laurel Davis, "A Postmodern Paradox?" in *Women, Sport, and Culture,* ed. Susan Birrell and Cheryl L. Cole (Champaign, Ill.: Human Kinetics Books, 1994), p. 150.

29 hit in the breast: Arabella Kenealy, *Feminism and Sex-Extinction* (London: T. Fisher Unwin, 1920), pp. 179, 120, and 139.

29 a-mazos: Barbara G. Walker, *The Woman's Encyclopedia of Myths and Secrets* (New York: Harper & Row, 1983), pp. 24–25.

Greek depictions do not show one-breasted Amazons. The missing breast concept, Walker says, "may have arisen from Asiatic icons of the Primal Androgyne with a male right half and female left half, echoed by a coalescence of the Amazon Goddess Artemis with her brother-consort Apollo."

29 France's 1917: Mary Leigh and Theresa Bonin, "The Pioneering Role of Madam Alice Milliat and the FSFI in Establishing International Track

and Field Competition for Women," *Journal of Sport History* (Spring 1977): 72–83. Cited in Costa and Guthrie, p. 125.

29 "able-bodied": Martha H. Verbrugge, *Able-Bodied Womanhood* (Oxford, England: Oxford University Press, 1988), p. 196.

31 "Rough and vicious": Senda Berenson, "The Significance of Basketball for Women," in *Line Basket Ball or Basket Ball for Women 1901,* ed. Senda Berenson (New York: American Sporting, 1901), pp. 20–27. Cited in Joan S. Hult, "The Story of Women's Athletics: Manipulating a Dream 1890–1985," in Costa and Guthrie, p. 87.

31 "an almost monopolistic": Hult, in Costa and Guthrie, p. 87.

32 This philosophy of "modified" sport marginalized female athletics, but as Messner points out, "it also ensured that, for the time being, the image of the female athlete would not become a major threat to . . . male athleticism, virility, strength and power," and they were able to continue. Despite its limits, then, the first wave of athletic feminism challenged sport as an uncontested arena of male dominance.

32 H. Lefkowitz-Horowitz, "Before Title IX." Paper presented at Stanford Humanities Center Sport and Culture meetings, April 1986.

32 Lou Henry Hoover: Hult, p. 90.

32 National Amateur Athletic Federation: Ibid.

32 "recreational" model: Ibid.

34 "When I was young": Margaret Carlson, "Why It Was More Than a Game," *Time,* July 19, 1999, p. 64.

34 "By developing": Ann Crittendon Scott, "Closing the Muscle Gap," *Ms.,* September 1973, p. 89.

36 The document stated: Reported in N. N. Gauthier, "Guidelines for Exercise During Pregnancy: Too Little or Too Much?" *Physician and Sportsmedicine* 14, no. 4 (1986): 162–69.

37 preventing health problems: L. A. Wolfe et al., "Aerobic Exercise in Pregnancy: An Update," *Canadian Journal of Applied Physiology* 18 (1993): 119–47.

37 "the unprecedented obviousness": Elizabeth Arveda Kissling, "When Being Female Isn't Feminine: Uta Pippig and the Menstrual Communication Taboo in Sports Journalism," *Sociology of Sport Journal* 16 (1999): 79–91.

38 "reading closely": Ibid., p. 84.

38 "Uta Pippig was sick": J. Hodges, "Tannui, Pippig Celebrate the 100th," *Los Angeles Times,* April 16, 1996, p. C1. Cited in Kissling, p. 85.

38 "There is no delicate": Dan Shaughnessy, "Passing into History," *Boston Herald,* April 16, 1996, pp. 41, 46. Cited in Kissling, p. 85.

39 "Pippig's victory": Ibid., p. 88.

Chapter 2

43 That was a body: *Newsweek,* July 19, 1999.

46 kept us hopping: See Colette Dowling and Patricia Fahey, "The Quest for the Quality Orgasm," *Esquire,* June 1966.

46 The originator: It wasn't only male psychoanalysts who fanned the flames of female sexual insecurity. Marie Bonaparte was a vaginal-orgasm-pushing protégée of Freud's who offered women maddeningly elusive methods of getting the goods. Essentially the idea was that you had to turn yourself inside out if you wanted to have any fun in bed. The famed psychoanalyst Helene Deutsch, in her classic *The Psychology of Women,* offered the technique of using a pencil eraser to "trace" the nerve endings from the clitoris to the vagina to train it into responding maturely—a kind of shortcut, as it were, to the orgasm of true womanhood.

47 "[T]he clitoris must give up": Sigmund Freud, *New Introductory Lectures on Psycho-Analysis* (London: Hogarth Press, 1946), pp. 151–52.

47 "women's . . . physiological": William H. Masters and Virginia E. Johnson, *Human Sexual Inadequacy* (Boston: Little, Brown, 1970), p. 214. See also the earlier study by the same authors, *Human Sexual Response* (Boston: Little, Brown, 1966).

48 few significant data: Anne E. Beall, "A Social Constructionist View of Gender," in *The Psychology of Gender,* ed. Anne E. Beall and Robert J. Sternberg (New York: Guilford Press, 1993), p. 141.

49 "Overall": M. E. Johnson, G. Jones, and C. Brems, "Concurrent Validity of the MMPI-2 Feminine Gender Role (GF) and Masculine Gender Role (GM) Scales," *Journal of Personality Assessment* 1 (February 1966): 153–68.

49 40 percent: Bernice Lott, "Dual Natures or Learned Behavior," in *Making a Difference: Psychology and the Construction of Gender,* ed. Rachel T. Hare-Mustin and Jeanne Marecek (New Haven: Yale University Press, 1990), p. 73.

49 People's actual: In the past decade some mavericks began suggesting we get rid of "masculinity" and "femininity" altogether and use "gender identity" instead. Why not simply stick to the basic acceptance of maleness or femaleness that comes when a child first acknowledges his or her basic biological sex—but attach no frills to this concept, no personality traits; that is, no behaviors, no "roles," only the fact of one's sex, and the rest is up for grabs?

50 strength as "a feeling of dominion": Friedrich Nietzsche, *Will to Power.*

50 "project a physical presence": David Whitson, "Sport in the Social Construction of Masculinity," in *Men, Sports and the Gender Order,* ed. Michael A. Messner and Donald F. Sabo (Champaign, Ill.: Human Kinetics Books, 1990), p. 23.

51 "emphasized femininity": *How Schools Shortchange Girls,* a study of major findings on girls and education commissioned by the AAUW Educational Foundation and researched by the Wellesley College Center for Research on Women (New York: Marlowe and Company, 1992); Orenstein, 1994; Pipher, 1994.

51 power and force: Tonya Toole and Judith C. Kretzschmar, "Gender Differences in Motor Performance in Early Childhood and Later Adulthood," *Women in Sport and Physical Activity Journal* 2, no. 1 (Spring 1993): 43.

52 "Parents are not": Bernice Lott and Diane Maluso cited the study in their chapter "The Social Learning of Gender" in the influential 1993 text edited by Beall and Sternberg, *The Psychology of Gender* (p. 109), although the study itself was published in 1978. ("The Influence of Sex of Child on Parental Reactions to Toddlers and Children," *Child Development* 49: 459.)

52 "One's sense": Young, pp. 140–42.

52 *I, I can,* and *I cannot:* Ibid., pp. 146–48.

52 Children begin using: B. E. Hort, M. D. Leinbach, and B. I. Fagot, "Is There Coherence Among the Cognitive Components of Gender Acquisition?" *Sex Roles* 24 (1991): 195–207.

53 cross-sex activities: Ibid.

53 By age four: K. R. Bailey, *The Girls Are the Ones with the Pointy Nails* (London, Ont.: Althouse Press, 1993).

53 shrink girls' physical expectations: Margaret Carlisle Duncan, President's Council on Physical Fitness and Sports Report, Section III: Sociological Dimensions, p. 2.

53 Seventy percent: Jean Zimmermann and Gil Reavil, *Raising Our Athletic Daughters* (New York: Doubleday, 1999), p. 46.

53 "Stereotype threat": C. M. Steele, "A Threat in the Air: How Stereotypes Shape Intellectual Identity and Performance," *American Psychologist* 52 (1997): 613–29. Steele's work was cited by Judith Rich Harris in *The Nurture Assumption* (New York: Free Press, 1998), p. 251.

54 specific . . . repertoire: Sandra Lee Bartky, "Foucault, Femininity and the Modernization of Patriarchal Power," in *Feminism and Foucault: Reflec-*

tions on Resistance, ed. I. Diamond and L. Quinby (Boston: Northeastern University Press, 1988), p. 64.

54 Preschool boys: J. Kahle, "Why Girls Don't Know," in *What Research Says to the Science Teacher—The Process of Knowing,* ed. Rower (Washington, D.C.: National Science Teachers Association, 1990), pp. 655–57.

54 A study of the playground: The Melpomene Institute, a research and educational association based in St. Paul, conducted the study, reported by Mary Duffy in "Making Workouts for the Strengths of Girls," *The New York Times,* June 13, 1999, p. A21.

54 In one study: Studies of toddlers reported in Zimmermann and Reavil, p. 42.

55 Even in preschool: B. I. Fagot, "Teacher and Peer Reactions to Boys' and Girls' Play Styles," *Sex Roles* 11: 691–702.

55 Preschool girls: Ibid.

55 Girls must be encouraged: *How Schools Shortchange Girls,* AAUW Educational Foundation and Wellesley College Center for Research on Women, p. 32.

55 The teachers' perceptions: J. Hay and P. Donnelly, "Sorting Out the Boys from the Girls: Teacher and Student Perceptions of Student Physical Ability," *Avante* 2 (1996): 36, 52.

55 The teachers she interviewed: Sheila Scraton, *Shaping Up to Womanhood: Gender and Girls' Physical Education* (Buckingham/Philadelphia: Open University Press, 1992). Scraton's central ideas were discussed in a review of her book, which appeared in *Women in Sport and Physical Activity Journal* 3, no. 2 (Fall 1994): 86.

56 Parents as well as teachers: H. Lytton and D. M. Romney, "Parents' Differential Socialization of Boys and Girls: A Meta-Analysis," *Psychological Bulletin* 109 (1991): 267–96.

56 sense of entitlement: S. L. Meyer, C. M. Murphy, M. Cascardi, and B. Birns, "Gender and Relationships: Beyond the Peer Group," *American Psychologist* 46 (1991): 537.

56 "inhibited intentionality'": Iris Young, *Throwing Like a Girl,* p. 355.

56 "Constrictive clothing": Jackie Hudson, "It's Mostly a Matter of Metric," in *Women and Sport,* ed. D. Margaret Costa and Sharon R. Guthrie (Champaign, Ill: Human Kinetics Books, 1994), p. 154.

57 only half: Lyn Phillips, *The Girls Report: What We Know and Need to Know About Growing Up Female* (New York: National Council for Research on Women, 1998), p. 18.

By comparison, 74 percent of the boys were into vigorous use of their bodies.

57 "disciplinary practices": Cited in Bartky.

57 Wex found them: Marianne Wex, *Let's Take Back Our Space: "Female" and "Male" Body Language as a Result of Patriarchal Structures* (Berlin: Frauenliteraturverlag Hermine Fees, 1979). Wex's work is discussed in Sandra Lee Bartky, "Foucault, Femininity and the Modernization of Patriarchal Power," in *Revealing French Feminism: Critical Essays on Difference, Agency and Culture,* ed. Nancy Fraser and Sandra Lee Bartky (Indiana University Press, 1992), p. 67.

58 "If she has subjected": Ibid. In a footnote Bartky quotes from *Femininity,* in which Susan Brownmiller says that women's "smaller steps and tentative, insecure tread" are seen as sexual, "but the overall hobbling effect" suggests "the restraining leg irons and ankle chains endured by captive animals, prisoners and slaves." (New York: Simon & Schuster, 1984, p. 184.)

58 Victorian females: David Whitson, "The Embodiment of Gender: Discipline, Domination and Empowerment," in *Women, Sport and Culture,* ed. Susan Birrell and Cheryl L. Cole (Champaign, Ill.: Human Kinetics Books, 1994), p. 356.

58 "Physical sport and activity": "Physical Activity and Sport in the Lives of Girls," President's Council on Physical Fitness and Sports Report, Overview of the Report, p. 13. Summary and full report can be accessed on-line or downloaded from http://www.coled.umn.edu/KLS/crgws/.

59 "Instead of": Howard Gardner, *Multiple Intelligences* (New York: Basic Books, 1993), p. 169.

Gardner theorizes that there are seven intelligences and grants that more could be identified in the future. Besides what he calls body-kinesthetic intelligence, he names musical intelligence, logical-mathematical intelligence, linguistic intelligence, spatial intelligence, interpersonal intelligence, and intrapersonal intelligence.

Gardner developed his theory of multiple intelligences at Harvard Graduate School of Education, when he was researching ways to assess the scientific knowledge concerning human potential and its realization.

60 Or, like a brilliant: Malcolm Gladwell, "The Physical Genius," *The New Yorker,* August 2, 1999, p. 57.

60 "You don't get born": Robin Finn, "Hingis and Venus Williams Do Not Bend to Wind," *The New York Times,* September 8, 1999, p. D1.

63 "degrees of freedom": Nikolai A. Bernstein was among the first to understand that both physical and neural activity are involved in motor move-

ment. He and the German scientist Erich von Holst published a number of seminal papers in the 1930s and 1940s that have had a significant impact on motor control theorizing today. But many scientists were mainly ignorant of the contributions of Bernstein and von Holst until translations of their work appeared in English in the late 1960s and 1970s.

63 That was Hillary's: Hillary threw this way with her *dominant* arm, which indicates serious lack of practice.

64 Videotapes were made: Kathleen Williams et al., "Environmental Versus Biological Influences on Gender Differences in the Overarm Throw for Force," *Women in Sport and Physical Activity Journal* 5, no. 2 (Fall 1996): 42.

64 In the academic field of sports studies that has emerged in colleges across the country in the last decade, sport is now regarded by social scientists as a lens on human behavior. It has become a rich, multidisciplinary field, with marketing professors investigating it as a growth industry, psychologists and gender scholars exploring it as a microcosm for the treatment of men and women in the larger society, and feminists considering it as a potential agent for social change. "Sport is such a wonderful empirical site to take on a lot of ideas," said Michael Messner, former president of the American Society for the Sociology of Sport. "It has become a place for a lot of our most sophisticated thinking."

66 Two social scientists: The kids were drawn from a school in southeastern Maine and ranged in age from four to fourteen.

67 First, the researchers: S. A. Butterfield and E. M. Loovis, "Influence of Age, Sex, Balance, and Sport Participation on Development of Throwing by Children in Grades K–8," *Perceptual Motor Skills* 76, no. 2 (April 1993): 459–64.

The study was produced by the Department of Health, Physical Education, Recreation and Dance, at the College of Education of Cleveland State University.

67 "mature catching": E. M. Loovis and S. A. Butterfield, "Influence of Age, Sex, Balance, and Sport Participation on Development of Catching by Children in Grades K–8," *Perceptual Motor Skills* 77, no. 3, part 2 (December 1993): 1267–73.

68 Kicking was: S. A. Butterfield and E. M. Loovis, "Influence of Age, Sex, Balance, and Sport Participation in Development of Kicking by Children in Grades K–8," *Perceptual Motor Skills* 79, no. 1 (August 1994): 691–97.

This study was sponsored by the Division of Health, Physical Education and Recreation, University of Maine, Orono.

68 Last but not least: E. M. Loovis and S. A. Butterfield, "Influence of Age, Sex, Balance and Sport Participation on Development of Sidearm Striking by Children in Grades K–8," *Perceptual Motor Skills* 81, no. 2 (October 1995): 595–600.

69 "Muscle maturation": J. P. Lin, J. K. Brown, and E. G. Walsh, "Physiological Maturation of Muscles in Childhood," *Lancet,* June 4, 1994, pp. 1386–89.

69 An inch-for-inch: Jackie Hudson, "It's Mostly a Matter of Metric," in Costa and Guthrie, p. 149.

70 Do girls: Research that will lead to better understanding of muscular effects on motor development is under way. A 1996 study, which supports the *Lancet* observations, found that the speed of alternating movements at the ankle and wrist joints doubles between ages three and eleven. An earlier study showed a parallel increase in the speed of calf muscles over the first ten years of life.

70 "The sum of the scores": Gladwell, p. 57.

72 "Girls generally": Tonya Toole and Judith C. Kretzschmar, "Gender Differences in Motor Performance in Early Childhood and Later Adulthood," *Women in Sport and Physical Activity Journal* 2, no. 1 (Spring 1993): 5.

72 Latia Robinson: "Mini Driver," *People,* June 8, 1998, p. 96.

73 The brain: Tim Gallwey, *Inner Tennis* (New York: Random House, 1976), as quoted in *Multiple Intelligences.*

74 major caveats: Toole and Kretzschmar, p. 51.

75 77 percent: Ibid., p. 67.

76 In a survey: Eccles and Harold, 1991. The survey included 875 elementary school children.

77 virtually identical: Michael Chia, Neil Armstrong, and David Childs, "The Assessment of Children's Anaerobic Performance Using Modifications of the Wingate Anaerobic Test," *Pediatric Exercise Science* 9, no. 1 (February 1997): 80.

   The study was performed with the Monark cycle ergometer. Pedal revolutions were measured with a voltage generator attached to the flywheel. The main contribution of this study, which was performed at the Children's Health and Exercise Research Centre, School of Education, University of Exeter, England, was establishing that more accurate data for children is arrived at when accounting for flywheel inertia and internal resistance of the ergometer.

77 better self-esteem: Constance Marie Weber, "It's Not Enough to Be Smart: Distinctions Among Female High School Peer Groups As They

Narrate Their Gender Identity Construction in the Context of Extracurricular Activities" (dissertation, State University of New York, Buffalo, 1997, Dissertation Abstracts Index, vol. 07A), p. 288.

77 "I discovered": Melissa Joulwan, "The River Wild," *Go, Girl!* May 1998, http://www.gogirlmag.com/profile.htm.

77 A 1994 study: N. Fejgin, "Participation in High School Competitive Sports: A Subversion of School Mission or Contribution to Academic Goals?" *Sociology of Sport Journal* 11 (1994): 211–30.

77 Girls in sports: *Gender Gaps* (Washington, D.C.: American Association of University Women Educational Foundation, 1999), p. 76.

77 lower rates of both sexual activity and pregnancy: Sabo, Farrell, Melnick, and Barnes, 1996.

78 jeopardize their immune systems: M. M. Kramer and C. L. Wells, "Does Physical Activity Reduce Risk of Estrogen-Dependent Cancers in Women?" *Medicine and Science in Sports and Exercise* 28 (1996): 322–34.

78 Chronic diseases: J. P. Depres, C. Bouchard, and R. M. Malina, "Physical Activity and Coronary Heart Disease Risk Factors During Childhood and Adolescence," *Exercise and Sport Sciences Reviews* 18 (1990): 243–61.

78 Children who: D. P. Williams et al., "Body Fatness and Risk for Elevated Blood Pressure, Total Cholesterol and Serum Lipoprotein Ratios in Children and Adolescents," *American Journal of Public Health* 82 (1992): 358–63.

79 that require the presence of estrogen: Barbara B. Sherwin, "The Impact of Different Doses of Estrogen and Progestin on Mood and Sexual Behavior in Postmenopausal Women," *Journal of Clinical Endocrinology and Metabolism* 72, no. 2 (1991): 336.

The statement about the interaction of estrogen with brain chemicals like serotonin is also based on a personal interview with Barbara Sherwin.

79 *decline steadily*: Message from Donna E. Shalala, "Physical Activity and Sport in the Lives of Girls," President's Council on Physical Fitness and Sports Report (Spring 1997).

This report was the first time an interdisciplinary approach was used in a government document to examine the impact of sport and physical activity in the lives of girls.

The decrease in strength and endurance is most striking when girls enter puberty. The endurance decline reverses with aerobic training. Anaerobic power—the capacity to perform strenuous activity in short bursts of time (for example, the ability to perform a vertical jump)—increases through early childhood, then *decreases* in adolescence and young adulthood. But anaerobic power, too, improves with training. Studies of children between ten and thirteen have shown they are able to improve anaerobic power up to 20 percent through systematic exercise. Interestingly, endurance performance—assessed in a timed-mile run—improves by about 15 percent in spite of a 20 percent decrease in aerobic power, probably because of an improvement in movement economy.

80 "In order for bones": Kimm and Kwiterovich, 1995, cited in Bunker and Freedman.

80 The effect: Mary Jane De Souza, Joan Arles Arce, John C. Nulzen, Jacqueline L. Puhl, "Exercise and Bone Health Across the Life Span," in *Women and Health,* p. 217.

80 Those who reach: Ibid., p. 215. The authors cite C. H. Chestnut, "Is Osteoporosis a Pediatric Disease? Peak Bone Mass Attainment in the Adolescent Female," *Public Health Reports* 104 (Suppl.): 50–54.

80 "These findings": De Souza et al., "Exercise and Bone Health Across the Life Span"; Costa and Guthrie, p. 215.

81 "ideal time": Carol Krucoff, "You're Never Too Young for Strength Training," *The Washington Post,* June 22, 1999, p. 19.

81 at greater risk: The American Orthopedic Society for Sports Medicine, in Rosemont, Illinois, reports that each year ten thousand female college athletes sustain debilitating knee injuries, as do twenty thousand female high school athletes.

81 dramatic changes: H. Van Praag et al., "Running Enhances Neurogenesis, Learning, and Long-Term Potentiation in Mice," *Proceedings of the National Academy of Sciences USA* 96, no. 23 (November 9, 1999).

H. Van Praag et al., "Running Increases Cell Proliferation and Neurogenesis in the Adult Mouse Dentate Gyrus," *Natural Neuroscience* 2, no. 3 (March 1999): 266–70.

81 A 1997 "meta-analysis": Jennifer L. Etnier et al., "The Influence of Physical Fitness and Exercise upon Cognitive Functioning: A Meta-Analysis," *Journal of Sport and Exercise Psychology* 19 (1997): 249–77.

81 Jean Piaget: J. Piaget, *The Origins of Intelligence in Children* (New York: New York University Press, 1936).

82 higher grades: Research Report, Section III, "Physical Activity and Sport in the Lives of Girls," President's Council on Physical Fitness and Sports Report (Spring 1997).

83 They want to be *big*: Stephen S. Hall, "The Bully in the Mirror," *The New York Times Magazine,* August 22, 1999, p. 31.

83 50 percent: The Melpomene Institute, *The Bodywise Woman.*

83 It's hard for parents to conceive: Lott, in Hare-Mustin and Marecek.

Chapter 3

86 Recent studies: The study on girls was done by Jaffee and Manzer, 1992. The studies on adolescents were done by Jaffee and Ricker, 1993, and Jaffee and Wu, 1996.

86 "It appears to be": Diane Wiese-Bjornstal, Research Report, "Physical Activity and Sport in the Lives of Girls," Section II: Psychological Dimensions, President's Council on Physical Fitness and Sports Report.

86 "Better perceptions": These findings aren't the same for all cultures. The Women's Sports Foundation Report: Minorities in Sport found that Hispanic, Caucasian, and African American high school females who engage in athletics perceive themselves as more popular than their nonathletic counterparts.

86 *expectations*: In contrast to a 1970s and 1980s emphasis on "need to achieve."

86 "That is": Diane L. Gill, "Psychological Perspectives on Women in Sport and Exercise," in *Women and Sport,* ed. D. Margaret Costa and Sharon R. Guthrie (Champaign, Ill.: Human Kinetics Books, 1994), p. 264.

86 Boys as young as four: C. Rees and F. Andres, "Strength Differences in Young Children: Real or Imagined? Implications for the Physical Education Teacher," *Motor Skills: Theory into Practice* 5 (1981): 117–21.

86 boys had a higher: B. Ulrich, "Perceptions of Physical Competence, Motor Competence, and Participation in Organized Sport: Their Interrelationships in Young Children," *Research Quarterly for Exercise and Sport* 58 (1987): 57–67.

86 Girls predicted lower: A. Lee et al., "Success Estimations and Performance in Children as Influenced by Age, Gender, and Task," *Sex Roles* 18 (1988): 719–26.

86 "Indeed, this gender influence": Diane L. Gill, "Psychological Perspectives in Women in Sport and Excercise," in Costa and Guthrie, p. 265.

87 major increase in testosterone: C. Ankarberg and E. Norjavaara, "Diurnal Rhythm of Testosterone Secretion Before and Throughout Puberty in Healthy Girls," *Journal of Clinical Endocrinology and Metabolism* 84, no. 3 (March 1999): 975–84.

88 "If prepubescent": Susan Wilkinson et al., "Gender and Fitness Standards," *Women in Sport and Physical Activity Journal* 5, no. 1 (Spring 1996): 17.

89 "Many parents": J. R. Thoms and K. T. Thomas, "Development of Gender Differences in Physical Activity," *Quest* 40, no. 3 (1988): 219–29.

89 "perceived cause": J. S. Eccles and R. D. Harrold, "Gender Differences in Sport Involvement: Applying the Eccles' Expectancy-Value Model," *Journal of Applied Sport Psychology* 3 (1991): 7–35.

89 lack of ability: Ibid. Caucasian females, Hispanic athletes, and Navajo athletes attribute failure to low ability. Caucasian males attribute it to low effort; they just didn't try hard enough.

90 In younger girls: Studies of nine- to twelve-year-olds and twelve- to seventeen-year-olds were sponsored by the Melpomene Institute and cited in Wiese-Bjornstal.

91 Girls who display: Hasbrook, p. 19.

91 "Our original": Melissa A. Landers and Gary Alan Fine, "Learning Life's Lessons in Tee Ball: The Reinforcement of Gender and Status in Kindergarten Sport," *Sociology of Sport Journal* 13 (1996): 87–93.

91 "The coaches' views ": Ibid., p. 90.

92 "As early": Michael Oriard, *The End of Autumn* (Garden City, N.Y.: Doubleday, 1982), pp. 18–19.

93 "Tonya, you": "Georgia Schoolgirl Makes the Points," *The New York Times*, November 1, 1998, sec. 8, p. 6.

93 Tawana Hammond: "National Federation of State High School Associations 1989–1990 Handbook" (Kansas City, Mo., 1989), p. 71.

94 "A female playing": Frank Huges, "Female Football Player Files Suit on Injury," *The Washington Post*, October 29, 1992, p. D3. Nelson reports this in *The Stronger Women Get*, p. 71.

94 21 percent: Mariah Burton Nelson, *The Stronger Women Get, the More Men Love Football* (New York: Avon Books, 1994), p. 78.

94 The average life: According to the National Athletic Trainers Association, 37 percent of U.S. high school football players had been injured during the previous year badly enough to be sidelined for at least the rest of the day. And each year about eight high school football players die from football-related injuries. These figures reported by Judy Oppenheimer in *Dreams of Glory: A Mother's Season with Her Son's High School Football Team* (New York: Summit Books, 1991), p. 67.

94 "teaching them": Harvey Araton, "Soccer Moms Who Play Set Example for Children," *The New York Times*, May 23, 1999, sec. 8, p. 13.

96 "It wouldn't be proper": "Such arguments reveal more about the fevered imaginations of those who invoked them than any objective reality," comment Zimmermann and Reavil, who quote Dr. Hale in *Raising Our Athletic Daughters* (New York: Doubleday, 1999), p. 82.

96 "This issue": Ibid., p. 82.

 The attorney who defended the girls was Jean Weis. She won her case, and on July 12, 1974, the national organization of Little League Baseball officially abandoned its boys-only policy. It promptly set up a diversionary tactic by organizing Little League Softball, "to provide young girls with the same opportunity to participate in organized ball as their male counterparts in Little League Baseball."

96 "The sooner little boys": Mariah Burton Nelson, "Introduction," in *Nike Is a Goddess*, ed. Lissa Smith (Boston: Atlantic Monthly Press, 1998), p. xv.

97 The boys resisted: Jerry Kirshenbaum, "Scorecard," *Sports Illustrated*, July 1993, p. 10. The girls' team was the Middleburg Diamond Football Club.

97 "just trying to skate around": Becky Beal, "Skateboarding: Alternative Masculinity and Its Effects on Gender Relationships." Paper presented at the North American Society for the Sociology of Sport Conference (Toledo, Ohio, November 4–7, 1992).

98 "We were to climb": Kevin McMurray, "Climbing a Mountain Can Prove Family Fun," *The New York Times,* July 5, 1998, sec. 8, p. 8.

101 "Are you sure": David Halberstam, "Ice Breakers," *Condé Nast Sports for Women,* February 1998, p. 91.

102 "Coaches who haven't": Ibid.

103 "Don't set": Araton.

103 It's extraordinary: Ibid. More extraordinary, even, than the percentage of American girls playing soccer is the heartening close of this male sportswriter's column: "In the endgame, a more important trophy is the son who grows up not thinking he's the sun, and that women are in orbit around him."

103 "Junior may not": Ibid.

103 "There is still": Anna Seaton Huntington, "All Sugar and Competitive Spice," *The New York Times,* May 17, 1998, sec. 8, p. 11.

107 "We want them": Marie C. Franklin, "Girls Say Outward Bound Helps Them Feel Strong and Able," *The Boston Sunday Globe,* July 31, 1994.

107 Elizabeth McLeod told me: Personal interview.

108 "In my group": Elizabeth McLeod in a paper, "Connecting with Courage: Learning About Self Through Relationships with Others," for a course called Rethinking Adolescence, December 1995, at Harvard University.

108 "When you get out": Hang Lam, "Project Courage Pioneers Speak Their Minds by Telling All Their Hearts," *At the Center,* Newsletter of the Bay Area Girls Center, April 1998.

109 "We know": Zimmermann and Reavil, p. 69.

110 "Anybody": Ibid., p. 121.

110 "These days": Ibid., p. 52.

111 "about 20 boys and girls": Anne Driscoll, "Giving Girls a Sporting Chance," *The Boston Globe,* October 24, 1999, p. 18.

111 A survey: Miller Lite Report, 1985.

112 "They are more confident": Ibid.

Chapter 4

113 "Precisely what menstruation is": Discussion of Victorian medicine is drawn from Joan Jacobs Brumberg, *The Body Project* (New York: Random House, 1997), pp. 7–11. Brumberg cites Edward Clark, *Sex in Education; Or, A Fair Chance for Girls* (New York, 1873), and Carol Smith Rosenberg and Charles Rosenberg, "The Female Animal: Medical and Biological Views of Woman and Her Role in Nineteenth-Century America," *Journal of American History* 60 (September 1973): 332–56.

114 Cloves, pickles: Joan Jacobs Brumberg, "Chlorotic Girls, 1870–1920: A Historical Perspective on Female Adolescence," *Child Development* 53 (1982): 1468–77.

114 girls weren't given much: A study of high school girls in Boston in 1895 found 60 percent to be ignorant when their first periods arrived. Cited by Brumberg in *The Body Project,* p. 15.

115 Sexy dresser: Monique P. Yazigi, "A Sweet-16-Going-on-25 Party," *The New York Times,* February 7, 1999, sec. 9, p. 1.

117 "The ego is": Sigmund Freud, "The Ego and the Id," *Standard Edition of the Complete Psychological Works of Sigmund Freud,* vol. 19 (Oxford: Hogarth Press), pp. 13–66.

117 Inwardly they may shrink: Elizabeth Debold et al., *The Mother Daughter Revolution* (Reading, Mass.: Addison-Wesley, 1993), p. 241.

117 "varies with the ideas": Jacques Lacan, "Some Reflections on the Ego," *International Journal of Psychoanalysis* 34 (as quoted in Elizabeth Grosz, *Space, Time, and Perversion* [London: Routledge,1995], p. 86).

118 A publicist I know: Personal interview.

120 "it *always* denotes": Alexander Lowen, M.D., *The Betrayal of the Body* (London: Collier Books, 1967), p. 72.

122 Up to 25 percent: Jane E. Brody, "Girls and Puberty: The Crisis Years," *The New York Times,* November 4, 1997, p. F9.

122 according to a Seattle: Ibid.

123 before adolescence: Physical abuse of the boys in the Commonwealth survey, though far less prevalent than of girls, was not uncommon: 12 percent of high school boys and 8 percent of those in fifth through eighth grades had experienced abuse.

124 "Although these rates": Tamar Lewin, "Sexual Abuse Tied to 1 in 4 Girls in Teens," *The New York Times,* October 1, 1997, p. A24.

125 "[T]here is that knee": Simone de Beauvoir, *The Second Sex* (New York: Vintage, 1989), p. 319.

126 "lose their vitality": Carol Gilligan and Lyn Mikel Brown, *Meeting at the Crossroads* (New York: Ballantine, 1992), p. 2.

126 sexual abuse of girls: *How Schools Shortchange Girls* (New York: Marlowe and Company, 1992), p. 136, based on a study reported in J. Gans and D. Blyth, *America's Adolescents: How Healthy Are They?* (Chicago: American Medical Association, 1990), p. 20.

126 "Sexual harassment occurs": *How Schools Shortchange Girls,* p. 129.
 Studying fifteen- to nineteen-year-olds from various backgrounds (including homeless girls and college girls), the Oregon Research Institute found that across all samples, 44.4 percent had been forced into some form of sexual activity against their will and that these experiences were consistently related to risky sexual behavior.

127 Seventy percent of girls: *Hostile Hallways,* the AAUW report on sexual harassment in America's schools, 1993, pp. 9–11.

127 "It made me confused": Ibid., p. 10.
 One in four harassed girls says that a school employee was the perpetrator.

127 Five times: AAUW News Release, "National Scientific Survey Reveals Sexual Harassment Rampant in Schools," AAUW Educational Foundation, June 2, 1993.

127 "There are some": Maria Alvarez, "Victims in Quiet Agony," *New York Post,* November 7, 1999, sec. RR, p. 5.

128 "These cases": Ibid.

129 "repeatedly attempted": Linda Greenhouse, "Sex Harassment in Class Is Ruled Schools' Liability," *The New York Times,* May 25, 1999, p. A1.

129 "teach little Johnny": Ibid.

130 "It took": Cynthia Gorney, "Teaching Johnny the Appropriate Way to Flirt," *The New York Times Magazine,* June 13, 1999, p. 47.

130 "What infuriated": Ibid. In 1991 Katy Lyle (the graffiti victim from Duluth, Minnesota) won a $15,000 settlement from her high school. The following year Tawnya Brawdy won $20,000 in an out-of-court settle-

ment because Kenilworth Junior High School, in Petaluma, California, hadn't stopped boys who "mooed" at her and jeered about her breast size.

131 "In teaching children": Katie Roiphe, *The Morning After* (New York: Little, Brown, 1993), p. 163.

131 "The AAUW is at it again": John Leo, "Gender Wars Redux," *U.S. News & World Report,* February 22, 1999.

132 "intimidation is nonsexual": Christina Hoff Sommers, "The Preteen Sexual Harasser," *The New York Times,* January 9, 1999, p. A15 (op-ed).

133 "boys insulting": Peggy Orenstein, *SchoolGirls* (New York: Anchor Books, Doubleday, 1994), p. 112.

133 "They don't see": Ibid., p. 113.

134 "We want to make": Ibid., p. 119.

134 "That happened": Ibid.

134 "when we were playing": Ibid., p. 120.

134 "Girls think that": Ibid., p. 121.

135 "They're taking it": Ibid., p. 122.

135 "The girls don't": Ibid., p. 129.

136 masturbate: Maria Laurino, "A Word the Town Did Not Want to Hear: Rape," *The New York Times,* May 9, 1999, Arts and Leisure section, p. 33. Mr. Lefkowitz's book is *Our Guys: The Glen Ridge Rape and the Secret Life of the Perfect Suburb.* Ms. Laurino, author of the *Times* essay about a film on the subject, is the sister of Bob Laurino, an assistant prosecutor who spent four years working on the case.

137 "It could have been me.": Laurino, ibid.

137 And so it could: Some studies have found that over half of middle and junior high school kids have had intercourse at least once. Daniel P. Orr, Mary L. Wilbrandt, Catherine J. Brack, Steven P. Rauch, and Gary M. Ingersoll, "Reported Sexual Behaviors and Self-Esteem Among Young Adolescents," *American Journal of Diseases of Children* 143 (1989): 86.

137 "Nothing my boy": Jill Smolowe, "Sex with a Scorecard," *Time,* April 5, 1993, p. 41.

137 "identity foreclosure": Pamela Manners and David Smart, "Moral Development and Identity Formation in High School Juniors: The Effects of Participation in Extracurricular Activities." Paper presented at April 1995 meeting of American Educational Research Association, San Francisco, California, ERIC Document ED385496.

138 Becca: Orenstein, p. 78.

138 "Much as feminists": Wardell Pomeroy, *Girls and Sex,* 3rd ed. (New York: Laurel Leaf Books, 1991).

139 "I hate my looks": Mary Pipher, *Reviving Ophelia* (New York: Ballantine, 1994), p. 55.

139 "girls are taunted": Ibid., p. 69.

140 "the attack": Ibid., p. 38.

140 mild by comparison: Personal interview. "Theresa" didn't want her name used.

140 In the 1990s: Millicent Lawton, "Sexual Harassment of Students Target of District Policies," *Education Week*, February 10, 1993, p. 1. Cited in Orenstein, p. 116.

140 "afford to ignore": One out of three girls has an unwanted sexual encounter with an adult male before the age of eighteen, and roughly a quarter of the abuse occurs before puberty, according to Judith Herman, *Father-Daughter Incest* (Cambridge, Mass.: Harvard University Press, 1981), p. 12.

141 A $762 million lawsuit: "Tennis Players Settle Lawsuit," *The New York Times*, March 27, 1999, p. D4.

   The amount awarded to the former players, Dacia Kornechuk and Kirsten Ericson, and their families was kept confidential.

142 "participated": S. L. Price, "Anson Dorrance," *Sports Illustrated*, December 7, 1998.

143 "Anson cultivates": Ibid.

143 an arbitration hearing: Steven Goiff, "Women's World Cup Roster Set," *The Washington Post*, May 18, 1999, p. D3.

144 "She was shaking": Robin Finn, "Growth in Women's Sports Stirs Harassment Issue," *The New York Times*, March 7, 1999, p. 24.

144 "He didn't want me": Ibid.

144 "I was starting to be afraid of him": Ibid.

145 "the walk of shame": Sharon Bohn Gmelch, *Gender on Campus* (New Brunswick, N.J.: Rutgers University Press, 1998), p. 202.

146 "in jokes": Deborah Johnson, "Women Who Trust Too Much: What AIDS Commercials Don't Tell You," *On the Issues* 5 (Summer 1996): 26.

146 At Cornell: "Sexist E-Mail Circulates at Cornell," *Monthly Forum on Women in Higher Education* 3 (December 1995): 8.

146 "If my penis": A. Ayres Boswell and Jean Spade, "Fraternities and Rape on Campus," *Gender and Society* 3 (December 1989): 457–73.

147 At three midwestern: Gmelch, p. 207.

147 "Yet in a way": Kim Hubbard, Anne-Marie O'Neill, and Christina Cheakalos, "Out of Control," *People*, April 12, 1999, p. 52.

148 more "forcible sex offenses": "Massachusetts Campus Tense After Attacks on Women," *The New York Times*, November 21, 1999, p. 32.

149 "they all look crazy": Pipher, p. 59.

149 "threaten the mental": A. Rothenberger and G. Hunther, "The Role of Psychosocial Stress in Childhood for Structural and Functional Brain Development: Neurobiological Basis of Developmental Psychopathology," *Prax Kinderpsychol Kinderpsychiatr* 46, no. 9 (November 1997): 623–44.

Chapter 5

151 "One of the great": Senator Birch Bayh.

151 "no person in the United States shall": 20 U.S.C. Section 1681 of Title IX of the Education Amendment Act of 1972.

152 girls were expelled: Many high schools prohibited boys from taking home economics. Girls could not take auto mechanics. Some schools even forbade girls to serve on the safety patrol. The Gender Equity "Report Card."

152 lagged significantly: In 1971, the year before Title IX was passed, only 18 percent of women completed four or more years of college, compared with 26 percent of men. By 1994 this gap had closed and 27 percent of both men and women finished college. Similarly, in 1972 only 9 percent of medical degrees went to women. By 1994 that percentage had increased to 38.

154 By 1986: Barry D. MacPherson et al., *The Social Significance of Sport* (Champaign, Ill.: Human Kinetics Books, 1989), p. 229.

154 By 1982: Susan Durrant, "Title IX—Its Power and Its Limitations," *Journal of Physical Education, Recreation and Dance* (March 1992): 102.

156 In 1992: *Empowering Women in Sports,* The Empowering Women Series, no. 4. A Publication of the Feminist Majority Foundation, 1995.

156 the Supreme Court held: Ibid.

156 Hundreds of girls: Ibid.

157 a small group: Ellen J. Staurowsky, "Critiquing the Language of the Gender Equity Debate," *Journal of Sport and Social Issues* 22, no. 1 (February 1998): 7–26.

158 "With the court's finding": *Brown Daily Herald,* the Title IX Library, www.netspace.org/herald/library/titleix/homepage.html.

158 "with repercussions": Ibid.

158 On June 23: Mark Asher, "Brown Resolves Final Issues; University's Preliminary Plan Approved in Title IX," *The Washington Post,* June 24, 1998, p. C2.

158 "women's sports enhancement programs": *Brown Daily Herald,* the Title IX Library, www.netspace.org/herald/library/titleix/homepage.html. School officials put their own glossy spin on their catch-up actions. The editors of the *Brown Daily Herald* advised readers that if they wanted the school's "party line" on the *Cohen* case, they could get it from the Brown news bureau.

159 *female college athletes: Brown Daily Herald,* ibid. On a per athlete basis, female athletes received $4,100, $2,000, and $1,900 per student athlete in Divisions I-A, I-AA, and I-AAA, respectively, compared with the $8,000, $2,400, and $2,500 received by their male counterparts in 1997.

159 NCAA GENDER EQUITY: Cedric W. Dempsey, "NCAA Gender Equity Figures Improving," *The Washington Post,* October 26, 1999, p. D5.

159 "rigorous criteria": Jim Naughton, "Clarification of Title IX May Leave Many Colleges in Violation over Athletes," *Chronicle of Higher Education,* July 31, 1998, p. A34.

160 For many years: Durrant, p. 60.

160 "To be able": Ibid., p. 61.

162 "No matter": Coubertin, quoted by Cashmore, who cited Snyder and Spreitzer, 1983, pp. 155–56.

162 "In public competitions": E. W. Gerber et al., *The American Woman in Sport* (Reading, Mass.: Addison-Wesley, 1974), p. 137.

162 In Paris: Robert Dunn, "The Country Club: A National Expression, Where Woman Is Really Free," *The Outing Magazine* 42 (November 1905), p. 69. Country clubs, in fact, were a main vehicle for women gaining access to sports.

163 In 1904: Ibid.

163 The AOC, too, was against: *The New York Times,* July 13, 1913, part IV, p. 2.

163 this supremely antifemale: Some, at least, were beginning to sing a different tune about the female as athlete. "Her steps in politics have been infantile, in business quite subordinary. . . . But on the golf and tennis field, and as a huntswoman, she has leaped to equal place with man," one male writer reported in *The Outing Magazine.*

163 When Sweden: *The New York Times,* July 19, 1913, p. 5. Cited in Paula Welch and D. Margaret Costa, "A Century of Olympic Competition," in *Women and Sport,* ed. D. Margaret Costa and Sharon R. Guthrie (Champaign, Ill.: Human Kinetics Books, 1994), p. 125.

164 On August 25: "Swimming (Women)," Report on the American Olympic Committee Seventh Olympic Games, Antwerp, Belgium (Greenwich,

Conn.: Condé Nast Press, 1920), p. 320. Cited in Welch and Costa, in Costa and Guthrie, p. 126.

164 Another winner was: "1896–1919: Emergence," www.usatoday.com/ olympics/atlanta/olya020.

164 "Where sport": Susan K. Cahn, *Coming On Strong* (Cambridge, Mass.: Harvard University Press, 1994), p. 114.

165 "are essentially masculine": Frederick Rand Rogers, "Physical Education Programs for Girls," May 1928, p. 354. Cited in Cahn, p. 114.

165 "This Paris meet": Mary Henson Leigh, "The Evolution of Women's Participation in the Summer Olympic Games, 1900–1948" (Ph.D. dissertation, Ohio State University, 1974), 249. Cited in Cahn, p. 58.

165 "It is more surprising": Press reports in the 1920s compared female athletes with chorus girls, movie stars, and beauty queens. A citywide track meet in which five thousand girls participated was described by the *Baltimore Sun* as "a girly show if ever there was one." Women's basketball players were similarly portrayed by the *Pittsburgh Courier* in the headline WASHINGTON, PA., LASSIES, FAMED FOR BEAUTY AND ABILITY, HAVE BEEN TERMED THE "ZIEGFELD FOLLIES" OF THE BASKETBALL WORLD BY ADMIRERS.

166 "The cinder track": Cited in "1920–1947: New Beginnings," www .usatoday.com/olympics/atlanta/olya021.htm.

166 "women who": Ibid.

166 the damage: The great endurance controversy had officials debating until 1964 about whether cross-country skiing was too formidable for women. That year thirty-five women from twelve nations entered the 10-kilometer cross-country event. Luge for women was also added to the Olympic program.

166 Betty Robinson: Paula Welch and D. Margaret Costa, "A Century of Olympic Competition," in Costa and Guthrie, p. 127. Robinson was from Riverdale, Illinois.

167 "animalistic": John R. Tunis, "Women and the Sport Business," *Harper's Monthly Magazine,* July 1929, p. 213.

167 "Manly women": Rogers, p. 194. Cited in Cahn, p. 114.

167 "If ever": Ibid., Cahn, p. 63.

167 "lacking": Ibid., p. 56.

168 "Play Days": Ibid., p. 66.

168 three women: "Women's Track and Field Team," Report of the United States Olympic Committee 1948 Games XIV Olympiad, London, England (Greenwich, Conn.: Walker-Rackliff, 1948).

168 THE MARVELOUS MAMA: "1948–1971: Conflicting Images," www.usatoday .com/olympics/atlanta/olya022.htm.

168 In 1952: Welch and Costa, in Costa and Guthrie, report (p. 130) that after Tuskegee set the standard for athletic programs that refined female track-and-field talent, Tennessee State's Ed Temple began attracting some of America's best black talent. Tennessee State eventually supplanted Tuskegee as the prime producer of track-and-field Olympians. Among Temple's athletes were such talented women as Wilma Rudolph and Wyomia Tyus.

169 In 1964: Ibid., p. 129.

170 "I knew it might": "The Battle of the Sexes," *Newsweek*, September 21, 1998.

170 How good: R. S. Wood, "Sex Differences in Sports," *The New York Times Magazine*, May 18, 1980, p. 33.

170 chauvinism: "Come the Revolution: Joining the Game at Last, Women Are Transforming American Athletics," *Time*, June 26, 1978, quotes pp. 54 and 59.

171 "Even as I": *Running Tide* was coauthored by Sally Baker and published in 1987.

171 For American women: Discussion of women's Olympic events in the 1980s from Welch and Costa, in Costa and Guthie, p. 132.

173 "Even after": "Walk, Ladies, Don't Run," *St. Louis Post-Dispatch*, January 15, 2000, p. 30.

173 In February of 2000: Vicki Michaelis, "U.S. Women's Boycott Nets Respect for Team," *The Denver Post*, February 6, 2000, p. C3.

173 "sex tests": Deborah Larned, "The Femininity Test," *WomenSports*, July 1976, p. 10.

174 no vaginal opening: A. Ljungqvist and J. L. Simpson, "Medical Examination for Health of All Athletes Replacing the Need for Gender Verification in Sports; The International Amateur Athletic Federation Plan; Commentary," *Journal of the American Medical Association* (February 12, 1992): 267, 850+ (Lexis/Nexis transcript).

174 advanced scientific standard: A. Serrat et al., "Gender Verification in Sports by PCR Amplification of SRY and DYZ1 Y Chromosome Specific Sequences: Presence of DYZ1 Repeat in Female Athletes," *British Journal of Sports Medicine* 30, no. 4 (December 1996): 310–12.

175 "one chromosome too many": Larned, p. 11. Kłobukowska's particular chromosome abnormality occurs in six women in a thousand.

175 "It is a dirty": "Records of Polish Girl Sprinter Who Flunked Sex Test Barred," *The New York Times*, February 26, 1968, p. 50.

175 "errors in interpretation": J. L. Simpson et al., "Gender Verification in Competitive Sports," *Sports Medicine* 16, no. 5 (November 16, 1993): 305–15.

175 These women: Ibid.

175 "genetic anomalies": J. Rodda, "Sex-Test Row Hits Olympics," *The Guardian,* January 29, 1992, p. 13 (Lexis/Nexis transcript).

176 "We have reached": "IOC Will Not Give In to Sex Test Protests," Agence France Presse, January 28, 1992 (Lexis/Nexis transcript).

176 "After the test": G. Kolata, "Ideas and Trends: Who's Female? Science Can't Say," *The New York Times,* February 16, 1992, sec. 4, p. 6.

176 "I was crying": Alison Carlson, "Chromosome Count," *Ms.,* October 1988, p. 43.

177 "I could barely": Ibid., pp. 24–29.

177 "I was scared": P. Vignetti et al., " 'Sex Passport' Obligation for Female Athletes, Consideration and Criticism on 364 Subjects," *International Journal of Sports Medicine* 3 (April 17, 1996): 239–40.

177 "In fact, there is no advantage": "Gender Testing at Olympics Is Faulty," *All Things Considered,* National Public Radio, February 7, 1992.

177 "I knew": Carlson, p. 27.

177 the first woman: L. Ewing, *Calgary Herald,* January 12, 1992, p. F6.

177 "Women must": Carlson, p. 29.

179 "The old test": P. Holmes, "Olympic Chiefs Brush Off Sex Test Storm," *The Reuters Library Report,* January 29, 1992.

179 "We won't": Ibid.

179 Controversy erupted: S. Zipay, "Women Boxers Take Unfair Hit," *Newsday,* April 18, 1995, p. A54.

181 "Jammed into": Leland J. Rosenberg, D. Van Boven, and T. T. Gegax, "Up in the Air," *Newsweek,* September 1, 1997, p. 57. Cited in Sarah Banet-Weiser, "Hoop Dreams: Professional Basketball and the Politics of Race and Gender," *Journal of Sport and Social Issues* 23 (4): 413–20.

182 "Hey, Sheryl!": K. Whiteside, *WNBA: Commemorating the Birth of a League* (New York: HarperCollins, 1998), p. 3.

182 "When I'm playing": A. S. Huntington, "So I Wanna Be a Superstar. You Got a Problem with That?" *Women's Sport and Fitness,* November 21, 1996, p. 50.

183 "The champ": *GQ,* June 1998.

183 overemphasizing: Nancy Theberge and Susan Birrell, "The Sociological Study of Women in Sport," in Costa and Guthrie, p. 323.

183 "The WNBA is to the": Columnist cited by B. Wilson, the Ethical Spectacle Web site, December 1997.

185 "the good apple": Rosenberg et al., "Up in the Air."

185 "the wonder girl": Ibid.

186 "They're both pretty": Ibid.

188 Over a quarter: Susan L. Greendorfer, "Title IX Gender Equity, Backlash and Ideology," *Women in Sport and Physical Activity Journal* 7, no. 1 (Spring 1998): 87.

Chapter 6

191 Sport is: Susan L. Greendorfer, "Title IX Gender Equity, Backlash and Ideology," *Women in Sport and Physical Activity Journal* 7, no. 1 (Spring 1998): 79.

192 the goal is: The backlash against female athletes is most brutal in nations where the oppression of females is most visible in general. In Algeria, Olympic gold medalist Hassiba Boulmerka was spat upon, pelted with rocks, and threatened with death by Muslim fundamentalists, who issued an official denunciation of her for "running with naked legs in front of thousands of men." This, in spite of (or because of) the fact that Boulmerka, who runs the 1,500 meter, is the first Algerian woman world champion. Mary A. Boutilier and Lucinda San Giovanni, *The Sporting Woman* (Champaign, Ill.: Human Kinetics Books, 1983), p. 102.

193 Army Corps of Engineers: J. E. Vader, "Sex Play," *M*, February 1992, pp. 41–47.

193 In archery: Also, in bowling tournaments men and women are separated on the pretext that men require different lane conditions. All pro bowlers use the same size and weight balls, but men's lanes are conditioned with what's known as "longer" oil.

193 rules were being changed: The whole notion of "girls' rules" confines females to "a ghetto of inequality, leaving unchallenged stereotypes about women's supposed frailty," observed Michael A. Messner and Donald Sabo, editors of *Sport, Men and the Gender Order* (Champaign, Ill.: Human Kinetics Books, 1990).

193 Zhang Shan: "Quick Facts: Looking Through the Female Olympic Lens," www.feminist.org/other/olympic/fact.

193 International Shooting Federation: Margaret Murdoch tied teammate Lanny Bassham for first place in 1976. The gold medal was given to Bassham based on a tie-breaking rule. At the awards ceremony he graciously invited Murdoch up onto the winner's platform with him. Mariah Burton Nelson, *The Stronger Women Get, the More Men Love Football* (New York: Avon Books, 1994), p. 65.

194 Young boys: Kal Muller, *National Geographic*, December 1970, pp. 786–811.

194 bobbing on her line like a yo-yo: Edwin McDowell, "Travel Industry Finds Adventure Is Now Ageless," *The New York Times*, February 20, 1999, p. C1.

195 They affect: Margaret MacNeil, "Active Women, Media Representations and Ideology," in *Women, Sport and Culture*, ed. Susan Birrell and Cheryl L. Cole (Champaign, Ill.: Human Kinetics Books, 1994), p. 282.

197 perhaps the final: Ellis Cashmore, *Making Sense of Sport* (London and New York: Routledge, 1990), p. 140.

198 "the most masculine interest": Jack Pollack, "How Masculine Are You?" *Nation's Business* 38 (June 1950): 49–55.

198 "potential homosexuality": Susan K. Cahn *Coming On Strong* (Cambridge, Mass.: Harvard University Press, 1994), p. 226.

198 "slightly less": Ibid.

198 scientific validity: Miriam Lewin, "Rather Worse Than Folly?: Psychology Measures Femininity and Masculinity," part 1, *In the Shadow of the Past*, ed. Lewin (New York: Columbia University Press, 1984), pp. 155–78. Cited in Cahn, p. 339.

199 eighteen grand slam singles: "Martina and Chrissie: At the Top for a Decade," *Ms.*, May 13, 1985, p. 72.

199 "some kind of hulking": Frank Deford, "The Smartina Show, or Tennis in a Lethal Vein," *Sports Illustrated*, April 4, 1983, p. 34.

200 "chromosomic screw": "The Best of All Time," *Time*, July 16, 1984, p. 61.

200 "punch out": "Our Lady Golfers Take the Cup, but Let the British Title Go," *Literary Digest*, June 18, 1932, pp. 34–35.

200 "cold, tense": "Little Mo Grows Up," *Time*, July 14, 1952, p. 44.

200 "was almost as though": *Literary Digest*, June 18, 1932, pp. 34–35.
Losers, by the same token, were often described in feminine terms—"towheaded and fluffy helplessness," one loser was called; a "slender, little Los Angeles matron" was the moniker given another. Carolyn Babcock, who came in a mere second at the 1932 U.S. Open, showed "the smile of a beaten, somewhat bewildered little girl." (Cahn, p. 212.)

201 "It gets my goat": Babe Didrikson, "I Blow My Own Horn," p. 103.

201 the press spent less time celebrating: Cahn, p. 216. Women athletes are still labeled as nonwomen, even by other women athletes. A great storm of protest arose in 1998, when Martina Hingis described a competitor as "half a man." Homophobia in women's sports is "like the McCarthyism of the 1950s," said Christine Grant, University of Iowa athletic director. "The fear is paralyzing."

201 Natasha Dennis: Mariah Burton Nelson, p. 77.

202 "I could pick up": Laura L. Noah, "A Former Coach's Primal Scream over a Stubborn Stereotype," *The New York Times,* October 24, 1999, p. D15.

203 "grossly unfair": S. Birrell and C. Cole, "Double Fault: Renee Richards and the Construction and Naturalization of Difference," *Sociology of Sport Journal* 7 (1990): 1–21.

203 "[T]hat the floodgates": R. Richards with J. Ames, *The Second Serve* (New York: Stein and Day, 1983), p. 345.

204 In the new edition: Cited by Peter J. Dorsen in a review of the *Oxford Textbook of Sports Medicine,* in *Journal of the American Medical Association* 282, no. 23 (December 15, 1999): 2264–66. *Oxford Textbook of Sports Medicine,* ed. Mark Harries et al. (New York: Oxford University Press, 1998).

204 between 1964 and 1995: Cashmore, p. 129.

205 record of 9.92 seconds: Seoul Olympian Entries, 1988.

205 "In other words": J. L. Hudson, "Prediction of Basketball Skill Using Biomechanical Variables," *Research Quarterly for Exercise and Sport* 56 (1985): 147.

206 fifty-seven women: Seoul Olympian Entries, 1988. P. Kennedy, P. Brown, S. N. Chengalur, and R. D. Nelson, "Analysis of Male and Female Olympic Swimmers in the 100-Meter Events," *International Journal of Sport Biomechanics* 6 (1990): 187–97. Cited in Hudson, ibid.

206 "In every case": Kennedy et al., ibid., p. 56.

207 Jackie Hudson's research found": Hudson, pp. 115–21.

207 She deduced: R. C. Nelson and P. E. Martin, "Effects of Gender and Load on Vertical Jump Performance," in *Biomechanics IX-B,* ed. D. A. Winter et al. (Champaign, Ill.: Human Kinetics Books, 1985), pp. 429–33.

209 "It is a preemptive": Susan Faludi, *Backlash* (New York: Doubleday, 1991), p. xx.

209 "I had things": A personal communication to Lisa Rubarth, reported by her in "Twenty Years After Title IX: Women in Sports Media," *Journal of Physical Education, Recreation and Dance* (March 1992): 53.

209 "a sign of weakness": Ibid.

210 Four months later: Nancy Theberge and Susan Birrell, "The Sociological Study of Women in Sport," in *Women and Sport,* ed. D. Margaret Costa and Sharon R. Guthrie (Champaign, Ill.: Human Kinetics Books, 1994), p. 343.

210 amused themselves: Bella English, "Fenway Bound? Take a Hatpin," *The Boston Globe,* June 19, 1991. Symbolic mockeries of the female body must have been in that year. I attended a New Year's Eve party given by some

New York men at their country house in the Hudson Valley. At midnight they strung up an effigy of a woman in a big oak tree in their front yard while men and women stood around in the cold, in black tie, cheering.

211 "It's not a matter": Ibid. That was the year the first woman made it onto the *Monday Night Football* broadcast team. Apparently Frank was getting nervous.

211 "loathsome": Nelson, p. 88.

211 "Fuck you": Steven P. Schacht, "The Sadomasochistic Ritual of Male Rugby Players and the Social Construction of Gender Hierarchies." Paper presented at the annual meeting of the North American Society for the Sociology of Sport (Toledo, Ohio, November 5, 1992), p. 20.

These observations were made at two university-based rugby clubs Schacht observed.

211 "All of us, collectively": Nelson, p. 30.

213 "the weaker sex": Patricia A. Vertinsky, *The Externally Wounded Woman* (Urbana: University of Illinois Press, 1994), p. 2.

Indeed, she says, the "weaker sex" perception continues to affect responses to demands for equity in the provision of competitive sporting opportunities, employment practices in jobs involving physical activity and/or strength, commercial approaches to sport, fitness, and recreation, media portrayal of women exercising, at sport, and at play, as well as perceptions of female health and disease and evolving public, educational, medical, and health practices and policies.

213 Dr. Arne Ljungqvist: Christopher Clarey, "A Winner Before the Race Is Won," *The New York Times,* August 16, 1999, p. D4.

214 "The animal data": Nancy Stedman, "Estrogen May Curb Women's Muscle Pain," *The New York Times,* August 24, 1999, p. F8.

213 "Estrogen seems": Ibid.

213 "may be able": Ibid.

213 "Women may": Ibid.

215 "This is surprising": Susan Gilbert, "Weak Bones Among Men Are Linked to Estrogen," *The New York Times,* December 8, 1998, p. F6.

215 a fascinating study: T. R. Lord and J. Garrison, "Comparing Spatial Abilities of Collegiate Athletes in Different Sports," *Perceptual Motor Skills* 86, no. 3, part 1 (June 1998): 1016–18.

217 "She stayed with": Chris Ballard, "On the Blacktop, a Kid of Sweat Equity," *The New York Times,* July 16, 1999, p. E40.

217 "It's a pleasure": www.freshandtasty.com/nicola, May 24, 1998.

219 In marathon: According to Bob Duenkel, creator of the International Swimming Hall of Fame.

219 Shelley Taylor-Smith: Randy Kennedy, " 'Ordinary Girl' Until She Enters the Water," *The New York Times,* July 16, 1998, p. B2. Diana Nyad is the only athlete to have completed the swim from Bimini to Florida. Lynne Cox holds the records for swimming the straits of Bering and Magellan. The first person to swim all five Great Lakes and the first ever to cross Lake Superior (in 1988) was Vicki Keith. (Nelson, p. 57.)

219 "Once you get going": Korky Vann, *The Hartford Courant,* June 30, 1998, p. F7.

220 medical studies: *The New England Journal of Medicine.*

220 As the century turned: Earl Hodges, "Girl Breaks Line, Takes Spot on Football All-Stars," *The Times-Picayune* (New Orleans), December 9, 1999, p. ID2.

220 "The world as we knew it": Steve Lopez, "A Fullback Picks Her Gown," *Time,* November 15, 1999.

220 "This is a dream": Associated Press, "Football May Be Next Frontier for Women," *St. Louis Post-Dispatch,* December 14, 1999.

221 "These were warriors": Robert Lipsyte, *The New York Times,* February 22, 1998, sec. 8, p 1.

222 "Being a professional woman": Lena Williams, "Teamwork off the Court," *The New York Times,* August 21, 1999, p. D6.

223 "Breast-feeding": Jere Longman, "U.S. Team Redefines 'Soccer Mom,' " *The New York Times,* May 9, 1999, sec. 8, p. 1.

223 "Seeing our players": Ibid.

223 "It's tough": Ibid.

224 "They had sacrificed": Ibid.

Chapter 7

225 "If 25 percent": Katie Roiphe, *The Morning After* (New York: Little, Brown, 1994), p. 52.

226 "Obsession": Betty Friedan, *The Second Stage* (New York: Summit Books, 1981), p. 362.

226 "Considering": Roiphe, p. 45.

227 "There is power": Ibid.

228 A third: S. Riger and M. T. Gordon, *The Female Fear* (New York: Free Press, 1989).

228 under thirty-five: M. Warr, "Fear of Rape Among Urban Women," *Social Problems* 32 (1985): 239–50.

228 More than half: Riger and Gordon, *The Female Fear.*

228 "special burden": Ibid.

228 one in four: Mary P. Koss et al., *No Safe Haven* (Washington, D.C.: American Psychological Association, 1994), p. 119. The statistics were earlier reported by Koss in "The Underdetection of Rape," *Journal of Social Issues* 48 (1992): 63–75.

230 "She was a journalist": Personal interview.

230 recent national study: Rape statistics from a study by the Centers for Disease Control and Prevention and the National Institute of Justice.

231 930 women: Report to the President's Council on Physical Fitness and Sport, Doreen Greenberg of Fairleigh Dickinson University and Carole Oglesby of Temple University. Cited in McGrath et al.

231 startling "regression": Lori Stern, "Disavowing the Self in Female Adolescence," in *Women, Girls and Psychotherapy,* ed. Carol Gilligan, Annie G. Rogers, and Deborah L. Tolman (New York: Haworth Press, 1991), pp. 105–6.

   Lori Stern is a Clinical Fellow in psychology at Harvard Medical School.

231 "I hate": Deborah A. Miranda, "Silver," in *Bad Girls/Good Girls,* ed. Nan Bauer Mayer and Donna Perry (New Brunswick, N.J.: Rutgers University Press, 1996), p. 129.

231 Some people forget: Shockingly, in cities, the prevalence of the disorder is 23 percent. *In fact, the prevalence of PTSD in young people growing up in cities is greater than that among wounded combat veterans.* Rates of post-traumatic stress disorder are highest among the young—23 percent of young adults in cities. Cited in David Baldwin's trauma information, www.trauma-pages.com/pg.2.html.

232 "the Spur Posse": The "posse" was a group of popular white high school boys who competed with one another using a point system for their sexual "conquests." When, finally, girls complained, several of the Spur Posse were charged with crimes ranging from sexual molestation to rape. Some parents excused, and even defended, their sons' behavior. "Nothing my boy did was anything any red-blooded American boy wouldn't do at his age," one father insisted. Jill Smolowe, "Sex with a Scorecard," *Time,* April 5, 1993, p. 41.

232 one out of five: Statistics provided by the Corporate Alliance to End Partner Violence, an advocacy group in Bloomington, Illinois.

232 The culture of date rape: A 1998 study traced the relationship of rape to suicidal ideation and behavior in the victims. As compared to one in twenty women who hadn't been raped, *one in four rape victims had engaged in a suicidal act.* The strongest predictor of suicidal behavior was

vaginal penetration following the threat or use of physical force (as compared to penetration without the use of force and/or force without penetration). S. Stepakoff, "Effects of Sexual Victimization on Suicidal
Ideation and Behavior in U.S. College Women," *Suicide and Life Threatening Behavior* 28, no. 1 (Spring 1998): 107–26.

232 "I know young girls": Simone de Beauvoir, *The Second Sex* (New York:
Vintage, 1989), p. 335.

233 a medical symptom: Two other symptoms of trauma are "hyperarousal"
(the uncomfortable and reality-distorting state of constant readiness for
danger) and "intrusion," in which shards of memory blast through, shattering any temporary sense of safety.

234 "throwing": S. Freud, "Charcot" (1893), in *Standard Edition of the Complete Psychological Works of Sigmund Freud,* vol. 3, trans. J. Strachey
(London: Hogarth Press, 1962), p. 19.

234 "Little by little": Ibid.

234 "people of the clearest intellect": J. Breuer and S. Freud, "Studies on
Hysteria" (1893–95), in *Standard Edition,* vol. 2, trans. James Strachey
(London: Hogarth Press, 1955).

235 "at the bottom of every case": S. Freud, "The Aetiology of Hysteria"
(1896), in *Standard Edition,* vol. 2.

235 "contemporary clinical": Judith Lewis Herman, M.D., *Trauma and Recovery* (New York: Basic Books, 1992), p. 13.

235 "Hysteria was so common": Ibid., p. 14.

235 Buckling under social pressure: Ibid. The case of the famous Dora became
the swan song of the psychoanalytic theory of sexual trauma. While Freud
acknowledged that as an adolescent his patient Dora had been used as a
pawn by her father (essentially her father had offered her to his friend as a
sex toy), Freud wouldn't validate her feelings of humiliation and degrada-
tion. He thought it would be more helpful for her to acknowledge her
erotic excitement during the traumatic experiences and to talk about them.
Repressed sexuality was her problem, he thought, not abused sexuality.

236 "without ever offering": Herman, p. 14.

236 "I was at last": S. Freud, "An Autobiographical Study" (1925), in *Standard
Edition,* vol. 20, trans. J. Strachey (London: Hogarth Press, 1959), p. 34.

237 "Many soldiers": Herman, p. 51.

238 "Hysteria is": Ibid., p. 32.

238 all symptoms resembling: A. W. Burgess and L. L. Holmstrom, "Rape
Trauma Syndrome," *American Journal of Psychiatry* 131 (1974): 981–86.
Burgess and Holmstrom's study is discussed in Herman, p. 31.

238 A sophisticated epidemiological: D.E.H. Russell, *Sexual Exploitation: Rape, Childhood Sexual Abuse, and Sexual Harassment* (Beverly Hills, Calif.: Sage, 1984).

Diana Russell, a sociologist and human rights activist, used a random sampling of nine hundred women, interviewing them in depth about their experiences of domestic violence and sexual exploitation.

238 For females, the likelihood: D. G. Kilpatrick et al., "Prevalence of Civilian Trauma and Posttraumatic Stress Disorder in a Representative National Sample of Women," *Journal of Consulting Clinical Psychology* 616, no. 6 (December 1993): 984–91.

239 one in approximately two: Koss et al., p. 119. The authors cite Fitzgerald and Schulman, "Sexual Harassment: A Research Analysis and Agenda for the 1990s," *Journal of Vocational Behavior* 42 (1993): 5–27.

240 "Sometimes, it's when": Christian Berthelsen, "Women Are Speaking Out to Heal Trauma and Rape," *The New York Times,* April 4, 1999, p. A17.

242 "grab the hand": William Underwood, *Self-Defense for Woman: Combato* (Garden City, N.Y.: Blue Ribbon Books, 1944).

The quote is from Martha McCaughey, *Real Knockouts* (New York: New York University Press, 1997), p. 51.

242 "Clearly these books": Martha McCaughey, *Real Knockouts.*

243 more likely to injure: Richard B. Felson, "Big People Hit Little People: Sex Differences in Physical Power and Interpersonal Violence," *Criminology* 34, no. 3 (August 1996): 433. The study was based on interviews done in 1980 in Albany, New York. People were asked to self-report their involvement in violent episodes prior to that date. While men were twice as likely as women to engage in a violent attack and over four times as likely to injure the respondent in incidents not involving the use of a weapon, women were more likely than men to "produce injury" when armed.

243 "Yes, it pays": Mary Conroy and Edward Ritvo, *Every Woman Can: The Conroy Method to Safety, Security, and Self-Defense* (New York: Grosset and Dunlap, 1982), pp. 96–97.

243 don't enrage: Kathleen Keefe Burg, *The Womanly Art of Self-Defense* (New York: A and W, 1979).

243 "how are you to know he's skinny": Frederick Storaska, *How to Say No to a Rapist and Survive* (New York: Random House, 1975), p. 42.

Storaska became known among feminists for advising women to dignify the assailant as a way to try to escape assault.

244 "Boldness": Lisa Sliwa with Keith Elliott Greenberg, *Attitude: Commonsense Defense for Women* (New York: Crown, 1986), pp. 31–32.

245 "Tribe 8 does not": McCaughey, *Real Knockouts,* p. 5.

246 "not a job": Ann Jones, "Is This Power Feminism?" *Ms.*, May–June 1994, pp. 38–44.

248 Four out of five: Pauline B. Bart and Patricia H. O'Brien, *Stopping Rape: Successful Survival Strategies* (New York: Pergamon Press, 1985).

Data on women putting up a fight are in Sarah E. Ullmann and Raymond A. Night, "The Efficacy of Women's Resistance Strategies in Rape Situations," *Psychology of Women Quarterly* 17 (1993): 23–38.

248 University of Nebraska: Cited in Sharon Bohn Gmelch, *Gender on Campus* (New Brunswick, N.J.: Rutgers University Press, 1998), p. 272.

252 "the myth that makes itself": Another myth of male supremacy is the idea "that sexual power . . . originates in the penis." Andrea Dworkin, *Intercourse* (New York: Free Press, 1987).

254 "I learned to jab": Martha McCaughey, "The Fighting Spirit: Women's Self-Defense Training and the Discourse of Sexed Embodiment," *Gender and Society* 12, no. 3 (June 1998): 277–300.

255 "Women do not perceive": Ibid.

255 "They develop a new self-image": Ibid.

255 "From birth": Elizabeth Swasey, "NRA Woman's Voice," *American Rifleman* 18 (1993).

255 "On the playground": Ibid.

257 "frightened me more": Rene Denfeld, *Kill the Body, the Head Will Fall* (New York: Warner Books, 1997), p. 24.

257 "Somehow": Ibid.

258 "It felt great": McCaughey, *Real Knockouts*, p. 132.

258 "They end unhealthy": Ibid., p. 122.

258 "I felt like I was": Ibid.

258 "I have a right": Ibid.

Index

Index

Janet, Pierre, 234, 239
Jennings, Melissa, 142, 143
Joan of Arc, 11
Johnson, Virginia, 47
Jones, Ann, 246
Jones, Mrs. Francis, 10–11
Jong, Erica, 218
Journal of Sport and Social Issues, 158,
   181
jumping, assessment of, 207

Keller, Debbie, 142–43
Kelly, E. Lowell, 198–99
Ken and Barbie dolls, 45
Kennedy, Anthony M., 129, 150
Kiam, Victor, 210
kickball, 110–11
kicking, research in, 68
kinesthetic intelligence, 59–60, 73
King, Albert F., 113
King, Billie Jean, xviii, 169–70
Kiniery, Nancy, 263–64
Kissling, Elizabeth, 37–39
Klein, Helen, 219
Kletz, Ann, 109
Kłobukowska, Ewa, 175
Koop, C. Everett, 229

Lacan, Jacques, 117
Ladies' Home Journal, 28
Lady Cyclist magazine, 26
Lancet, 69
Landers, Melissa A., 91–92
LeDoux, Joseph, 239
Lefkowitz, Bernard, 136, 137
legislation:
   California, 133
   trickle-down effect of, 111
Leo, John, 131–32, 133, 150
lesbianism, fear of, 182, 198–99,
   201–3
Leslie, Lisa, 182
Levy, Bruce, 173
Lewis, Carl, 205
Lewis, Lyn, 220
Life magazine, 201
Little League, 96–97, 99, 159
Ljungqvist, Arne, 213–14

London Games (1948), 168
Loovis, E. M., 66–70
Loroupe, Tegla, 37, 172, 195
Lowen, Alexander, 119, 120
Ludtke, Melissa, 209
Lyle family, 130–31

McCaughey, Martha, 242–43, 245–46,
   252, 254–56
McGee, Michael, 38–39
McGee, Pamela, 222
McKee, Alice, 141
MacKinnon, Catherine, 252
McLeod, Elizabeth, 105–9
McLish, Rachel, 196–97
McMurray, Keven, 97–98
Madonna image, 30
male backlash, 208–11, 261
male bodies, as instruments of power,
   192, 252
mannish woman, myth of, 198–204
Manuel, Theresa, 168
marathons, 35, 37–39, 171–73, 204,
   218–19
martial arts, 257–58
Martínez Patino, María José, 176–78
masculinity:
   he-man mystique in, 24
   identity and, 50, 139, 199, 201
   measurements of, 48–50, 198–99
   Olympic competition and, 163,
      164–65
   as social construct, 48–50
   stereotype threat and, 53,
      200–201
   stringent requirements of, 46
   women's strength as threat to,
      22–25, 194, 195–204, 208–9,
      211
   and women's work, 261–64
masculinization, in women's sports,
   15
Masters, William, 47
Mattel Toys, 45
maturation:
   and motor skills, 62, 68–69
   strength and, 79
Mayer, Helene, 193–94

Index

About the Author

COLETTE DOWLING is an internationally known writer and lecturer whose books have been translated into twenty languages. She is the author of numerous books, including *Maxing Out, Red Hot Mamas, You Mean I Don't Have to Feel This Way?*, and *The Cinderella Complex*, which has been in print since it was first published in 1981. Her articles have appeared in many magazines, including *The New York Times Magazine, New York*, and *Harper's*. She lives in Woodstock, New York.

About the Type

This book was set in Fairfield, the first typeface from the hand of the distinguished American artist and engraver Rudolph Ruzicka (1883–1978). Ruzicka was born in Bohemia and came to America in 1894. He set up his own shop, devoted to wood engraving and printing, in New York in 1913 after a varied career working as a wood engraver, in photoengraving and banknote printing plants, and as an art director and freelance artist. He designed and illustrated many books, and was the creator of a considerable list of individual prints—wood engravings, line engravings on copper, and aquatints.